THE SALARIED PROFESSIONAL

How to
Make the
Most of
Your Career

by
Joseph A. Raelin

PRAEGER

PRAEGER SPECIAL STUDIES • PRAEGER SCIENTIFIC

New York • Philadelphia • Eastbourne, UK
Toronto • Hong Kong • Tokyo • Sydney

Library of Congress Cataloging in Publication Data

Raelin, Joseph A., 1948—
    The salaried professional.

    Includes index.
    1. Professions. 2. Vocational guidance. I Title.
HD8038.A1R34 1984   331.7'02   83-24756
ISBN 0-03-068918-X (alk. paper)
ISBN 0-03-068919-8 (pbk.)

Published in 1984 by Praeger Publishers
CBS Educational and Professional Publishing
a Division of CBS Inc.
521 Fifth Avenue, New York, NY 10175 USA

© 1984 by Joseph A. Raelin

456789 052 987654321

Printed in the United States of America
on acid-free paper

To JEREMY

who keeps me so willing
to make the most of
my career with him.

Preface

This book has been written for a growing segment of the population which unfortunately has not been given enough attention in self-development circles. I am referring to salaried professionals. That is — those scientists, engineers, accountants, lawyers, teachers, and other professionals who are working within organizations as opposed to engaging in private practice.

One common factor among all professionals, whether self-employed or salaried, is the relative dearth of training they receive regarding their career development. So much time is spent learning the technical aspects of their profession that these individuals have scant opportunity to learn how to make the most of their careers. Career development, if given any attention by professionals, is assumed to signify getting a job that makes use of their highly developed skills. It is, however, much more than that. Once on the job, you need to know how to shape it to fit your needs for growth and development. You need to know the leverage available in your organization for moving to new and different jobs. You need to know how to work with your management to ensure that you meet your needs in addition to the needs of your organization. Further, any changes you make from your first job experience should match your expectations, many of which are dependent upon personal values, abilities, and potential. You may be able to fulfill a good number of your goals and ambitions within your own organization. Unfortunately, many professionals, untrained in career development techniques, leave their organization without having sufficiently explored internal opportunities. There may be a time when you will in fact have to leave your organization, but that should be done only after a careful analysis of in-house options. Indeed, during times of economic recession or industry-specific shortfalls when professional mobility is dampened, it behooves you to explore internal opportunities to their fullest before attempting to tackle an unreliable marketplace.

This book will help you examine these and many more issues regarding your personal career development as a salaried professional. Through a carefully designed sequence of chapters accompanied by multiple personal exercises, you will come out of the experience of this book equipped with a personal career development strategy which will guide your career choices hopefully throughout the rest of your professional life.

The basic premise of the book, which is introduced immediately in the first chapter, is that as a professional you can make effective choices regarding your personal career development once you have a thorough understanding of two critical elements: (1) your self, especially the abilities, values, and developmental attributes which guide your goals and ambitions, and (2) your work environment, which would incorporate an analysis of your job and organizational climate. These two elements are combined to produce a realistic and attainable plan for change. Indeed, the book, by using skills which as a professional you have already acquired, can lead you to a productive strategy for personal career development in a relatively short time and, perhaps, without the need for additional self-development courses or seminars (although many of these are quite good).

Finally, I have written this book keeping in mind some of the things which professionals already know and as a result don't need — conducting a job search, writing a resume, and so on. There are already hundreds of available resources on these subjects. Rather, I wanted to write about those things which have been left out of your career training, to wit, how to make your way once you find yourself in an organization. The language and style used are also geared to the professional audience; facts are backed up by appropriate references, explanations are given in concrete language with useful examples, and technical information is provided rather than avoided. It is my hope that this book will in some small measure contribute to our human resource productivity to the extent professionals will use it to keep themselves fulfilled in both their organization and in their profession.

Acknowledgments

Much of the material used in this book was developed for some of my classes and workshops. Through these experiences, I have been able to shape the presentation and content to convey greater meaning to my readers. Therefore, my students and trainees deserve a good deal of credit for any clarity shown in the ensuing pages. In particular, many of the exercises are used in a workshop called "Career Motivation Within the Organization," which was co-designed with my friend and colleague, Albert Savitsky. I am sincerely grateful to Al not only for his partnership in this venture but for his inspiration through the many years of our collaboration.

I have also been fortunate to have had some outstanding research assistance in the preparation of this volume. Jessica Rodrigues was there to lend some great insights at the project's inception and Maureen Murphy held it together at the end. Andy Majewski, however, saw it through from beginning to end, providing selective topical research and overall manuscript management, always with a wonderful sense of humor.

Four other individuals provided expert typographical assistance at various phases of manuscript preparation. They are, in sequence, Mary McCourt, Rosanne Colocouris, Fritz Ross, and Gertrude Dolin.

Finally, to my wife Abby, I owe the greatest debt, not only for the time she allowed me in order to prepare this book, but for her comments and reactions as a successful professional who, unlike so many of us, already knows how to make the most of her career.

Contents

LIST OF ILLUSTRATIONS

TABLES

FIGURES

EXHIBITS

LIST OF EXERCISES

ONE: The Salaried Professional and the Need for Career Development

INTRODUCTION AND PLAN FOR THIS BOOK

Career development, or the process of formulating steps one would consider in pursuing alternative work situations, is not typically a formal consideration among professionals. Nevertheless, professionals, once obtaining their first job in an organization, are not content to remain on that job forever. Like most people, they will aspire to learn new skills and responsibilities ordinarily through a progression of other jobs in the same organization, or perhaps in different organizations. What is different about career development for the professional is the notion of systemically mapping one's next steps. As Sarason[1] has suggested, professionals are imbued with the prospect of having "one career to live," and are perhaps accustomed to believe, in their training and in their observation of leading figures in their field, that the career sort of takes care of itself.

Of course, we all know that it doesn't. As this book is about and for the salaried professional within the organization, what I shall attempt to point out in this first chapter is that although respected for their background and potential contribution, professionals are not by nature completely comfortable in the organizational setting. And aside from the help a mentor or sponsor may provide, professionals cannot expect that their management is going to plan their career for them. So, if it isn't just going to "happen," there has to

1

be some way professionals can directly affect their career within the organization.

This book is designed especially for the salaried professional as an aid in this process of personal career development. The book's plan or conceptual framework is depicted in Figure 1-1. It begins with an overview of you — the reader — who is most likely a salaried professional. In addition to talking about who you are as a professional, the first chapter will devote considerable attention to some concerns you may have about your organization, your management, and, of course, your career. The first chapter will also highlight how the professional copes with the pressures of transition to management.

The process of career development will then be detailed in the ensuing chapters. In Chapters Two and Three, you will be invited

FIGURE 1-1

Conceptual Framework for this Book: A Personal Career Development Plan for Professionals

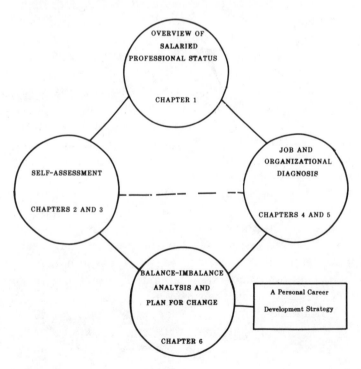

OVERVIEW OF SALARIED PROFESSIONAL STATUS

CHAPTER 1

SELF-ASSESSMENT

CHAPTERS 2 AND 3

JOB AND ORGANIZATIONAL DIAGNOSIS

CHAPTERS 4 AND 5

BALANCE-IMBALANCE ANALYSIS AND PLAN FOR CHANGE

CHAPTER 6

A Personal Career Development Strategy

to conduct a self-assessment which entails examining yourself, your values, skills, and aspirations, and your development as a person and as a worker. In Chapters Four and Five, you will perform a job and organizational diagnosis in order to obtain a clear reading of your current career situation. This will entail delving into such questions as how to do a personal job analysis, how to develop a career path, how to work more effectively with your boss, whether and how to find a mentor, and how to analyze your organizational climate. These two steps, the self-assessment and the job and organizational diagnosis, are presented sequentially in the book, but are essentially concurrent processes and are so indicated in Figure 1-1 with a broken line. In Chapter Six, all of this prior analysis is integrated through the vehicle of the balance-imbalance analysis. This will incorporate a plan for change or a strategy for putting in motion a systematic program for fulfilling your personal needs within the context of your present or perhaps a new organization. The plan for change will lead you to the product which this book is designed for — a strategy for personal career development.

In order to get you to that end point, it is critical that you work through the material in the prior chapters. Starting with Chapter Two, you will be asked to engage in a variety of exercises which will help you conduct the preliminary analyses of yourself and your career situation so that you can make the best choices when developing your personal career development strategy. Given a variety of contingencies, such as your previous exposure to career development, your time and commitment to this process, etc., I occasionally present some optional exercises which can either supplement or replace the principal exercises. To obtain the greatest benefit from this book, it is advisable that you work through all the principal exercises and reflect very carefully on the reading material. If you do so, your plan for change developed in the last chapter will become a meaningful document which you should be able to implement immediately and carry forward throughout the next important years of your career.

Before getting into the analytic components of the framework, let us begin with an elaboration of those particularities of professional status which make you and your work patterns different from other workers. This will suggest why your career needs are different from others, which will in turn explain why a fresh approach to career development is required in your case.

PROFESSIONAL STATUS: ITS MEANING AND SIGNIFICANCE IN CAREER DEVELOPMENT

It may seem redundant to talk about "professional" career development in this book since so many individuals who happen to work in organizations call themselves professionals these days. To the extent we think of professionals as having superior intellectual training on the level of higher education, as maintaining their own standards of excellence and success, and as being supported by associations which maintain the quality of the profession, indeed many individuals today could say that they fall into the category of "professionals." Yet, there needs to be some kind of distinction which qualifies an individual for professional status, assuming professionalism can still make an important contribution to organizational development and social change.

Who, then, are the professionals? Sarason defines them as follows:

> Individuals whose choice of work requires at least a college education giving them specific knowledge and skills, to be applied under supervision for a period of time, at the end of which they are entitled to a "label" which carries credentials for independent activity.[2]

As this definition, though well articulated, is unlikely to limit the category, we turn to other means of classification.

Definitional Approaches

Professional taxonomies are typically built around occupational status; however, a functional approach may also be used. This may be further broken down into an individual level of analysis which has structural and attitudinal attributes. These classifications are each discussed respectively below.

The occupational approach, which is by far the most familiar, simply selects occupations which are presumed to fall into the professional category. Most of the extant occupational classifications are based upon either prestige or socioeconomic status. Since there has been no agreement on these classification criteria, and since the changing nature of many occupations make these taxonomies somewhat crude to begin with, at the risk of excluding some legitimate members, I offer an arbitrary list, representing the occupations I have been commonly thinking about in writing this book for professionals in organizations.

Accountants
Airline pilots and controllers
Architects, artists, and writers
Clergy
Doctors and veterinarians
Engineers and computer scientists
Foresters
Lawyers
Nurses
Pharmacists
Psychologists, counselors, and social workers
Scientists — physical, mathematical, and life
Teachers, librarians, and professors
Urban planners

As was indicated above, the occupational approach is clearly limited by the crudeness of the criteria used in defining membership in the class. Therefore, an alternative approach, which I call *functional* has been used to add precision to the classification. According to the functional approach, membership as a professional is conditional upon doing the things (or functions) which professionals do, or having the characteristics of professionals. Although the functional approach is subject to some arbitrariness, there is quite a bit of research backing up the listing of characteristics. Kerr, Von Glinow, and Schriesheim[3] in reviewing this research, came up with six characteristics which the literature has acknowledged as representing professional status:

1. *expertise* — engaging in prolonged specialized training in a body of abstract knowledge.
2. *autonomy* — possessing the freedom to choose the examination of and means to solve problems.
3. *commitment* — showing primary interest in pursuing the practice of one's chosen specialty.
4. *identification* — identifying with the profession or with fellow professionals through formal association structures or through external referents.

5. *ethics* — rendering service without concern for oneself or without becoming emotionally involved with the client.
6. *standards* — commiting oneself to help in policing the conduct of fellow professionals.

One can, of course, use the functional approach to draw up an occupational listing. However, as Ritzer[4] points out, the revised occupational approach may still be inadequate at an individual level of analysis. In other words, there may be some individuals who do not possess professional traits in a supposed professional occupation, and conversely, there may be some individuals who act like professionals but who are not members of a recognized professional occupation. Hence, in every occupation, there are some individuals who are more professional than others.

The individual level of analysis may even be further broken down by structural and attitudinal aspects. According to Hall,[5] the structural attributes consist of such aspects as formal education, standards, and entrance requirements which are part of the structure of the profession; whereas the attitudinal attributes represent such aspects as disposition towards other colleagues in the field, sense of autonomy, etc. These structural and attitudinal attributes may also be applied at the occupational level of analysis.

Professionals vs. Quasi Professionals

Although not necessarily reflected in their financial remuneration, professionals have consistently been rated by public opinion surveys as having the greatest amount of prestige in our society. Hence, it is not unusual that some occupations aspire to professional status even though the majority of their members may not fulfill the functional conditions as outlined in the previous section. Nevertheless, such occupations may clearly qualify as professions on many of the key functions or may have a sufficient number of professionally disposed members to qualify then as emerging or quasi professions. Among the occupations which I noted previously which might fall into this middle ranking category might be: accounting, engineering, library work, pharmacy, and urban planning. The truth of the matter, though, is that using the functional approach, one could probably scale all of the occupations in order of their increasing professionalism, suggesting that professionalism is a matter of degree and cannot be defined as a discrete category.

Nevertheless, it is useful to consider the quasi professionals as a separate group since their career concerns may be different from those of the professionals. In fact, a number of researchers have found a variety of differences between these two groups. Most of the studies have looked at engineers as representative of the quasi-professional occupational category and scientists as representative of the pure professional category. Kerr et al.[6] used the six functional characteristics to differentiate the two occupations, so their work is again referred to in what follows.

1. *Expertise* – Engineers are not found to have as rigorous an educational background. In fact, some studies have found practicing engineers with less than a four-year undergraduate engineering degree. Engineers are also thought to treasure the practical and pragmatic components, as opposed to the basic components of knowledge. Finally, engineers value interpersonal skills more highly than scientists.
2. *Autonomy* – Scientists are unrelenting in their support of this characteristic. Hence they tend to look with disfavor upon conformity or adherence to organizational norms. They consequently seek the freedom to select the problems they will study, whereas engineers are typically given the problems and even the procedural guidelines for solving them.
3. *Commitment* – This characteristic has the most implications for career development. Basically, scientists are seen as interested in pursuing a career in their field, whereas engineers think in terms of a career in their company. Similarly, career dissatisfaction or alienation among scientists might manifest itself as a lack of autonomy to pursue their work, whereas among engineers, it typically results from lack of power and participation in organizational affairs. This characteristic, then, has implications for career progression for the two-role occupants. As I shall point out, the transition to management is much more accepted among engineers whereas scientists will have a tendency to remain with their technical specialty.
4. *Identification* – Engineers do not maintain an identification with their profession, in terms of dealings with associations and external referents, to the same extent as scientists. However,

engineers with Ph.D. degrees were found to participate more actively in professional activities than those with less formal education, although engineers with doctorates constitute under 5 percent of all practicing engineers.

5. *Ethics* — Given their socioeconomic origin, specialization, and fragmentation, engineers are not considered to have a strong enough foundation in the values of professionalism to maintain a service ethic. Smaller percentages of engineers would seek to make a contribution to society than percentages indicating an interest in contributing to their organization.

6. *Standards* — A number of both formal and informal mechanisms exist in the sciences for certification, review of practitioners' competence, and censure; yet, these activities are typically beyond the power and interest of engineering associations. Further, it is not evident that engineers value peer control. In fact, many feel that their manager would be an appropriate judge of their professional performance. Yet, notwithstanding the fact that the forces of change in a given profession may come from leaders who do not fully represent the membership, there are pressures in the quasi professions, such as engineering, to police themselves more, to strengthen their professional associations, and to express a community orientation and code of ethics.[7]

In spite of the foregoing discrepancies between professionals and quasi professionals, it is clear that the individual approach must apply in determining the ultimate criterion of membership. In other words, some engineers will act like professionals; others may not. In the material which follows, individual readers will have to keep these distinctions in mind and determine for themselves whether particular strategies and discussions are immediately applicable to them. The so-called quasi professionals are considered to be professionals in this book. Nevertheless, since we are addressing the audience of professionals *within* organizations, there are going to be limits to the amount of autonomy and identification feasible within the recognizable constraints of one's organizational setting. I shall examine these constraints in detail later on but for now, it should be apparent that salaried professionals face pressures on their professional identification which would likely be of little consequence to self-employed professionals.

Growth and Erosion of Professionalism

Statistically, in terms of the way our labor analysts refer to professionals, this component of the labor force is growing for every professional occupation with the exception of teachers, professors, and social workers. As Table 1-1 demonstrates, the percent of professionals employed in our civilian labor force is now approaching 16 percent (from 8.4 percent in 1950) and some projections have forecast a proportion of 20 percent sometime in the 1990s. Further, if one breaks down the professional cohort by salaried versus self-employed individuals, there is an overall trend toward finding increasing numbers of professionals working in industry, government, universities, and hospitals. Table 1-1 indicates that although now stabilized at about 75 percent of total professional employment, salaried professional employment from 1950 to 1975 grew even at a faster pace than overall professional employment. The growth trend among salaried professionals was demonstrated by Kornhauser[8] as being even more remarkable in the first half-century, between 1900 and 1950. This trend can be explained in two ways. First, some of the quasi professionals, such as engineers, are found almost uniquely within organizational borders and hence depend upon the organization itself, or an external government bureaucracy, for their financial security.[9] Secondly, a growing number of the "old" professionals, such as lawyers and doctors, are finding employment in large organizations.

What are the underlying reasons for the change among professionals from self-employment or private practice to organizational membership? Everett C. Hughes[10] supplied some convincing arguments. Due to the increasing complexity of our society, in particular, the emphasis on specialization of work as well as advances in technology, today's professional is trained to work in organizational settings such as courtrooms, hospitals, etc. Specialization also makes professionals more interdependent. In order to serve the client better, but also as a practical matter for the professional, many specialists locate within the same organizational setting. The professional also needs to supervise the work of many paraprofessionals as well as control sophisticated technological apparatus, activities which essentially constitute part of the system of professional service. So, today, even those from the so-called old professions, in order to affiliate with other professionals but also to continue

TABLE 1-1   Professional and Salaried Professional Employment Growth for Selected Years, 1950-79

	1950		1960		1970		1975		1977		1979	
	Number[a]	Percent[b]	Number	Percent	Number	Percent	Number	Percent	Number	Percent	Number	Percent
All Professionals	5,000	8.4	7,336	10.8	11,018	13.7	12,748	15.0	13,692	15.1	15,050	15.5
Salaried Professionals[c]	3,200	5.4	4,920	7.2	7,332[d]	9.1	9,494	11.2	10,067	11.1	11,102	11.5

[a]Raw totals, expressed in thousands, represent civilian labor force, 16 years and older, employed in professional occupations.
[b]Percentages represent proportion of total employed.
[c]Salaried professionals represent following occupations: accountants, computer specialists, engineers, librarians, nurses, personnel workers, scientists, systems analysts, technicians, teachers, vocational counselors.
[d]The 1970 salaried data are projected from prior and later years since complete disaggregate figures were not available.

Sources: U.S. Bureau of the Census, *Historical Statistics of the United States, Colonial Times to 1970*, Part I, 1976; and U.S. Bureau of Labor Statistics, *Handbook of Labor Statistics*, 1980.

to work in population areas which can support private practice, are turning more and more to group and organizational forms of practice.[11]

The growth trend of professionals and salaried professionals aside, the mere prestige of professionalism in our society is sufficiently powerful that many occupations, which have not traditionally been classified as among the professions, have asserted their claim to professionalism. It is therefore an intriguing question whether the classification of professional has grown to a point where it has become a meaningless label. Conversely, since, as I pointed out earlier, most professionals can now be found working in organizations which by their nature threaten professional autonomy and ethical standards, one might also wonder whether the professional classification might erode to a point where its membership would be insignificantly small.

In terms of the first challenge to professionalism — its insurmountable growth — Harold Wilensky in his classic piece, *The Professionalization of Everyone?*[12] argued convincingly against such an occurrence. A number of threats, according to Wilensky, exist to dampen such growth. For example, professional status is unlikely to be conferred on occupations where the work is supervised largely by nonprofessionals. In other cases, such as real estate brokers, professionalism cannot ensue since the service provided is so commercialized that the meaning of the service ethic is reduced. Other occupations, such as sales or personnel work on one hand, or technical specialties on the other, rest on a base of knowledge which is either (1) too general or vague, or (2) too narrow or specific for achievement of the autonomy of the profession. Finally, Wilensky, although applauding the development of associations which establish higher levels of training and standards of performance among a number of occupations, suggests that these structural adaptations fall short of the expertise typically obtained in programs of higher education, associated with the traditional professions.

As for the erosion of professionalism, it is simply not the case that most professionals who happen to work in large organizations will be swallowed up by those bureaucracies. Although management needs to integrate the services of the professional with the other activities of the organization, management is at the same time dependent upon the professional for those same services and recognizes its limited control over the regulation of technical performance. Further, as I shall soon demonstrate, a number of accommodative mechanisms, such as the creation of the role of professional administrator, have alleviated the potential conflict between the need for integration by management vs. the need for autonomy by the professional.[13] Yet, to the extent the results of professional expertise and research are dependent upon market strategy, the professional's autonomy and independence can be sharply curtailed. However, if the productivity of our society in recent years has indeed been thwarted by a research lag[14] or a dearth of creativity, the role of the professional will be protected, for our policymakers are coming to understand that the necessary search for new knowledge is dependent upon the integrity of professional endeavors.

THE MAJOR CONCERNS OF SALARIED PROFESSIONALS

The Professional vs. the Organization

A great deal has been written about the strain salaried professionals experience when working within large organizations. While most of the literature is in agreement that the strain is considerable, although some believe it to be overplayed,[15] there is also agreement that sufficient accommodative mechanisms exist within organizations to lessen this strain.

In this section, I shall identify the sources of strain based upon the values or functional characteristics of professionals, previously presented, and for each potential conflict which might ensue between the professional and the organization, discuss the accommodative mechanisms which exist. In this way, professional readers can learn to anticipate these potential conflicts and take advantage of the organizational mechanisms of accommodation. Further, identification of the sources of conflict with the organization should help you, the professional, diagnose first yourself, then your job and organization, and finally, the intersection between the two (that is, you in your organization). This process constitutes the essence of the career development framework presented in the introduction and to be applied in the chapters to follow.

Perhaps the most apparent source of strain between professionals and organizations derives from the specialized *expertise* which the professional brings to the organization. Management is often found to have little patience with the elegant procedures practiced by the professional and frequently applies pressure on the professional for faster results or more immediate applications. The professional in turn resists these pressures on the basis of his or her special competence which, in many cases, is not sufficient to resist market uncertainties which largely govern the behavior of management.

The most common accommodative mechanism used by organizations to respond to the potential crisis over expertise is the creation of specialized roles or departments for professionals, such as research laboratories, where they can pursue their research interests in a relatively unrestricted fashion. Of course, management is still left with the problem of seeing that other parts of the organization make adequate use of the work produced in these specialized units. The separate institution of the university can function as a source of basic research and may be the most compatible locus of employment for those professionals who cannot withstand even the slightest market or administrative constraint.

Recently, professionals have come under increasing pressure from the public to consider the consequences of their action in the form of a "technological assessment." This term suggests that professionals have a responsibility to consider the social costs of their inventions and research forays including how the research is to be used (for example, for peaceful or nonpeaceful purposes). Consequently, like it or not, professionals will continue to be expected to participate in the integration of their research with the preparation of end products.

Autonomy has been shown to be a critical dimension of professional life. As in the case of expertise, professionals wish to maintain self-control over the development of the applications of knowledge in their field. Yet the organization, and in particular its management, in order to coordinate the diverse activities it undertakes to accomplish its goals, needs to maintain control over all the individuals in the organization, professional or not, who contribute to organizational task performance. This condition results in professionals being supervised by nonprofessionals who happen to occupy supervisory positions. Although this may seem normal, it runs counter to the value system of many professionals who expect to establish their own agenda and be controlled certainly by no less than their own peers. The need to determine the problems to be examined and the means to be used is compromised where professional personnel can virtually be hired, promoted, and fired at the will of the manager.

The potential conflict regarding the autonomy of the professional within the organization is minimized under certain organization types. Where there is a high degree of receptiveness to professional expertise, where the professional's services are in much demand, or where administrators are knowledgeable about professional concerns (or even have come from professional backgrounds), professionals may be granted an acceptable level of autonomy or control over their own work. A further accommodation is the creation of the role of the professional administrator. A hierarchy of such roles may be created such that professional administration near the top of the ladder may take on near normal administrative trappings, whereas at the lower, front-line level, supervision may approximate colleague control.[16]

Besides seeking autonomy over one's work, the professional also displays a *commitment* to a chosen specialty and maintains an *identification* with the profession such that personal research and discoveries draw the attention and recognition of one's peers. This commitment and identification to the profession may be inconsistent, however, with the requirements for success and advancement in the organization. Management desires its employees to be loyal to the organization and not to consider it a mere place of work. Loyalty is, in turn, induced through organizational incentives which beyond salary and benefits normally contain the opportunity for the assumption of managerial responsibilities. The most committed of professionals, however, will look to external referents and to their professional associations for recognition, support, and stimulation. Also, professional unions may be relied upon to support professional interests, although their interests tend to lie more in protecting economic rights and benefits than in preserving the norms of professionalism.

The most popular accommodative mechanisms which are used to reduce the strain along the lines of commitment and identification address the issue of incentives directly. Organizations that employ professionals might simply allow them to achieve professional rewards along with their expected contribution to the organization. This can come in the form of an opportunity to participate in professional association meetings, to publish, research, and patent new discoveries, to work almost exclusively on projects making full use of one's professional methodology, to continue one's training and education, and to collaborate with peers in a common work group. Some organizations have further created *dual track* ladders (to be discussed in detail in Chapter Four) wherein beyond the traditional managerial ladder, a professional ladder exists, allowing professionals to gain financial benefits as well as status, without having to give up their chosen technical specialty for managerial responsibilities. Finally, organizational type may also be considered an accommodative factor. Certain professional service organizations, such as accounting firms, as well as universities, hospitals, and some government agencies, allow for greater professional identification in their jobs than most industrial organizations.

Considering the last functional characteristics, professionals are presumed to follow codes of *ethics*, usually established through formal associations, which establish *standards* of conduct. These standards are set apart from the requirements placed on professionals by the organization. Professionals are obliged to serve their client, who may also be the employer, according to standards set by the profession; hence, they may not consider themselves altogether subject to the direction of the management. Nevertheless, compared to professionals in private practice, salaried professionals are in a weaker position to influence the way their services are used, given the administrative imperative of managers to set standards for their organization.

Accommodation is achieved in the area of standards by the acquiescence of management to allow professionals and/or their associations to, if not actually determine membership in the respective organization, at least control the sources of recruitment and to establish standards of competency. A well-known example is the medical profession's system of accrediting medical schools.[17] Professional associations, in establishing certification, licensing, and other registration requirements, are typically unchallenged in their determination to set qualifications for membership in their profession.

Accommodation is perhaps most difficult to achieve in the area of ethics, especially the service ideal, due to the inevitable routines and impersonal exigencies of bureaucratic life. Large service organizations simply could not survive if each client were to receive the personalized service one might expect from a private attending professional, whether it be a teacher, doctor, or counselor. Although accommodation, then, in bureaucratic environments is especially trying for the professional espousing the service ideal, it is an area where there is likely to be a good deal of concurrence in values between manager and professional. Both are likely to understand the dilemma of serving more individuals, perhaps even more needy individuals, but with less personal attention. Service to large numbers, in this case, might be seen as the greater good. Further, professionals themselves provide their own source of accommodation in this situation if they willingly compromise their services in behalf of research ideals. This compromise is no better illustrated than in Caplow and McGee's famous depiction[18] of the academic professional, hired to teach, but evaluated on the basis of contribution to knowledge in a chosen discipline.

Deviant/Adaptive Behavior

Precursory Factors

In the preceding section, the strain experienced by the salaried professional resulting from the incompatible demands of management or from undue pressure to comply with organizational norms was detailed. Another way to refer to this strain is by using cognitive dissonance theory. According to Festinger,[19] cognitive dissonance results when two cognitions psychologically stand in each other's way. Dissonance creates tension within individuals, forcing them to reduce it usually by changing their attitudes or perceptions or even the environmental conditions causing the dissonance. In the case of salaried professionals, if faced with a dissonant work environment, they may justify putting up with it by attributing their behavior to factors outside their control. The professional employee may also reinterpret the job – value aspects previously considered unattractive – in order to make it appear more satisfying. However, some professionals, especially when they have little need to justify their decisions to stay with an unsatisfactory work environment, may engage in either adaptive, maladaptive, or even deviant behavior to reduce the dissonance.

At this time, little empirical research is available to assess the true extent of the so-called "deviant/adaptive" behavior of salaried professionals, although I have recently initiated a prototypical study. Yet, through years of observation combined with a rich but disparate literature on the subject, I have identified some of this behavior by professionals in organizations. Some of the specific behavioral responses will be described shortly in this first chapter, again for identification purposes, as well as for ultimate observation and introspection by the reader. The way to approach the next several pages, then, might be simply to ask yourself what part of the information, if any, sounds familiar to you personally. If so, simply make note of it for it will come in handy in the diagnoses which will be prepared in the forthcoming chapters.

Now before explaining the specifics of deviant/adaptive behavior, it should be noted at the outset that it and/or the dissonance creating it are in fact mediated by some of the accommodative measures of management, addressed earlier. There are also at least four other precursory factors that affect the emergence of deviant/adaptive behavior. First, as was pointed out in the beginning of the chapter, not all professionals are alike. Recalling the prior definition of the quasi professional, one can safely assume that most quasi professionals will be subject to less deviant/adaptive behavior than pure professionals. This is so because they are expected to experience less dissonance with organizational expectations. Hence, individual characteristics must be taken into consideration.

Secondly, organizational characteristics shape the behavioral responses of salaried professionals to organizational expectations. Professionals work in a variety of organizations and in different industries, and some organizations are more receptive to professional practices than others. Thirdly, job characteristics must be considered. As shall be discussed in Chapter Four, such job characteristics as skill variety, task identity, task significance, autonomy, and feedback[20] have been found to be particularly important to professionals. Of course, autonomy has been cited as being synonymous with the very concept of professionalism.[21]

Finally, information professional workers have about job prospects both inside and outside their source of employment affects their behavioral responses. The longer the stay of employment with a company, the more accommodative one might become, especially when internal job information is reasonably accurate. For example, if a staff engineer discovers through his internal information network that the chances of becoming a principal have become minimal, he might need to lower his initial expectations or change them to focus on other opportunities inside or outside the company. The availability and attractiveness of jobs outside the company may lead to deviant/adaptive behavior but this factor too will decrease in importance over time.[22] The only condition under which an external alternative will be pursued is obviously if it is expected to lead to a more positive outcome than one's current job.

Cognitive State

We have seen that potential deviant/adaptive behavior can be moderated by not only accommodative mechanisms introduced by management but also can be affected by individual, organizational, and job characteristics and job information. Persisting dissonance with the organization, however, may lead to behavioral responses although it should be recognized that a process of cognition may evolve before, after, or concurrently with the behavior.

Although not as well researched as the behaviors, the cognitive state is supported by Sarason's work[23] which suggests that professionals, when faced with self-doubt, uncertainty, or negative evaluations, are prone to resist candor regarding their underlying dissonant feelings. Elsewhere[24] I submitted that the first cognitive experience would be *confusion* which manifests the disappointment, disillusionment, or plain uncertainty regarding the source of dissonance. Confusion then makes way for identification or *awareness* of the source of dissonance. Psychologists might say that the second stage of cognition, awareness, simply brings into consciousness what may have previously been unconscious feelings or confusion. Finally, the last cognitive stage is *intention*. At this point, the professional, having identified the source of dissonance, plans some kind of behavioral response. Hence, intention is a very good predictor of behavior.

Behavioral Responses

As has been indicated, the professional ultimately needs to take some action to reduce the dissonance experienced in his or her organizational life. Of course, the option of leaving is available but depending upon a number of circumstances, such as the degree of seriousness of the dissonance with the organization, the availability and attractiveness of outside offers, or the psychological makeup of the individual, the professional may prefer to stay — at least for the time being. In staying, a commitment is made to face the dissonance in some way. One may simply decide to accommodate the situation perhaps by changing one's expectations to match those of the organization. Or, one may attempt to change the expectations of the organization to match one's own. Some specific accommodative measures such as job enrichment or trying to obtain a favorable transfer will be discussed in Chapter Six. Another one — transition to management — will be the focus of the next section of this chapter.

In this section, what I would like to critically explore are behavioral responses which are not particularly constructive to either the individual or the organization. These behaviors, if at all practiced by the professional, are indicative of strain and suggest the need for personal career development. This book will suggest a variety of methods to develop a personal career development plan. In order to obtain an overview of how deviant/adaptive behavior fits into an overall career development scheme, consider Figure 1-2. The behavioral responses of the professional are shown to be derived from dissonance and may be preceded by the cognitive state discussed above. Further, the precursory factors which affect dissonance as well as deviant/adaptive behavior are listed. Finally, the figure indicates that both the deviant/adaptive behavior and the cognitive state may lead to turnover.[25]

As I indicated above, the behavioral responses are almost always detrimental to either the individual or to the organization. Some of them might be considered to be only marginal detrimental or may constitute only short-run maladjustments. Others may constitute outright deviancies which can only cause harm. The response behaviors, then, form a continuum from adaptive to deviant. As Figure 1-2 suggests, they may be broken down into four categories: behavioral responses vis-a-vis the elements of management, job, self, and the career itself.

As for the notion of the continuum representing the severity of the behaviors from adaptive to deviant, a more thorough examination is provided in Figure 1-3. The figure lists the four career

FIGURE 1-2
A Model of Professional Deviant/Adaptive Career Behavior

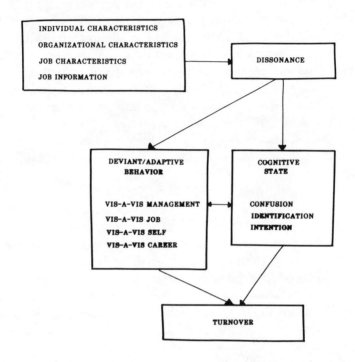

elements and the deviant/adaptive continuum with a suggested list of behaviors, arranged in approximate position along the continuum. Their relative position will eventually be pinpointed by some current empirical testing, but for now the figure represents a reasonable approximation. Below, I shall discuss these behaviors according to each of the four career elements.

Vis-a-Vis Management

Most of the response behaviors vis-a-vis management have been discussed by Kornhauser[26] and La Porte[27] as behaviors which have the potential to move to deviancy if an appropriate accommodation can't be reached with the organization. The impediment placed on professional conduct by the bureaucracy and the professional's resultant behavior of questing for freedom from structural

FIGURE 1-3
A Continuum of Professional Deviant/Adaptive Behavior

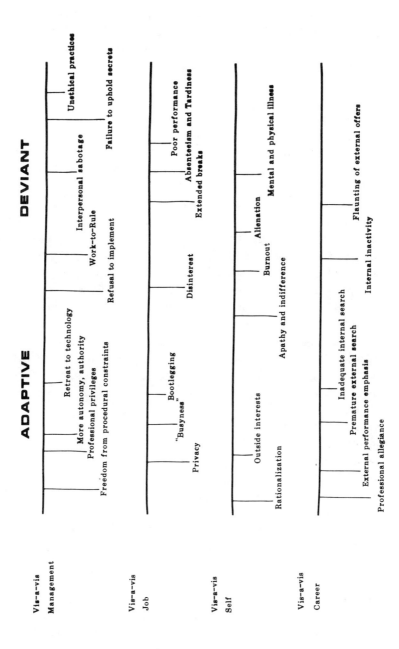

21

constraints have been well documented. This behavior is not serious if the professional shows willingness to accept some natural organizational imperatives, such as goals, rules, and communication structure. Similarly, some demands for greater autonomy and/or authority can be furnished to the professional although there is the danger that it may seem like not enough to the professional, but seem like too much to the manager. The demand for additional professional privileges might come in the form of an opportunity to participate in professional association meetings, to publish research and patent new discoveries, to work exclusively on projects making use of professional methodology, to continue training and education, or to collaborate with peers in a common work group. Again, these may be accommodated but they have a tendency to reduce the loyalty of the professional to the organization. The retreat to technology, first broached by Selznick[28] and then treated in depth by Argyris and Schön[29] as the inability to interpenetrate technical and interpersonal theories, depicts professionals as unwilling to make themselves available to management except for the technical purposes for which they are trained. Even more serious would be, first, their refusal to be concerned with the results or implementation — as in the production and marketing function — of their technical work. Secondly, under more severe dissonance, professionals in reaction to management's bureaucratic constraints, may choose to do things "only by the book," known also as *work-to-rule*.

Deviancy in the management area is clearly achieved when professionals seeking an outlet for their frustrations attempt to recruit others in spreading the word regarding managerial lack of faith. Since this behavioral vehicle is typically made illicit rather than open, it is a form of sabotage against the organization. Another approach to which professionals can turn presumably in the interest of the professional value of knowledge dissemination, is the failure to uphold corporate trade secrets. Beyond this act, there are numerous other unethical practices which professionals may perpetrate on the organization perhaps as a way to serve their exclusive self-interest, as in a bribe or extortion, or to retaliate against management for some past real or imagined indiscretion. The Tylenol murders in the fall of 1982 are thought to have been initiated by the latter motive.

Vis-a-Vis Job

In terms of job adaptations, an initial personal strategy may be to demand more privacy. This doesn't perforce lead to lack of job performance unless the professional eschews interaction necessary for task accomplishment. The professional may also become very busy. Busyness in and of itself is not a problem. In fact, the employee may be working long and hard hours on essential work. However, when he or she is no longer available for requisite tasks, overall job performance may suffer. A related but less formally sanctioned activity is that of bootlegging. As defined by La Porte and Wood,[30] bootlegging means engaging in projects not specified within one's scope of work or one's contractual obligations. Although bootlegging may ultimately benefit the organization, La Porte and Wood find that it tends to benefit the personal career of the professional more than contribute to the accomplishment of organizational goals. Yet, when successful, bootlegging may allow professionals a way out of the dissonance facing them.

Beyond these three behaviors lies disinterest. This behavior approaches deviancy as it implies that conditions within the organization have become sufficiently severe that one no longer can find fulfillment at least within the job. Whereas disinterest represents a passive dimension of deviancy, the next three behaviors take on an active dimension. An unauthorized work break extension can be viewed as a dishonest act since it goes against company policy. Although extended breaks constitute an extreme form of behavior, they may at least allow the worker to come back revived to the job, although this may not always be the case. On the other hand, the professional may choose to withdraw completely, manifested by excessive absenteeism or tardiness. Finally, a decision to stay in the organization (perhaps due to the unavailability of other opportunities) combined with extreme dissonance might lead to reduced or even poor performance on the job itself.

Vis-a-Vis Self

In terms of self, dissonance might be negotiated intrapersonally through the adoption of some kind of psychological defense mechanism, such as rationalization. Unless carried to excess, this kind of psychological process can help the individual adapt to current working conditions. Another adaptive mechanism is to focus on outside interests, such as family, leisure activities, or community affairs. Bailyn's research in this area[31] has revealed that professionals who react in this way can adjust to their work reasonably well; in other words, they become less concerned "about advancement, high earnings, or other signs of organizational power." However, such professionals are also seen as being more passive in their professional role. Less adaptive would be becoming apathetic and indifferent, for these traits could lead to markedly reduced functioning in the work place and could even carry over into home life. More serious than apathy and indifference is the strain of burnout, which Cherniss[32] has found to be particularly associated with professional work. According to Cherniss, burnout has both personal and work effects. It is associated, for example, with emotional detachment and an excessive concern with self-interest. Further, it tends to involve a lowering of personal standards and of personal responsibility for outcomes. In alienation, the individual actually experiences a sense of powerlessness and lack of control over life and work processes. Finally, when the strain and frustration experienced in the work setting become intolerable, mental and physical illness may result.[33]

Vis-a-Vis Career

In this last element, behavioral effects from the professional's dissonance and confusion surrounding the professional's role in the organization are traced in terms of the career itself. In order to emphasize one's professional identification which is challenged by the organization, an initial response may be to strengthen one's professional allegiance. This may take the form of increasing activity in one's professional association, forming closer ties with external professional colleagues, etc. Similarly, the professional may decide that his or her career may be better served by emphasizing work that is professionally, as opposed to organizationally, evaluated. Although this practice could work to the detriment of the organization, it can at times actually benefit the organization if the externally rated activity concurrently serves organizational goals. A clear example of this behavior is a professor's emphasis on research publications which might ultimately increase the reputation of the university.

Less adaptive certainly for the individual and to some extent for the organization is the professional's assumption of premature search activity, which will be defined as persisting in external search independent of the probability of finding an acceptable alternative. According to Mobley, Horner, and Hollingsworth,[34] this behavior is incited by a cognitive state, ending with an intention to quit. It can result in frustration for the individual, and if carried to excess, can limit the contribution the professional might make to the organization. However, it can also result in positive turnover. The converse, inadequate internal search, can be equally damaging to the individual and also has long-term, negative consequences for the organization. Although management may be at fault for not introducing the individual to career planning and development, the individual, too, as is the thesis of this book, has responsibility for shaping his or her own internal growth. A reaction to dissonance, however, among the professionals may be to limit the search of internal opportunities. This may result from what Argyris and Schön[35] refer to as a "self-sealing theory-in-use." Accordingly, professionals, already in doubt about their worth or value to the organization, withhold the search of information which might disconfirm their assumptions about themselves or their organization. While obvious that this kind of behavior restricts the individual, it also reduces the supply of competent human resources to fill new and challenging organizational positions. Beyond inadequate internal search, a more severe reaction by professionals would be to limit their participation in what might be called "extra-work" activities, that is, functions which might be nonmandatory but helpful to the organization. For example, the professional, in order to resist organizational pressures, might simply decide not to volunteer for any committees, might show little interest in entrepreneurial activity, or might refuse to work overtime regardless of the need. Although such behavior can indeed be harmful to the organization, it also limits the present and potential role of the individual in significant organizational activities. Finally, as was pointed out earlier in the discussion regarding behavior vis-a-vis self, a decision to stay in one's organization due to such constraints as closed external opportunities may result in a variety of deviant reactions. In terms of the professional career, a potential reaction is the flaunting of external offers. In this instance, the disheartened professional, whose self-esteem has already been battered by the lack of external opportunities, tries to save face by resorting to inflated statement of fact. Naturally, this kind of behavior unnecessarily heightens the expectations of colleagues and can serve to dampen morale in the respective work unit.

Turnover

The model that has been presented above regarding deviant/ adaptive behavior ends with turnover which results when the professional resigns his or her job. All indications point to a serious turnover problem in our country among professionals. For example, the reputed turnover rate among engineers and scientists in the San Francisco Bay area averages about 30 percent. Now, of course, this figure is generally higher than other less selective labor pools in the country. Further, not all turnover is negative. Some companies, for example, are happy to rid themselves of some poor performers, to get an infusion of new ideas through replacements, to provide for increased internal mobility, or to find an opportunity for a cost-reduction program, all of which might be made available through turnover.[36] Nevertheless, it is safe to say that much turnover is premature or even unnecessary, and that some of the negative consequences experienced by professionals who quit organizations – such as loss of certain benefits and perquisites, family disruption, disillusionment – can be avoided.

In terms of deviant/adaptive behavior, all dissonant responses are, of course, temporarily suspended at the point of turnover since the organizational restraints causing dissonance are released. However, these same behaviors are very prone to surface again in the next organizational position unless role expectations on the part of the professional or the new organization are modified, or more suitable methods of accommodating the potential dissonance are found. Hence there is a need for professionals to carefully monitor their career aspirations and values especially in the context of their employing organization. The ensuing chapters are designed for this express purpose. Before moving on, however, one other immediate concern of the salaried professional needs to be addressed: the transition to management.

Transition to Management

Some professionals, either through their organizational experience or as an original aspiration, choose to enter the management ranks in their respective companies. The latter reason is especially pertinent in the case of quasi professionals who might see the transition to management as a natural progression of responsibility from exclusive and limited professional practice to managerial authority. Other professionals become socialized to management work through experience in their organization. However, many of these individuals may never become completely content with a managerial position. For some of them, it may simply be an alternative to an unrewarding professional life perhaps resulting from dissonance with managerial expectations, as pointed out in the previous section. For others, it may be a more attractive alternative than either transition to another job or potential obsolescence in one's current job.

Before delving into some of these issues, the subject of transition in general is one which merits an introductory discussion. Naturally, obtaining one's first job entails a transition. Since I expect most of the readers of this book to be in an organization and to have already experienced their first job, the next transition or set of transitions of interest would entail job, organization, or career changing. It is well known that professionals as an occupational group change jobs and organizations relatively frequently. Further, Haber[37] found that a subset of "selected professional wage and salary workers," which his listing reveals to be very close to what I have referred to as "salaried professionals," had the highest mobility of all occupational subgroups. In five years, for example, he found the transition rate to out-of-state jobs to be 31.7 percent. The reasons for this high transition rate were hypothesized to be the relatively low cost of job search for professionals, their taste for mobility acquired through college and professional training, and their access to teachers, societies, and journals which could stimulate the desirability of job or career change.

Another less tangible reason for high professional transition rates was articulated by Hall[38] in his reference to the notion of the "protean career." Compared to the career model of the past wherein individuals made the initial transition to an organization and then allowed circumstances or management to propel them up the ladder, the protean career model allows for greater personal freedom of choice. What Hall is suggesting is that professional and other salaried employees today wish to assume both the problems and responsibilities that coincide with making their own career choices. Sheppard's research[39] confirmed Hall's observations as he found his sample of career and job changers to have high achievement values but low autonomy and independence and low opportunities for promotion in their current jobs. Similarly, Gerstenfeld and Rosica[40] in their research reported that most engineers who change jobs do so first in order to change the direction of their career, and then to find more interesting work and opportunities for advancement.

Another value treasured by engineers and scientists who change jobs is that of autonomy. Earlier this value was defined as being consonant with professional practice. An engineer or scientist who chooses to work for a company may not find the assignment of projects to work on objectionable. However, once assigned the project, professionals most likely will want sufficient independence to complete it on their own.

If autonomy or discretion over one's work is not forthcoming, the professional may choose to change jobs or organizations. However, a different outlet may be to move into management which at least offers the level of responsibility which was heretofore lacking as a professional. The transition to management has been a particularly attractive career alternative for engineers. However, most engineers do not start out thinking in terms of this transition. In fact, as Jay Gould[41] has explained, since it takes less training to become an engineer than some of the other professions such as law or medicine, engineering, especially for intelligent children of working-class families, is seen as a very attractive career option. However, from the time engineering school is entered through the duration of the technical career, the engineer is encouraged to aspire to positions in management. The technical aspects of engineering are in many instances seen as a means to an end – transition to management. In fact, engineers are often viewed as failures if they don't become managers.[42]

There are other reasons which might explain the movement of engineers to management positions besides the emphasis of their professional training. Three other reasons relate to the organizational circumstances surrounding the engineer's work. First, since engineers typically work in large bureaucracies, it is not uncommon that the inherent stress on efficiency results in work characterized by microdivision of labor. Although this environment might provide an initial challenge, the fact that it is removed from the "grander picture" of what the company is doing can lead to feelings of personal insignificance and, subsequently, disinterest. Becoming a lower or middle-level manager, for example as a project leader, can provide at least a greater sense of one's contribution to the company's mission. Second, the more specialized the engineer becomes in doing technical work, the greater the risk of eventually becoming redundant as new generations of technology and methodology gradually replace prior technical knowledge. Faced with this reality, the professional might choose either to get updated or simply move into management which, in many cases, is an easier or less troublesome alternative.

Finally, with the exception of companies which have instituted so-called dual ladder systems (which I shall discuss in some depth in Chapter Four), there are real limitations in terms of earnings and status by staying in engineering as opposed to making the transition to management. Further, aggravating this condition is the fact that as professionals become more obsolete in their skills and resultingly more dependent on their organization, they tend to sublimate their professional interest in autonomy in favor of the desire for greater security and financial well-being.[43] Hence, with enough foresight, they can make the shift to management to avoid the stigma and financial insecurity of becoming a professional castaway.

The Transition Dimensions

In an important report by the National Aeronautics and Space Administration (NASA),[44] three dimensions of the transition from science and engineering into management were detailed: the management tasks to be performed, the skills to be used in performing the tasks, and the motives entailed in the managerial role. Of the three, the skills dimension produced the greatest challenge to the professional in making the transition to management.

The tasks of management, such as reporting, supervising, planning, and program assessment were found generally acceptable to the scientists and engineers in the NASA sample who had made the transition to management. They especially liked the prospect of having greater influence in their organization. Further, the tasks were not found to be particularly new, but rather broader in scope. There were more tasks to be done, policies were broader based and longer range, and one had to maintain contact with many more individuals.

In terms of the skills required in management, the NASA sample experienced little problem with the technical skills, but expressed great concern about the people-oriented skills. Decision making, problem solving, or applying fundamental technologies were of no difficulty. However, the transition to management became particularly difficult when it came to such interpersonal, leadership, and coping skills as working with diverse individuals, coordinating group efforts, operating within the organizational system and its subsystems, relying on subjective judgment, using political expediency as a factor in a decision, and dealing with uncertainty.

In terms of the motives of management, although the interests and rewards were identified as being different between professionals and management, most of the sample reacted favorably to the reward systems and motivations entailed in management. Table 1-2 lists these differences in motives. As revealed in the table, overcoming difficult obstacles was a common motivation between professionals and managers and financial advancement was a common reward factor. However, the latter has been shown to be discrepant in private industry, reflecting here the comparability in salary potential between professionals and managers in the NASA environment.

A minority of the professionals in the Bayton and Chapman study reacted unfavorably to the idea of becoming managers. In particular, they feared loss of opportunity to perform their technical skills and displayed anxiety over whether they had the interpersonal skills necessary to perform as managers. Bayton and Chapman concluded that there are three types of professionals:

Type I – manager motivated, expected to actively pursue transition to management
Type II – professional motivated, initially reluctant to make the transition to management but ultimately adaptable
Type III – professional motivated, expected to be dissatisfied with and oppose a transition to management

They found 65 percent of their sample to be Type I.

TABLE 1-2   Motivations and Systems of Rewards for Professionals vs. Managers

	Professionals	*Managers*
Motivations	Enjoying new and different activities	Enjoying leadership and detailed planning
	Direct attack on problems	Helping one's colleagues
	Association with intellectually competent co-workers	Association with congenial coworkers
	Exercise of technical knowledge and skills	Risk taking in making decisions
	Wanting independence and recognition	Wanting to exercise authority and contribute to the organization's goals
	Overcoming difficult obstacles	Overcoming difficult obstacles
Systems of Rewards	Satisfaction derived from the successful completion of tasks	Satisfaction derived from directing others
	Recognition by one's peers and colleagues	Increased authority
	Independence of action	Pride in position attained
	Making a contribution	Participating in a wide scope of activities
	Making creative use of one's abilities	Involvement in policy decisions
	Financial advancement	Financial advancement

Source: Adapted from James A. Bayton and Richard L. Chapman, "Making Managers of Scientists and Engineers," *Research Management*, Vol. 16, 1973, pp. 34-35.

Coping with Transition

The problems of transition to management are not unique to scientific and engineering professionals. Greiner and Scharff[45] cite similar difficulties faced by accountants who work for large public accounting firms, and who make the expected transition to middle management positions and then ultimately to partner. They point out that beyond the problems of personal adaptation, young professional accountants have to further withstand the lack of attention given to managerial transition by the organization. In particular, four problems are discussed.

1. There is relatively little attempt to develop managers as managers; the emphasis is rather on their technical expertise.
2. There is an absence of fixed superior-subordinate relationships; consequently, it is difficult to measure the professional's strengths and weaknesses. A strong *project orientation* causes supervisors to feel a closer association with their clients than with their changing subordinates.
3. Senior management is divorced from many of the traditional management functions, having delegated them to lower-level managerial subordinates.
4. There is a reluctance to create a hierarchy among senior management (perhaps a carry-over from professional tradition); hence, less senior managers are unlikely to get much coaching on their job performance.

Such organizational barriers as these are not uncommon among other non-industrial organizations, such as hospitals, schools, and universities, manned largely by professionally trained employees. Even in industrial organizations which are more managerially structured, one has to learn how to diagnose the organizational/political climate in order to map out a successful strategy of transition. Of course, this must be preceded by a thorough diagnosis of one's own skills, values, and motives to assess whether one is both oriented to and trained for management practice. These diagnostic needs will be addressed in detail in the chapters to follow with the accompanying personal development tools needed to make better transition decisions.

With respect to specific steps to consider in contemplating a career transition — whether it be to management or any other job opportunity — Meryl Reis Louis' action steps[46] can be very helpful. Most of these will also be subsequently addressed in greater detail in the chapters to follow.

1. Learn to anticipate the transition experience, that is, prepare for the feelings of being overwhelmed or surprised and begin to appreciate the potentially new frame of reference.
2. Learn how to make the transition in the terms that are right for you, namely, are you going to require considerable time to get oriented to the new job, or do you want an immediate challenge? Who are the people who can best guide you through the experience?
3. Analyze the transition situation in terms of your new boss; your predecessor; other key personnel, such as your new subordinates; and the new position itself, including its history, its long-range potential, the reputation of the work unit of which it is a part, etc.
4. Highlight potential problems and resources specific to the transition, such as organizational resistances to prior professional status in the case of the former or management development programs in the latter.
5. Review essential transition tasks such as mastering the basics of the job, building a role identity whether it be status quo or change oriented, building good working relationships, finding out what's appropriate and expected in the new setting, mapping the relevant players and where one fits in, learning the local language, and assessing how well the job is currently being done in one's new work unit.
6. Set priorities based upon an analysis of the transition situation, knowledge of the essential tasks, and personal preferences.
7. Select strategies and take action based upon the above prior analysis.

In addition to these seven action steps, I offer three others which are considered to be particularly important for technical professionals who are considering a transition to management.

1. Begin by ensuring that you have an adequate support group of both like professionals and managers who appreciate your interest in transition and will assist in making the transition

a deliberate, reasoned, and supportive process.

2. Search for and then apply those principles which are called for in the new management setting and which helped you become a successful professional. For example, you might experience little burden (in fact, even enjoy) picking up the accounting tools which will be essential for you as a manager in controlling your operation.

3. Learn where established professional dimensions have to give way to managerial methods. For example, if as a professional you were accustomed to doing all the work yourself, now you must learn to trust others and, in so doing, delegate authority. As was pointed out earlier, you may well need practice in interpersonal and coordination skills.

TWO: Self-Assessment

INTRODUCTION

As was stressed in the first chapter, the salaried professional has a responsibility to guide his or her own career development. Ideally, an organization will provide as many resources and opportunities within its means to assist in the personal career development process. However, management cannot perform career planning for employees. The latter must not only take what's given to them, but also take steps to ensure their own career fulfillment. Hence, this chapter initiates what Storey[1] has referred to as "person-directed" as opposed to "manager-directed" career development. Note that the discussion will be in terms of career fulfillment and not necessarily career advancement. As I shall emphasize later on in Chapter Six, advancement is not the sole ticket to success. Many other options, including the mere process of self-exploration — which is the thrust of this chapter — offer opportunities for fulfillment in a professional career.

When it comes to career choice, uncertainty is minimized in the case of professionals by their rather career-specific training. Nevertheless, the choice of organization as well as their current job and future prospects typically represent areas of uncertainty. For some professionals, this uncertainty might even provoke a reevaluation of an original career choice. Perhaps some readers might be fortunate enough to be fully satisfied, or minimally, relatively satisfied (as against expectations) with their current job and career prospects.

For such readers, the following account might serve as a check against perceived reality. Or perhaps it will serve to enlighten or categorize what one already knows — the benefit being an intellectual and emotional confirmation of one's original choices.

For what I suspect represents the typical reader (given the interest in consulting this book in the first place), this chapter is devoted to the individual still in search of career satisfaction. Its purpose is to provide the tools for you, the professional, to undertake a reevaluation of your career through an examination of those aspects of the self which relate to work and career choice. The framework to be used consists of an examination of knowledge and values. A review of your knowledge base extracts those cognitive abilities which have led you to particular career pursuits. A clarification of values extracts the attitudes which have framed your career choices.

You will begin with a self-interview, which will produce a work autobiography, to be based on both preinstitutional as well as formal, postschool work experiences. An educational history will be prepared as well. Both work autobiography and educational history will constitute a personal data base from which a number of subanalyses will be derived to examine the abilities and attitudes making up your professional career orientation. First, an interest and skills assessment will be presented followed by an analysis of learning style. These sections are primarily concerned with the development of your knowledge base and knowledge processes. The remaining sections focus on values, also referred to as psychological needs. Included is an examination of the context of need fulfillment, referred to as need orientation. The development of personality style is considered, especially the impact it has on professional career choice and fulfillment. Finally, the chapter closes with a pertinent discussion of the role of the career in the total life space, acknowledging the contribution that other components of your life make to your development, and how these relate to your career.

The self-assessment should equip you with all the necessary tools to get a good look at yourself through your career present, past, and future. The chapter contains a number of exercises which you are urged to work through. As I stressed at the outset, successful completion of the exercises and textual material is essential. Here, the exercises will help you to move on to a second aspect of self-assessment to be presented in Chapter Three, your career stage of development.

WORK AUTOBIOGRAPHY

The self-assessment process cannot be undertaken without first preparing a personal data base of work experience. The focus on work experience stems from the whole notion of career which may be defined as the sequencing of *work*-related components of our life. Hence, the data base should be limited to work experiences or related phenomena affecting our work such as our family's financial condition. In order to develop this personal data base, it will be essential to complete some form of work autobiography as a principal exercise. A work autobiography serves to bring into consciousness the many experiences which either in a haphazard or planned way got us to the career point in which we find ourselves today. As the initial experience of this chapter, it will be presented with a variety of options, the selection of which will depend upon the time available or the completeness which is desired.

It is advisable to begin the autobiographical account before the first job experience. Hence, the work autobiography is much more than a resume. My own research[2] has shown that although the first job is clearly the key to later employment success, that first job and its sequels are largely affected by family and educational background and other qualitative experiences affecting one's aspirations. For example, the impact made by a model teacher or the personal success enjoyed through a creative hobby could have established important career patterns or direction. The exercises which follow, then, provide for the collection of work-related data necessary in conducting the self-assessment.

EXERCISE 2-1

A. SELF-INTERVIEW. This first exercise is simply a self-interview which can be either recorded and later transcribed, or written down from the start. It should take at least an hour of your time, perhaps longer depending upon the amount of reflection required. It should address your work history, namely, as complete a description as possible of the key aspects of the work experiences you have had over the course of your life. Keeping in mind our aforementioned concern with describing work experience in a broad sense, you can go as far back in your work history as you can recall – jobs you had as a child, volunteer work, etc. I am purposely not providing guidelines for the preparation of your self-interview since it is important that you establish the criteria for your autobiographical account. That way, what will be highlighted will be events and experiences which you value. Subsequently, I will provide some methodologies for analyzing the rich data produced in this exercise. These analyses will instigate the diagnosis of patterns which have one way or the other led you to your current career state.

The way to attack this exercise is to let it flow. If you belatedly realize that you've left something out, put it down as you think about it. You should produce a rough manuscript for your own use. No one else has to see it.

B. TWO-WAY INTERVIEW (Option #1). Although the self-interview is the preferred vehicle for generating the work autobiography due to its unrestricted nature, it may be easier for some of you to be interviewed rather than conduct the interview on yourself. In the two-way interview, you would normally choose someone close to you to actually conduct the full work autobiographical interview. This person should be instructed to go back as far as possible in your worklife and to dig into the details of your work history right up to the present. As before, a recording could be made and later transcribed, or the interviewer could write down your responses as the interview proceeds. The former procedure is ordinarily less interruptive.

Although the two-way interview can be conducted as the interviewer sees fit, within the constraints that it develops your work autobiography, I offer a few questions that might be asked:

1. Tell me about the key work experiences you have had in your life, starting as early as you care to.
   (then, for each experience cited:)
2. What was significant about each of these experiences?
3. Were they positive or negative experiences? Why?
4. What aspects of the various activities you performed did you really enjoy?
5. What did each experience teach you, if anything?
   (after having completed the work history up to the present:)
6. As you reflect on your work experiences, can you identify any patterns which keep cropping up?
7. Are there certain work settings that you seem to prefer?
8. At this point, could you identify and describe your ideal job?

C. TABULAR WORK HISTORY (Option #2). Another option to the self-interview which might speed up the process, but which leaves out some anecdotal information is the tabular work history. This option provides a set format for recording your work history (see Table 2-1). You should remember in using this format to include every possible job you can remember and to give separate credit for jobs which, although under the same title, might require new or different tasks. The brief description of the jobs recorded on the table should later be expanded into a full description on a separate sheet of paper.

D. TIME LINE (Option #3). The final option in performing your work autobiography is to use a time line. Accordingly, you divide up a line into proper time segments representing years of your life (see Figure 2-1). You may extend the line at certain intervals to allow for discontinuous activity; that is, the line segments need not be symmetrical. You then draw a dot for each period when you undertook a new job or significant work activity (remember that jobs do not have to be construed as formal, organizational assignments). From the dot, draw a slanted line (upward or downward) on which you write the name of that work assignment. Once you fill in the time line, you should write separate descriptions on another sheet for each named assignment.

EDUCATIONAL HISTORY

Now that your work autobiography has been completed, it is important to incorporate noteworthy educational and training experiences in order to supplement your personal career data base. Apart from incidental summer and after-school jobs as well as evening and weekend avocations, most of our career-related experiences as children and adolescents take place in school. We are certainly aware, however, that after graduation, whether it be from high school, college, or graduate school, our education does not terminate. Education is a life-long experience. We are constantly learning new things from our job and homelife. Our continuing education can be formal or informal; it can be on the job or in the classroom. Clearly no one single activity contributes more to our occupational choice and ultimate work experience.

Professionals almost by functional definition have committed themselves to educational processes. Formal degree programs are typically required as gateways to the profession. After having earned

TABLE 2-1 Tabular Work History

Jobs	Organization or Location	Job Task and Title	Brief Description	Dates From	To
1.					
2.					
3.					
4.					
5.					

FIGURE 2-1
Time Line

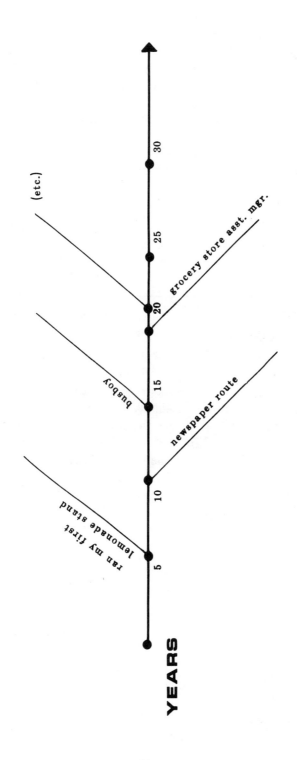

41

a degree, however, in order to remain current regarding the profession's state-of-the-art, constant updating is needed through practice as well as through formal and informal training experiences.

One's educational history is nevertheless typically more discrete than one's work history. Hence the exercises for this section may be completed through the use of a single table.

EXERCISE 2-2

TABULAR EDUCATIONAL HISTORY. On Table 2-2, write in your educational and training background, giving as much attention to the less formal training experiences as the formal educational programs. Examples of both formal and informal education are provided to get you started.

INTEREST AND SKILLS ASSESSMENT

Having developed a personal data base consisting of both work and education-related components, it is now appropriate to begin an analysis of your interests and skills relative to your career development. Interests and skills are the principal ingredients making up one's knowledge base. Interests are also supported by values or psychological needs. Since I shall pay extensive attention to values later on in this chapter, the coverage of interest assessment will be short. Skills, defined as physical and mental abilities emanating from formal and informal education and from work, and perhaps the most fundamental component of career potential, will be discussed in depth.

Interests

Interests do not have to be related to work or education, but it is expected that many of your interests have in the past or do now get carried out within the work environment. Interests are those activities to which participation is voluntarily committed. There are levels of interests such that some entail more or less commitment than others.

TABLE 2-2 Tabular Educational History

Program, Experience, or Degree	Learning Acquired	Organization or Location	Nature of Certificate (if any)	Dates From	To
B.S. in accounting	Complete undergraduate accounting education	Ledger State College Ledger, W. Va.	CPA	1972	1976
(EXAMPLES)					
Financial Officers Training Program: Part III – Debt Service	Learned how the co. defines financial risk, esp. regarding the level and use of its fixed-cost securities	On-site at the Pembroke Company	Corporate Certificate (after Part IV)	Spring 1983	
(BEGIN HERE)					

Work-related interests or vocational interests constitute those interests which can affect a career. Edward Strong[3] built an entire inventory of occupational choice based on the concept of vocational interest. The Strong Vocational Interest Blank, commonly used today in vocational guidance, measures the likelihood of vocational preference based upon the interests of people in chosen occupations.

Rather than use the Strong test here, an interest assessment exercise is offered to help you identify your work-related interests and put them in order of priority.

EXERCISE 2-3

INTEREST ASSESSMENT. Examine your work autobiography very carefully. As you go through it, consider the following questions, being sure to note your responses in the space provided.

1. What activities have I engaged in which really interest me? For example, have I been "turned on":
   by figuring out the optimal layout of a paper delivery route,
   by working on a new computer program to help the storeowner keep track of his inventory,
   by presenting papers in my chosen field,
   by working with a senior colleague in solving a particularly difficult aspect of a technical project,
   by putting in the necessary hours in order to make a new scientific discovery,
   by being awarded the responsibility to lead a team of professionals in a new investigation?

Also, note the setting in which key activities took place. Were they when you were alone, with a few others, with many others; which organization were you with at the time or was it preinstitutional; did they occur when you were younger or older, etc.

Interests   *Setting*

2. What activities stand out as particularly disinteresting to me; what was their setting?

Disinterests	*Setting*

After going through your work autobiography, consider the following question:

3. Are there interests which I have or am engaging in outside the work setting, but which I wish could somehow be incorporated into my work?

Interest outside work	*(√) if could be incorporated into work*	*(√) if desire them to be incorporated into work*

4. Now go back over your interest list from question 1 as well as your double-checked list from question 3. Are there repeated interests? If so, can you cluster them?

    Clustered Interests   *New label I shall give them*

become

5. Prioritize all your interests. If you have developed a massive list (greater than 10), it is not necessary to rank each one; you could group them into levels. Try to have about five levels. The determinants of your priorities should incorporate the following considerations:
    a. which interests am I willing to devote considerable time
    b. which interests exact a great deal of my energy
    c. which interests am I willing to spend a lot of money on
    d. which interests really represent who I am as a person
    e. which interests do I take particular pride in

Final Priority List of Interests

Level One

1.
2.
3.

Level Two

4.
5.
6.

Level Three

7.
8.
9.

Level Four

10.
11.
12.

Level Five

13.
14.
15.

6. Now, as the last part of this exercise and of specific concern to your self-assessment, consider these final two questions:
   a. Based upon your priority list of interests, how would you characterize yourself in terms of the things which really seem to capture and hold your interests? (for example, that I need to have clear goals and ways to measure them; that I seem to have a fascination with numbers; that I have had my "ups" and "downs," but my "ups" have occurred when my interests at work dovetail with my interests at home)
   b. What are the settings in which you particularly thrive? What are the settings which you need to avoid? (for example, I can't seem to get motivated by myself, but give me a few good people to work with, and I come alive!)

Skills

As stated earlier, skills are physical and mental abilities which emanate from education and work. They are also the most basic component of one's career in that they combine in various ways to form the tasks required in the jobs which one does. Performance of a wide variety of tasks in the jobs you have held throughout your career as well as through your education has already provided you with an array of skills.

This section will attempt to dissect your work and educational history in such a way that these learned skills will become more readily apparent, and consequently, of greater service to you in your career development.

The work of Sidney Fine[4] and Richard Bolles[5] is most helpful in analyzing skills. According to Bolles, skills may be divided into three categories: work-content skills, functional skills, and self-management skills. The work-content skills are most apparent to all of us as they relate to the substantive nature of our work and profession. They are derived from our professional training as well as from knowledge derived through our work experience. These skills constitute those specific abilities which demonstrate understanding of our professional subject matter, vocabulary, and procedures. Displaying general competence and dexterity in the design of digital and analog devices, organizing the financial records of a company to make up its balance sheet, pursuing research on a specific topic, are all examples of work-content skills.

The functional skills do not have a specific substantive base; that is, they are not tied to a line of work. Rather, they constitute abilities basic to our performance of three major functions: data, people and things. Fine's research distilled 30 verbs, arranged in Figure 2-2, from an examination of some four thousand job definitions. Note that these verbs are transferable from one occupation to another. Hence, they are especially critical to professional career development as they are not confined to fixed work environments or positions. Complete definitions of Fine's functional skills are provided in the Appendix. Professionals are more inclined to work with people or data. It may be helpful in order to get a better grasp of these skills to break down (as shown in Table 2-3) the people function into two subfunctions: service and management; and the data function into three subfunctions: numerical, creative, and abstract. It should be apparent that the functional skills are not necessarily derived from one's formal training, but also emanate from general education, experiences, and talent. Exchanging information with others on the results of one's research, computing logarithmic functions, operating machines, or supervising others in such operation are all examples of functional skills.

Finally, the self-management skills are the least obvious and tangible of the three skill categories but perhaps the most critical for career development. They entail a person's ability to get along

FIGURE 2-2
Summary Chart of Worker Function Scales

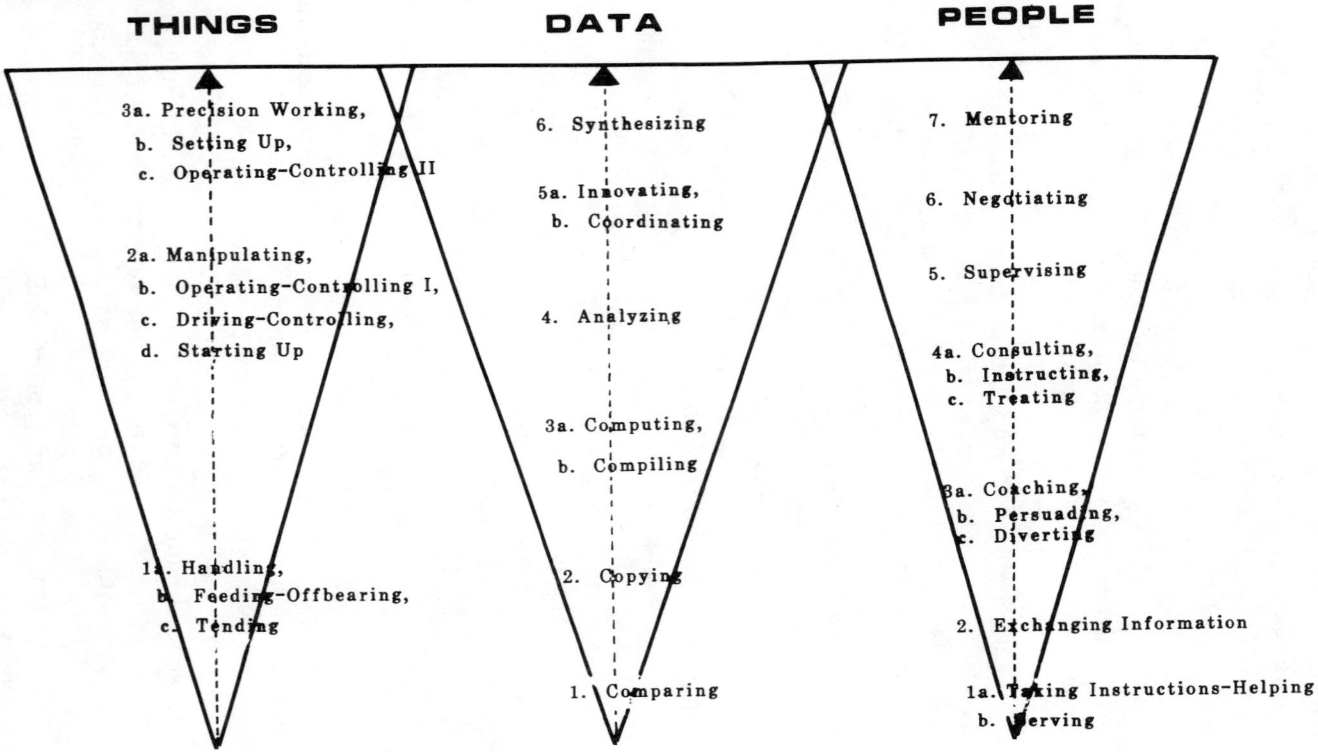

THINGS

3a. Precision Working,
b. Setting Up,
c. Operating-Controlling II

2a. Manipulating,
b. Operating-Controlling I,
c. Driving-Controlling,
d. Starting Up

1a. Handling,
b. Feeding-Offbearing,
c. Tending

DATA

6. Synthesizing

5a. Innovating,
b. Coordinating

4. Analyzing

3a. Computing,
b. Compiling

2. Copying

1. Comparing

PEOPLE

7. Mentoring

6. Negotiating

5. Supervising

4a. Consulting,
b. Instructing,
c. Treating

3a. Coaching,
b. Persuading,
c. Diverting

2. Exchanging Information

1a. Taking Instructions-Helping
b. Serving

Notes:

1. Each hierarchy is independent of the other. It would be incorrect to read the functions across the three hierarchies as related because they appear to be on the same level. The definitive relationship among functions is within each hierarchy, not across hierarchies. Some broad exceptions are made in the next note.

2. Data is central since a worker can be assigned even higher data functions although Things and People functions remain at the lowest level of their respective scales. This is not so for Things and People functions. When a Things function is at the third level, e.g., Precision Working, the Data function is likely to be at least Compiling or Computing. When a People function is at the fourth level, e.g., Consulting, the Data function is likely to be at least Analyzing and possibly Innovating or Coordinating. Similarly for Supervising and Negotiating. Mentoring is some instances can call for Synthesizing.

3. Each function in its hierarchy is defined to include the lower numbered functions. This is more or less the way it was found to occur in reality. It was most clear-cut for Things and Data and only a rough approximation in the case of People.

4. The functions separated by a comma are separate functions on the same level, separately defined. The empirical evidence did not support a hierarchical distinction.

5. The hyphenated functions, Taking Instructions-Helping, Operating-Controlling, etc. are single functions.

6. The indented functions in the Things hierarchy are machine oriented as opposed to the hand or hand tool oriented functions (Handling, Manipulating, or Precision Working). They can be considered as parallel hierarchies.

Source: Reprinted by permission of Sidney A. Fine, Copyright 1979.

TABLE 2-3   Functional Skills

A. DATA
1. Numerical Category
   a. organizing, classifying, processing
   b. copying, compiling, computing, inventorying
   c. budgeting, allocating
   d. analyzing, synthesizing
2. Creative Category
   a. imagining, innovating, creating
   b. symbolizing, designing
3. Abstract Category
   a. sensing, feeling
   b. observing, reflecting, estimating
   c. reasoning, abstracting, diagnosing
   d. clarifying, surveying, experimenting, researching
   e. inspecting, reviewing, critiquing, assessing, choosing

B. PEOPLE
1. Service Category
   a. speaking, writing, reading, communicating
   b. coaching, instructing, supervising
   c. influencing, motivating, negotiating
   d. caring, listening, understanding, helping
   e. performing, modeling, playing, singing, dancing, competing
2. Management Category
   a. initiating, leading, solving, risking
   b. planning, implementing, evaluating
   c. questioning, guiding, inspiring, reviewing, developing, mentoring
   d. consulting, informing, assisting, conferring, recommending

C. THINGS
   a. tending, feeding, washing, handling
   b. operating, manipulating, shaping
   c. adjusting, repairing
   d. lifting, moving

Source: Based on the work of Sidney A. Fine, *A Systems Approach to Manpower Development in Human Services*. Kalamazoo: The W. E. Upjohn Institute for Employment Research, 1969.

with others, to relate to authority figures, to act appropriately in different situations, to control one's impulses, to know when to be firm and when to be flexible, etc. In other words, they describe the capacity of individuals to adjust to varying environments. They are not typically part of formal learning; rather, they are usually derived from early experiences in family, school, and/or work. Although, as Bolles states, there is no authorized list of self-management skills, his is sufficiently complete so as to assess one's strengths and weaknesses in this area. The list is provided in Table 2-4.

TABLE 2-4   Self-Management Skills

Ability to choose, or make a decision	High energy level, dynamic
Alertness	Honesty, integrity
Assertiveness	Initiative, drive
Astuteness	Loyalty
Attention to details, awareness, thoroughness, conscientiousness	Openmindedness
	Optimism
Authenticity	Orderliness
Calmness	Patience, persistence
Candor	Performing well under stress
Commitment to grow	Playfulness
Concentration	Poise, self-confidence
Cooperation	Politeness
Courage, risk taking, adventuresomeness	Punctuality
	Reliability, dependability
Curiosity	Resourcefulness
Diplomacy	Self-control
Easy goingness	Self-reliance
Emotional stability	Self-respect
Empathy	Sense of humor
Enthusiasm	Sincerity
Expressiveness	Spontaneity
Firmness	Tactfulness
Flexibility	Tidiness
Generosity	Tolerance
Good judgment	Versatility

Source: From *The Three Boxes of Life* by Richard Nelson Bolles. Copyright 1981. Used with permission. Available from Ten Speed Press, Box 7123, Berkeley, CA 94707. $8.95 + .75 for postage and handling.

EXERCISE 2-4

A. SKILLS ASSESSMENT. Based upon the preceding theoretical presentation, this exercise is designed to have you identify your personal strengths and limitations vis-a-vis skills. For those readers who have already done some work in this area, there are two optional exercises which will surely supplement your previous experiences. The present exercise, however, is recommended as the principal methodology to perform a skills assessment.

To begin, you are once again requested to refer to your work autobiography and educational history. In this exercise, you may find it most useful to review your record three different times as you will be looking for skills in three different categories. Before working on each category, examine the definitions and charts in the text very carefully.

1. What are my key work-content skills? What support or evidence can I cite from my work autobiography to acknowledge their emergence? For example, did I develop these from one specific job, over time from reading, from a role-model in school, from a hobby, etc.?

       Work-Content Skills   *Support/Evidence*

2. What are my key functional skills?

       Functional Skills   *Support/Evidence*

3. What are my key self-management skills?

       Self-Management Skills   *Support/Evidence*

4. Examine the three lists of skills above. Which skills do I value the most? Which ones would I like to use more in my job? (Label the skill by placing one of three letters after each skill: "W" if work-content, "F" if functional, "S" if self-management.)

> *Skills Valued*   *Skills to Use More*

5. Can you identify any skills from any or all of the three categories which you currently do *not* have, but which you would desperately like to acquire? (Label these as above.) Indicate how you might acquire them. (For example, would you need to take a specific course, to consult a colleague, to join a committee, to study at home by yourself, etc.?)

> *Skills Desired*   *How to Acquire*

B. SKILLS ASSESSMENT (Option #1). Henry Pearson[6] has developed a list of skills, which seem to combine some of the principal elements of both the self-management and functonal skills and which he refers to as "transkills." They are so named because they are not confined to a special work or learning environment but can be transferred from one activity to another. Pearson agrees with the contention proposed earlier that the transferable skills (functional and self-management) are the ones most critical to career development. Pearson's list of skills are included in Table 2-5, in what he refers to as the Transkills Finder.

1. With the transkills finder in hand, review your work and educational histories. What are my key transkills?

> *Transkills*   *Support/Evidence*

2. Which transkills would I most like to develop? How might I acquire them?

Transkills to be Developed   *How to Acquire*

TABLE 2-5   The Transkills Finder

WORDS	Applying knowledge to	Improvising/inventing
Reading	technical things	Conceptualizing
Writing		**Intuitive Thinking**
Conversing	**THE BODY**	Sizing up
Interviewing	Coordinating eyes/body	Having insight
Reporting information	Being physically active	**Gaining Knowledge**
	Applying strength	Learning
NUMBERS	Moving around	Investigating/research-
Calculating	Coordinating eyes/hands	ing
Working with figures	Using hands	Memorizing
Estimating	Operating things/tools	Recalling
Handling money	Using fingers	Analyzing
Buying/shopping	Building/making	Evaluating
Economizing	Repairing/fixing	**Thinking Ahead**
		Planning/goal setting
ARTISTIC ABILITIES	**THE SENSES**	Using foresight
Using artistic talents	Observing	Being logical/reasoning
Being creative	Examining	Problem solving/deci-
Sensing beauty through	Inspecting	sion making involving:
eyes/ears	Visualizing	people, information,
Interpreting feelings,	Listening/hearing	things, ideas
ideas, sights, sounds	Touching/feeling	
		BEING ORGANIZED
MECHANICAL/TECH-	**THE MIND**	**Organizing**
NICAL ABILITIES	**Original Thinking**	Starting things up
Making machines and	Coming up with ideas	Scheduling
mechanical things work	Using imagination	Following up

Table 2-5, continued

Persisting	Raising/training living	**Taking Direction**
Getting result(s)	things	Getting and delivering
Meeting demands:	Dealing with elements/	things
quantity, quality, dead-	nature	Adapting to others
lines		Following directions
Attending to Detail	**RELATIONS WITH**	**Instructing**
Being thorough/careful	**OTHERS**	Training/coaching
Being accurate/exact	**Persuading**	Teaching
Using system	Influencing	Explaining
Being neat/orderly	Selling	Informing
Using clerical skills	Promoting	**Leading**
Keeping records	Negotiating	Directing others
Maintaining routines	Bargaining	Managing
	Performing for Others	Motivating
SELF-DIRECTING	Entertaining	Being responsible for
Asserting self	Speaking	others' actions
Taking risks	Using showmanship	**Associating**
Taking on responsibil-	Demonstrating	Cooperating
ity	**Helping Others**	Sharing
Being independent	Being of service	Contacting
Being self-disciplined	Serving	Consulting with
Keeping cool	Volunteering	Being tactful
Developing self	Doing favors	Socializing
	Meeting others' physi-	Being friendly
RELATIONS WITH	cal needs	Making joint effort
OUTDOOR AND	Being sensitive	Making team effort
NATURAL WORLD	Guiding/advising	**Being Competitive**
Taking care of living	Encouraging	Winning
things	Being patient	Contending

Source: The Transkill Finder, reprinted with the permission of the author, from *Your Hidden Skills: Clues to Careers and Future Pursuits*, by Henry G. Pearson, Mowry Press, Box 405, Wayland, MA 01778, 1981, $8.50.

C. SKILLS ASSESSMENT (Option #2). If, due to time constraints or previous exposure to skills assessment, you find it cumbersome to go through the complete analysis in the previous exercises, you should nonetheless review your principal strengths in five areas of personal skill development (technical, administrative, communications, social, and personal).[7] Which ones do you need to work on?

	Strengths	Skills Needing Development
1. Technical: scientific, engineering, computer, research, analysis, legal		
2. Administrative: operating, planning, organizational, problem-solving		
3. Communications: writing, speaking, foreign language, negotiating		
4. Social: conflict resolution, human relations, understanding others, ability to instill confidence		
5. Personal: memory, creativity, adaptability, force of personality		

Source: Reprinted with permission of the publisher from: Burack, Elmer H. and Mathys, Nicholas J. *Career Management in Organizations: A Practical Human Resource Planning Approach*. Lake Forest, IL: Brace-Park Press, 1980, pp. 223-24.

LEARNING STYLE

Up to this point, the self-assessment has focused on interests and skills — two elements which contribute to one's knowledge base. The intent of these initial phases of the self-assessment has been to assist the reader in examining the activities and abilities which contribute to his or her identity as a working professional. These phases, however, have not directly explored how knowledge is acquired. In this section, I expressly consider the process of knowledge acquisition, referred to here as one's learning style. Particularly given the pressures on professionals to keep updated in their field or face the threat of obsolescence (a subject which will be given explicit attention in the next chapter), the subject of how one continues to learn is of critical importance in professional career development.

Learning is also a critical phase of self-assessment as it provides the base for each individual's understanding of his or her world and his or her role in it. Indeed, learning is the vehicle through which one develops the capacity to move through the work-related sequences of one's life; hence, it is vital to personal career development.

It is apparent, however, that learning styles vary a great deal among professionals. Further, they get accentuated through repetition in one's line of work. Discontinuity between the learning style of the individual versus that of the organization can also become debilitating. Hence, it is critical that professionals correctly assess their learning style to better ensure a fit with their organizational environment as well as with their overall career.

To the extent learning is consonant with change, it typically requires some kind of behavioral manifestation. Behavior is caused; it results from an expression of need or from one's motivation. According to the psychology of operant conditioning,[8] if behavior succeeds in meeting a need, that behavior becomes reinforced. The quicker the reinforcement, usually the faster the learning of that particular behavior. This presents the usefulness of feedback in stimulating learning. Generally speaking, a compatible learning environment, compatible in the sene of style fit, is most conducive to growth for the professional. This is because it provides positive reinforcement which allows identification of the specific behavior which induced the learning. Negative reinforcement or punishment, which may be inflicted in an incompatible environment, doesn't often allow such identification. The exception to this situation is where the reinforcement does not provide for the occasional unfreezing of one's familiar behavior. We hear people sometimes talk of the benefit of being *shook up* every now and then, so that they can learn something new. An environment which presents general compatibility with one's style but which allows for some diversity and experimentation, for immediate feedback of performance, including occasional negative reinforcement, is conducive to productive learning.

The thrust of this section is that the assessment of learning style focuses not so much on learning outcome but learning process. What are the conditions most propitious to your personal learning as an adult professional? What specific climates induce learning among adults? What is your personal learning style and how will it affect your career development?

Beyond the more specific purpose of career development itself, adults appear to be highly motivated to learn due to their own self-esteem. However, once on the job and raising a family, there are many pressures on the individual which demand time. These pressures compete with time for study. Adulthood is also characterized by learning which becomes more and more specialized, as compared to the more generalized requirements of childhood. While working toward mastery of one's particular career tasks, time must also be allotted for experimentation.

Formal learning presents a certain amount of frustration to the adult, then, as it must compete with other life demands. Moreover, the adult, now out of the routines of daily schoolwork, may lack confidence in the ability to learn. To insure effective learning, the adult should be allowed to set the learning pace, to work on real problems as opposed to exercises which seem irrelevant, to set personal goals for learning, and as stated earlier, to receive immediate feedback on progress toward goal accomplishment.[9] According to the characterizations of professionals provided in Chapter One, the professional is also seen as someone who is committed to his field and who wishes to have the autonomy to choose not only the examination of but the means with which to solve problems.

Turning now to the appropriate climate for learning among professionals, it should preferably be supportive, person-centered, and spontaneous. Beyond this general setting there are at least seven specific climates in which learning can occur. As you review these seven climates, can you identify which one(s) characterize your optimal learning conditions?

1. Learning primarily by myself independently in an individualized fashion.
2. Learning through mutual study with a few others.
3. Learning within a group at the group's pace.
4. Learning through experience.
5. Learning with the aid of pictures and sounds and other audio-visual devices.
6. Learning by reading.
7. Learning by listening to others, for example, through lecture.

Having considered the conditions and climates conducive to learning, I would like to turn to the notion of learning style. As individuals, we each develop personal styles which emphasize some learning abilities over others. Although it is important to vary and thereby enrich our learning abilities, it is apparent from research that dominant styles do in fact persist over time. Kolb, Rubin, and McIntyre[10] identified four different kinds of abilities critical to learning: concrete experience (CE), reflective observation (RO), abstract conceptualization (AC), and active experimentation (AE). CE was defined as being able to involve oneself fully, openly, and without bias in new experiences; RO as being able to reflect on and observe these experiences from many perspectives; AC as being able to create concepts that integrate one's observations into logically sound theories; and AE as then being able to use these theories to make decisions and solve problems. Kolb,[11] although arguing that these abilities should be integrated for optimal learning, found in his continuing research that four styles emerged which characterize most people. These four styles, including their main characteristics, strengths and weaknesses, problem-solving modality, and dominant professional type, are depicted in capsule form in Table 2-6. The last category, dominant professional type, though drawn in part from Kolb's research, is purely hypothetical.

In brief, *convergers* show dominance in abstract conceptualization (AC) and active experimentation (AE). Their strength lies in the practical application of ideas. *Divergers* combine opposite abilities, namely, concrete experience (CE) and reflective observation (RO). Their strength lies in imaginative ability. *Assimilators* combine abstract conceptualization (AC) and reflective observation (RO) and consequently do well in creating theoretical models. Finally, *accommodators* combine concrete experience (CE) and active experimentation (AE), allowing them the facility to get things done.

Consistent with Kolb's contention that learning styles will persist for some individuals, Kolb and Plovnick[12] found that certain styles seemed to depict the career patterns of individuals. Using an instrument which detects dominant styles, Figure 2-3 displays the distributions of a sample of undergraduate majors.

Kolb and Plovnick found that these styles were accentuated during the early career; in other words, learning environments were sought consistent with one's learning style. Given the pressures

TABLE 2-6   Learning Style Capsules

CONCRETE EXPERIENCE

THE ACCOMMODATOR	THE DIVERGER
Main Characteristics: Likes doing things and getting involved in new experiences. Doesn't mind taking risks. Able to adapt to different environments. Operates on trial and error and "gut" reaction.	Main Characteristics: Likes to look at things from different perspectives. Uses imagination. Good at generating ideas. Oriented to relationships with people. Supportive.
Strengths: Goal-oriented action and accomplishment.	Strengths: Creativity and brainstorming.
Weaknesses: Work not completed effectively. Problem-Solving Modality: Deciding on one's goals and executing solutions. Dominant Professional Type: Nonprofessional.	Weaknesses: Inability to act on good ideas. Problem-Solving Modality: Identifying problems and opportunities based on reality. Dominant Professional Type: Psychologists.
THE CONVERGER	THE ASSIMILATOR
Main Characteristics: Likes to work on problems that have a single correct solution. Interested in practical applications of ideas. Uses reason and logic.	Main Characteristics: Likes to create theoretical models. Good at synthesizing. Is organized, precise, and careful.
Strengths: Design and decision making.	Strengths: Planning and theoretical insights.

ACTIVE EXPERIMENTATION

60

Weaknesses: Theories not tested. Insufficient focus.
Problem-Solving Modality: Evaluating consequences and selecting solutions.
Dominant Professional Type: Engineers, nurses.

Weaknesses: Unable to learn from mistakes.
Problem-Solving Modality: Building models and considering alternatives.
Dominant Professional Type: Scientists.

ABSTRACT CONCEPTUALIZATION

Source: Based on the work of David A. Kolb, esp. Chap. 2, pp. 27-54 in David A. Kolb, Irwin M. Rubin, and James M. McIntyre, *Organizational Psychology: An Experiential Approach.* Englewood Cliffs, N.J.: Prentice-Hall, 1979.

FIGURE 2-3
Learning Style by Undergraduate Major

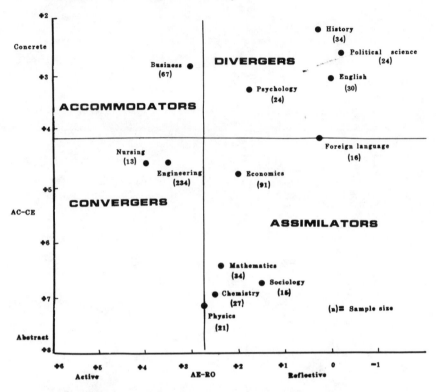

Source: "The Experiential Learning Theory of Career Development," by David A. Kolb and Mark S. Plovnick, in John Van Maanen (ed.), *Organizational Careers: Some New Perspectives.* Copyright © 1977, by John Wiley & Sons, Ltd. Reprinted by permission of John Wiley & Sons, Ltd.

in youth to find jobs, errors are naturally made, in which case, young workers are inclined to move from incompatible to compatible learning environments.

Keen's research[13] is consistent with that of Kolb and Plovnick but lends additional insight into the predominant styles of professionals. Keen contends that about 30 percent of the population has a dominant style and that specialized jobs seem to be associated with particular styles. Unfortunately, some of the problems encountered by professionals within organizations arise from learning style differences, especially between them and management. The pure professional, besides invariably being a cognitive specialist, typically relies on a systematic mode of problem-solving. The manager, besides being a generalist, tends to operate in the intuitive mode. A number of attributes characterize these two styles, for example, the systematic approaches a problem through an ordered sequence of search and analysis, whereas the intuitive prefers to keep the overall problem continuously in mind. Other cognitive differences are displayed below in Table 2-7; Keen's findings on the occupational choices of each style are displayed in Table 2-8. The critical point is that some professionals may be working under a learning style inconsistent with management and that recognition of this potential style difference may go a long way toward resolving operating problems otherwise outside the control of the affected parties.

TABLE 2-7   Characteristics of Systematic vs. Intuitive Cognitive Styles

---

Systematic thinkers tend to:
    Look for a method and make a plan for solving a problem
    Be very conscious of their approach
    Defend the quality of a solution largely in terms of the method
    Define the specific constraints of the problem early in the
        process
    Move through a process of increasing refinement of analysis
    Conduct an ordered search for additional information
    Complete any discrete step in analysis that they set out on

Intuitive thinkers tend to:
    Keep the overall problem continuously in mind
    Redefine the problem frequently as they proceed
    Rely on unverbalized cues, even hunches
    Defend a solution in terms of "fit"
    Consider a number of alternatives and options simultaneously
    Explore and abandon alternatives quickly

Source: "Cognitive Style and Career Specialization," by Peter G. W. Keen, in John Van Maanen (ed.), *Organizational Careers: Some New Perspectives*. Copyright © 1977, by John Wiley & Sons, Ltd. Reprinted by permission of John Wiley & Sons, Ltd.

TABLE 2-8   Occupation Preferred by Systematics and Intuitives

Systematics	Intuitives
Management science	Psychology
Production	Librarianship
Engineering	Law
Computer programming	Journalism
Finance	Advertising
Military	Arts

Source: "Cognitive Style and Career Specialization," by Peter G. W. Keen, in John Van Maanen (ed.), *Organizational Careers: Some New Perspectives*. Copyright © 1977, by John Wiley & Sons, Ltd. Reprinted by permission of John Wiley & Sons, Ltd.

A popular instrument has been developed by Kolb[14] to measure learning style. It is called the Learning Style Inventory or LSI and is available from McBer and Company of Boston. The LSI has come under some sharp criticism, however, in recent years, especially by Richard D. Freedman and Stephen A. Stumpf,[15] relative to its reliability and validity. A key question seems to be whether the LSI measures a stable property — learning style. Kolb contends that learning style might vary for any individual from situation to situation.

Rather than use the LSI, the next exercise asks you to rate yourself on the four abilities which in Kolb's research were found to be critical to learning. You will then construct a profile which might reveal a learning style preference. Although not as scientifically based as the formal LSI, the exercise should involve you in a direct examination of your personally developed process of learning.

EXERCISE 2-5

A. PERSONAL LEARNING STYLE ANALYSIS. According to Kolb's work just recently cited, effective learners rely on four principal learning activities or modes. Below, these four activities are briefly described. Following each activity is a seven-point rating scale in which you are to rate how you personally view your strength on that particular activity. If you don't use that activity at all, you would circle a one on the scale. If you use it fully, you would circle a seven. If you use it an average amount, you would circle a four, and so on. For purposes of the exercise, the four activities are to be viewed as independent of one another so that you should not feel, for example, that if you score highly on one, you would need to compensate by giving a lower score to another.

INSTRUCTIONS:
Circle the number on each scale which represents your strength in using the learning activity described.

Concrete Experience: I involve myself openly in new experiences; I use my feelings to understand new things.

    1   ②   3   4   5   6   7
not at all   fully

Reflective Observation: I observe and reflect on new experiences, often using a variety of perspectives.

    1   ②   3   4   5   6   7
not at all   fully

Abstract Conceptualization: I am able to create concepts or integrate my observations into logically sound theories.

    1   2   ③   4   5   6   7
not at all   fully

Active Experimentation: I'm a doer. I take theories and use them to make decisions and solve problems.

    1   2   ③   4   5   6   7
not at all   fully

Now that you have rated your key learning activities, you can use the profile matrix in Figure 2-4 to determine whether you have a dominant style. Simply place a dot corresponding to the rating given for each learning activity on the appropriate segment of the matrix. Then connect the four dots. Does any one line fill in a significant portion of any one quadrant? If so, you may have one or more learning style preferences. Be sure to review the textual material, especially Table 2-6, to see whether you agree with your style depictions.

If you have a dominant style, how can you build on your strengths? Do you need to improve on your weaknesses? If you're a converger, for example, is it true that you don't sufficiently test your theories? If so, how has that affected your career, if at all, as revealed in your work autobiography? Do you wish to assume more control over your theoretical applications?

If you don't have a dominant style, is it because you practice all learning activities equally well? Have you avoided certain learning modes? How critical are any deficiencies in performing your job? What steps can you take to make up for any deficiencies?

FIGURE 2-4
Learning Profile Matrix

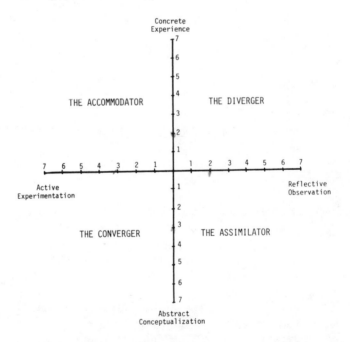

Source: Adapted from David A. Kolb, Irwin M. Rubin, and James M. McIntyre, *Organizational Psychology: An Experiential Approach*. Englewood Cliffs, N.J.: Prentice-Hall, 1979, p. 41. And through the advice of Professor Kolb.

B. LEARNING STYLE EVALUATION (Option). The following questions are designed to tap your learning style preferences as well as your learning capacity.

1. Which of the seven learning climates identified in the text are you most comfortable in? Have you attempted to learn under differing climates?
2. Which of the four learning styles identified in the text best characterizes your learning? Have you attempted to integrate the four principle learning abilities: (1) concrete experience, (2) reflective observation, (3) abstract conceptualization, (4) and active experimentation?
3. Are you motivated to learn right now? Do you have an inquiring mind? Are you willing to test your assumptions?
4. Are you capable of directing your own learning? Can you be objective? Are you open to feedback from others?
5. Are there any blocks to your learning? Can you release yourself from unproductive learning habits?
6. What resources are available to you in accomplishing your desired learning tasks? Are there people who can assist you?
7. Does your organization provide the facilities necessary to stimulate your continued learning?
8. What courses or educational activities, on-the-job or classroom, are available to you?
9. Do you prefer to focus your learning in nonwork-related areas? Why? Do these relate to your interests, identified in the previous section?

PSYCHOLOGICAL NEEDS

Having examined your knowledge base, the chapter now redirects the self-assessment to a diagnosis of your values and how they relate to your personal career development. Although values have been defined very broadly to include not only attitudinal but also spiritual aspects of our identity, I shall concentrate only on the former and in particular will examine attitudes which are thought to shape career behavior. I begin this section with a discussion of work-related psychological needs. Later in the chapter, I shall also review personality traits, career anchors, and life space concerns to round out the discussion of career values.

In the previous section, I explained that learning and its behavioral manifestations were derived from our needs. The inner organization of these needs forms the basis of motivation. If our inner or psychological needs are satisfied, we are happy and become motivated to continue to fulfill these and perhaps even higher needs. If our psychological needs are not satisfied, we become frustrated and may even lose interest in these needs, although we may continue to try to meet them, perhaps in different ways.

In pursuing a career, we engage in a variety of behaviors (in our job performance, our contact with others, our skill utilization, etc.) which hopefully will satisfy our needs. Our needs or, more broadly, values, represent things which contribute meaning to our lives. If there is congruency between our needs and job conditions, then we will tend to be satisfied with our job and contribute to the organization in which we are a part. Hence, need fulfillment becomes a key element of career development both from the individual and organizational point of view.

Pre-eminent in the study and identification of psychological needs is Abraham Maslow.[16] Maslow reasoned that our needs are shaped in a hierarchy such that it is possible to strive for higher needs only after accomplishment of those needs which are of a lower order. The familiar triangular model is presented in Figure 2-5.

Accordingly, the lowest needs are physiological, namely, needs for food, clothing, and shelter. On the job, this typically converts to demands for more pay. The next need is that of safety which in recent times is represented by the importance of job seniority or tenure, pension plans, insurance programs, and savings accounts. The third level, the social needs, represents people's desire to belong, to be loved and respected by others, to have friends. This can be represented in the work place by a bonus, by belonging to work groups, or by plain social interaction with colleagues. At the fourth level are the self-esteem needs which are represented by such attributes as responsibility, achievement, challenge, and recognition. This level has two components, an external and internal aspect. The external consists of one's sense of competence and achievement as seen by others. The internal aspect represents one's self-perceptions. Finally, the last and highest level is that of self-actualization, a state consistently attained by few individuals. At this level, the predominant attribute is self-acceptance and the realization of one's full potential.

Maslow's hierarchy has been subjected to a great deal of scrutiny over the years. Some observers believe that the two lower needs have virtually been accomplished by all adults except for our most

FIGURE 2-5
Hierarchy of Needs

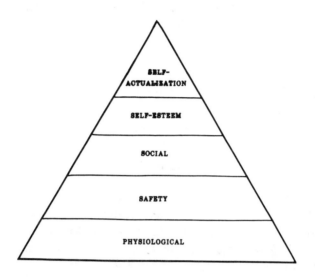

Source: Based on the work of Abraham Maslow, especially his "A Theory of Human Motivation" in *Motivation and Personality*, 2nd edition. New York: Harper & Row, 1970.

disenfranchised societal members. On the other hand, the needs represented at the lower levels may be represented by a greater array of requirements. In other words, the physiological needs may require a television in the home, a college education, or even a job in order to achieve fulfillment.

Maslow's hierarchical framework itself has been questioned. Does one really need to satisfy the lower-order needs to get to the higher ones? It may well be that each of the needs operates on us at different times with different relative strengths. Based upon some prior research efforts, Alderfer[17] combined the seven needs of Maslow into three levels and argued that his levels do not necessarily develop hierarchically. Alderfer's model was called ERG, after the three levels: (1) *existence*, combining Maslow's physiological and safety needs; (2) *relatedness*, combining the social and external aspect of Maslow's self-esteem needs; and (3) *growth*, combining Maslow's internal self-esteem and self-actualization needs.

Less complicated frameworks of needs identification have been proposed. Mitchell[18] identified four principal needs of man: (1) competence and curiosity, (2) achievement, (3) affiliation, and (4) power. Herzberg[19] discussed two principal needs — hygienes and motivators. There is approximate correspondence between Maslow's lower-order needs (the first three levels) and Herzberg's hygienic factors and Maslow's higher-order needs and Herzberg's motivating factors. However, Herzberg's research suggested that true satisfaction on the job could only be accomplished through the motivators, that is, through achievement, recognition, challenge, and responsibility. All the hygienic factors, namely, a good salary, safe working conditions, fair supervision, congenial colleagues, could do would be to prevent one from becoming dissatisfied.

Another way to view the hygiene-motivator dichotomy was demonstrated by Souerwine.[20] According to him, hygiene satisfaction tends to move a person away from the lower-order needs. On the other hand, motivator satisfaction tends to keep a person around the source of the satisfaction — the higher-order needs. For example, if you request a transfer and get it, then your need to get a new boss or new colleagues may be satisfied; you can now move on to other needs. However, if you are recognized for your fine work, you tend to want more of the same. Hence, the key to career satisfaction comes mostly from placing oneself in work environments which allow for the pursuit and satisfaction of the higher-order needs. Note the word "satisfaction" of higher-order needs. It is imperative that the professional obtain at least occasional satisfaction of these needs; otherwise, as was stated initially in this section, frustration will set in. The immediate response to the frustration tends to be a return to the lower-order needs and perhaps, as was discussed in Chapter One, the practice of deviant/adaptive behavior. For example, in a job which severely limits the discretion you have over your own assignments, you might become more concerned about salary, you might become more involved in gossip, etc. Avoiding nongrowth-oriented behavior, then, is vital to successful career development. It starts with careful identification of individual higher-order needs. Following identification, the choice can be made to pursue realization of one's needs, which in turn should lead to satisfaction.

In the ensuing exercise, you will have an opportunity to identify your principal psychological needs. An interpretation for professionals will be provided once you have finished.

EXERCISE 2-6

NEEDS IDENTIFICATION QUESTIONNAIRE. The questionnaire featured in this exercise was developed by Lyman W. Porter originally to measure managerial motivation. The questionnaire has since been used to measure needs in all types of people. All of Maslow's need levels are incorporated in this instrument except for the physiological needs, which I expect most professionals to have satisfied.

As you respond to the questionnaire, think about the importance to you personally of each characteristic described in terms of your current job. If you are not currently employed, respond in terms of your last job. If you have never worked, respond in terms of your expectations relative to the job you'll have when you start working.

Needs Identification Questionnaire

INSTRUCTIONS:
Given below are several characteristics or qualities connected with your job. For each such characteristic, rate how important this characteristic is to you.

Each rating will be on a seven-point scale, which will look like this:

(minimum)   1   2   3   4   5   6   7   (maximum)

You are to *circle the number* on the scale that represents the importance of the characteristic being rated. Low numbers represent low or minimum amounts, and high numbers represent high or maximum amounts. If you think there is very little or none of the characteristic that is important in your job, you would circle a one. If you think there is just a little, you would circle a two, and so on. If you think there is a great deal but not a maximum amount, you would circle a six. For each scale, circle only one number. *Please do not omit any scales.*

1. The feeling of self-esteem a person gets from being in my job position:

    1   (2)   3   4   5   6   7
    min   max

2. The opportunity for personal growth and development in my job position:

    1   2   3   (4)   5   6   7
    min   max

3. The prestige of my job inside the company (in other words, the regard received from others in the company):

1	(2)	3	4	5	6	7
min						max

4. The opportunity for independent thought and action in my position:

1	(2)	3	4	5	6	7
min						max

5. The feeling of security in my job position:

1	2	3	4	5	(6)	7
min						max

6. The feeling of self-fulfillment a person gets from being in my job position; that is, the feeling of being able to use my own unique capabilities, realizing potentialities:

1	2	(3)	4	5	6	7
min						max

7. The prestige of my job position outside the company (in other words, the regard received from others not in the company):

1	2	3	4	(5)	6	7
min						max

8. The feeling of worthwhile accomplishment in my job:

1	2	3	(4)	5	6	7
min						max

9. The opportunity, in my job, to give help to other people:

1	2	3	4	(5)	6	7
min						max

10. The opportunity, in my job, for participation in the setting of goals:

1	(2)	3	4	5	6	7
min						max

11. The opportunity, in my job, for participation in the determination of methods and procedures:

| 1 | 2 | ③ | 4 | 5 | 6 | 7 |
| min | | | | | | max |

12. The authority connected with my job:

| 1 | ② | 3 | 4 | 5 | 6 | 7 |
| min | | | | | | max |

13. The opportunity to develop close friendships in my job:

| 1 | 2 | 3 | ④ | 5 | 6 | 7 |
| min | | | | | | max |

Source: Adapted from *Experiences in Management and Organizational Behavior*, by Douglas T. Hall, Donald D. Bowen, Roy T. Lewicki, and Francine S. Hall. Copyright © 1982 by John Wiley & Sons, Inc. Reprinted by permission of John Wiley & Sons, Inc.

SCORING:
Compute your need score for each of the need categories, using the scoring form in Table 2.9.

1. Enter the number you circled for each question in the space next to that number.
2. Next, add up the numbers in each column to obtain your total score for each need.
3. Divide by the number of questions used to measure that need to obtain your score.
4. You can then compare your score against Porter's managerial sample.

Professional Needs

Since the norms in Porter's questionnaire were based on managerial positions, it would be more instructive for purposes of this book to compare against professionals. Seiler[21] administered a job needs questionnaire to newly hired professionals (mostly engineers) working

TABLE 2-9 Needs Identification Scoring Form

	SECURITY	SOCIAL	ESTEEM	AUTONOMY	SELF-REALIZATION
	5 =	9 = 13 =	1 = 3 = 7 =	4 = 10 = 11 = 12 =	2 = 6 = 8 =
Total	6	9	11	9	4
Divided by	1	2	3	4	3
Equals Score	6	4.5	3.67	2.25	3.67
National Mean[a]	5.33	5.36	5.28	5.92	6.35

[a]National means from Porter's sample of 1,916 managers.

Adapted from *Experiences in Management and Organizational Behavior*, by Douglas T. Hall, Donald D. Bowen, Roy T. Lewicki, Francine S. Hall. Copyright © 1982 by John Wiley & Sons, Inc. Reprinted by permission of John Wiley & Sons, Inc.

in 30 different manufacturing locations. Analysis of the question-naire revealed that professional aspirations, job freedom, freedom from supervision, and technical challenge scored highest on impor-tance. These needs, incidentally, are consistent with many of the functional traits described in Chapter One as associated with profes-sionalism. Next, in Seiler's study, financial aspirations and mana-gerial aspirations received moderate ratings, and professional recog-nition and security received the lowest ratings. Clearly the higher-order needs prevailed. Seiler went on to suggest that turnover would result if the organization did not match the needs of its young pro-fessionals. It should be kept in mind that Seiler's findings were for professionals at the very start of their careers.

Perrucci and Gerstl[22] queried young but more seasoned engineer-ing professionals. In their study, challenge was rated as the highest need, followed by advancement and autonomy. Colleagueship ranked fourth with professional community and knowledge a distant fifth and sixth. These findings are entirely consistent with Seiler's findings, except that pecuniary rewards as a component of advance-ment were rated substantially higher. Perrucci and Gerstl in a further analysis, however, discovered that engineers with doctorate degrees placed much less emphasis on pecuniary rewards and emphasized higher-order needs much more than engineers as a whole.

Professional Need Orientation

Besides identifying psychological needs, it is important to view the context of need fulfillment, which has also been referred to as one's need orientation. Professionals can be oriented toward the profession in which they have been trained, the organization for which they work, or both. Many authors, especially sociologists, have discussed this distinction in a variety of terms, but the most popular is Gouldner's "cosmopolitans" and "locals."[23] According to Gouldner, cosmopolitans are low on loyalty to their employing organization and high on commitment to their specialized skills. Locals are just the reverse, plus they tend to take an organizational reference group orientation, whereas cosmopolitans take a profes-sional reference group orientation. It is commonly thought that professionals, according to the precise definitions provided above, are clearly cosmopolitan in need orientation. Indeed, Chapter One pointed out that they engage in cosmopolitan behavior as opposed to local behavior — which is the preference of their managers — and this is the major cause of the strain or dissonance experienced by them when working within large organizations.

Research since Gouldner's initial work suggests that one need not be strong in one of these orientations or the other, but can be strong in both. Glaser[24] found the highest performers to be of this combined type. My depiction of the quasi professional in Chapter One corresponds to the notion of the combined type. Kornhauser[25] reasoned that the combined orientation as well as the two distinct types can make functional contributions to the organizations to which they are a part. For example, the cosmopolitan orientation tends to be good for producing technical results. The local orientation, on the other hand, plays a strong role in administering technical activities. Finally, the combined orientation is useful in applying and communicating the technical results.

Organizations obviously need all three of the above functions to be performed; so to that extent, it makes sense that they should provide opportunity for each of the three orientations. I shall discuss this organizational issue more fully in Chapter Five, but for now let us just say that most organizations, particularly industrial enterprises, favor the local as opposed to the cosmopolitan focus. Nevertheless, there are opportunities in many organizations for all three orientations. Further, consistent with the prior discussion of psychological need fulfillment, professionals must seek to satisfy their need orientations if they are to be content with their jobs and careers. How to do that and yet remain a productive member of an organization is really a question of balance or imbalance. I shall take that up in Chapter Six.

PERSONALITY TRAITS

Another set of characteristics which describe our values are personality traits. Although closely related to psychological needs, they deserve separate treatment as individual diagnostic elements. Whereas needs tend to be latent and emergent in a person, personality is more of a here-and-now description of who we are. Our personality traits constitute a collection of attributes which truly characterize us as individuals primarily based upon early life experiences. The importance of personality traits emanates from the contention of a number of scholars in the career development field who associate personality with career choice and with career fulfillment. Even without such an association, however, it is imperative that we know as much about ourselves as possible in order to make adequate career decisions.

Although this book should hardly be the appropriate incentive to the reader to take a psychological test, there are some rather simple tests which are not only quite accessible but which offer worthwhile insights into career choice and fulfillment. One such test is the Allport-Vernon-Lindzey (AVL) Study of Values, available from Houghton Mifflin Company. The AVL produces a profile of the relative strength of six personal values. These values include:[26]

1. *theoretical* — interested in the discovery of truth
2. *economic* — interested in what is useful
3. *aesthetic* — interested in form and harmony
4. *social* — concerned about people
5. *political* — interested in power
6. *religion* — interested in understanding the cosmos

In taking the AVL, a profile can be developed of the relative strengths of these six values or traits compared to national norms for a given occupational group.

Another test, the Myers-Briggs Type Indicator Test, produces a personality profile based upon one's score on four continual connecting pairs of opposite behavioral patterns. These behavioral pattern pairs are based upon Carl Jung's scheme of personality types:

1. *extroversion-introversion (E/I)* — extroversion deals with the outer world of people and things whereas introversion is concerned with the inner world of concepts, ideas and feelings.
2. *sensation-intuition (S/N)* — sensation is the direct awareness of a situation through the senses, whereas intuition represents an indirect perception of the deeper meaning inherent in any situation.
3. *thinking-feeling (T/F)* — thinking tends to be a logical, formalized process of judgment, whereas feeling tends to entail personal or subjective values.

4. *judgment-perception (J/P)* — judgment emphasizes nonimpulsive regulation of experience, whereas perception is inclined to be more open and receptive to all experience.

Doering[27] was able to characterize a number of diverse professional groups using the Myers-Briggs test.

Finally, Sperry, Mickelson and Hunsaker[28] have developed a personality style continuum which, like the Myers-Briggs, depicts end-points on a scale. Their profile, however, as seen in Table 2-10, suggests that the traits on the left-hand side tend to be psychologically unhealthy, whereas those on the right-hand side tend to be psychologically healthy. They further explain that it is unusual for anyone to exclusively occupy the right-side, and that we all must contend with our left-side elements in an effort to grow or to release the creative processes we possess.

The following exercise describes the end-points in the Sperry, Mickelson, and Hunsaker personality style continuum, providing a means to make a preliminary assessment of your personality traits.

EXERCISE 2-7

PERSONALITY STYLE ASSESSMENT. An individual's behavior is organized around a central theme or goal which serves as a unifying force for behavior. By examining the repetitive behaviors you engage in to achieve that goal, you can identify your personality style. As you think about yourself and your behavior in your everyday life (you may also wish to review your work autobiography), what personality styles seem to predominate?

Are you the *Overachiever* (the Overachiever is a "workaholic," a person who puts in an eight-day work week but who never seems satisfied with his or her accomplishments) or the
Achiever (the Achiever works as hard as the Overachiever, but when a task is successfully completed, he or she can relax and enjoy what was accomplished);
Are you the *Inadequate One* (Inadequate Ones do not believe in their abilities and hence need constant supervision) or the
Adequate One (the Adequate One acknowledges individual strengths and also recognizes personal limitations);

Are you the *Martyr* (the Martyr is ready to "die for a cause." Seeking injustice, a "prove-me" attitude and behavior is intended to attract sympathy from others and increase feelings of being victimized) or the *Compassionate One* (this individual willingly offers new ideas but respects the opinions of others and does not feel put down by them);

Are you the *Right One* (this is the "Monday-morning quarterback" who always has the right answers and who judges others as always being wrong) or the

Fair One (the Fair One doesn't focus on judging others but rather spends time trying to figure out what went wrong and what can be done about it);

Are you the *Poor One* (Poor Ones never have enough, but feeling "entitled," they will do anything to get what they feel they deserve) or the

Rich One (Rich Ones enjoy what they have and share willingly with others);

Are you the *Hero* (the Hero likes keeping others in an inferior position so that he or she can always come to the rescue; this entails making sure that everything is done his or her way) or the

Leader (the Leader is a developer of people who believes that everyone should participate in decisions and share in the responsibility of what happens).

Now, place an x in the continuum where you believe you stand for each of the personality styles. For example, in considering the first style, if you believe yourself to be an Overachiever, you would place an x at the left-side of the continuum near the Overachiever label. You may leave blank any style which doesn't fit you altogether.

TABLE 2-10   Personality Style Continuum

OVERACHIEVER	ACHIEVER
INADEQUATE ONE	ADEQUATE ONE
MARTYR	COMPASSIONATE ONE
RIGHT ONE	FAIR ONE
POOR ONE	RICH ONE
HERO	LEADER

Source: Based on the work of Len Sperry, especially *You Can Make It Happen* by Len Sperry, Douglas J. Mickelson, and Phillip L. Hunsaker. Reading, MA.: Addison-Wesley, 1977, Chap. 5.

As suggested earlier, although it is very unlikely that we can consistently demonstrate the personality which is represented by all the traits on the right-side of the continuum, we need to: (1) recognize and come to terms with our left-side predispositions and (2) make an effort to move to the right where possible. The right-side traits are healthier for career development in the sense that they not only represent more stable individual characteristics but are preferable for developing successful interpersonal or collegial relationships. For example, although there is a common misconception that one must be an Overachiever in order to get ahead, the Overachiever's characteristics are very prone to professional burnout. The Martyr is another unfortunate but common professional type. Some professionals believe that by virtue of their superior technical training, their cause is always right. The Compassionate One, however, demonstrates sensitivity to other people's opinions, communicates more effectively, and ultimately makes a better representation of self and profession with fellow colleagues and superiors.

The actual process of making personality adjustments is beyond the scope of this book, for in many cases it entails counseling or even psychotherapeutic interventions. However, in Chapter Five, the issues of managing relations with one's boss and developing a mentor or sponsor relationship will be addressed. Further, in Chapter Six I shall outline the necessary career, if not personality, adjustments one must make to undertake a specific personal career development strategy.

Career Types and Anchors

As I had indicated earlier, some personality theorists have made direct connections between personality traits and career orientations. One such theorist is John Holland who introduced six personality types which he then through exhaustive research associated with 456 occupations.[29] He found it necessary to utilize secondary or even tertiary classifications with these types, but always keeping one type dominant. The six Holland personality/occupation types are:

1. realistic (R) — involves physical activity requiring skill, strength, and coordination. (For example, forestry, surveying, automobile repair, architecture.)

2. investigative (I) — involves cognitive activity rather than affective activity. (For example, biology, mathematics, research.)
3. social (S) — involves interpersonal rather than intellectual or physical activities. (For example, education, social work, clinical psychology, foreign service.)
4. conventional (C) — involves structured, rule-regulated activities and subordination of personal needs to an organization or person. (For example, accounting, secretarial work, finance.)
5. enterprising (E) — involves persuasive, influential activities to attain power or status. (For example, business, law, public relations.)
6. artistic (A) — involves self-expression, artistic creation, and expression of emotion. (For example, art, writing, music.)

Holland's Self-Directed Search, the SDS, helps respondents develop a personality profile congruent with a range of occupations. The central thesis in Holland's work is that given the proper instrument, people can project their own personality orientation. This in turn will be a good predictor of present career aspirations or subsequent career choice. Finally, people tend to be more satisfied in environments congruent with their personality type.

Perhaps the most definitive work relating personality style to career choice and orientation has been the work of Edgar Schein. To emphasize the interconnections between personality and career orientation, he dispenses with any mention of the word, "personality," and substitutes the concept of "career anchor." Distinct from classical conceptions of personality, Schein's career anchor is broader in scope in that it entails the self-perceived talent, abilities, motives, needs, attitudes, and values of a person and also because he believes anchors develop over time through one's early career and not simply during the formative years. Consequently, it is not possible, according to Schein, to predict career anchors from tests. Rather, "the concept emphasizes evolution, development, and discovery through actual experience."[30] Further, Schein believes that the career anchor once formed remains relatively stable throughout a person's career.

The five career anchors are pretty much self-explanatory:

1. technical/functional — emphasizes challenge in a specific content area

1. managerial — is concerned with climbing the corporate ladder to a position of general management, wherein large amounts of responsibility may be exercised
3. security — is preoccupied primarily with organizational or geographical stability
4. autonomy — seeks to be free of organizational constraints in order to pursue career interests independently
5. creativity — seeks to build or create something that is one's own

Follow-up research by DeLong[31] confirmed the existence of the above five career anchors. However, three additional anchors or orientations were proposed and subsequently validated by DeLong:

1. service — is interested in using interpersonal skills to help others
2. identity — is interested in the status and prestige derived from belonging to certain companies or organizations
3. variety — desires a maximum variety of job assignments and work projects especially for the challenge involved

DeLong also found that career anchors may coexist. For example, a psychologist may value assisting others as part of the service anchor but may also value the autonomy resulting from being on a faculty or having a private practice. Combinations of career anchors may also occur. For example, Brooklyn Derr has suggested that a so-called "warrior" career concept may evolve from a combination of the technical/functional and autonomy anchors. An example of the warrior would be the fighter pilot who thrives on putting his life on the line.

Career Anchor/Work Environment Fit

Although I shall consider the problem of personality/environment imbalances in greater detail in later chapters, it might be well to introduce this problem in the context of career anchors. One particular issue which seems to plague professionals within organizations is the apparent conflict between their expectations and values and the norms and accompanying reward system of the organization in which they work. Although I have already discussed this conflict at the outset of the book, in Schein's terminology, the problem emerges as a conflict between the technical anchor of the professional (especially the science or engineering professional) and the managerial anchor of his or her administrators. For example, professionals, interested in the finer details of their technical area, cannot understand or accept management's drive to proceed on the basis of partial information. They need to work systematically to develop their field, whereas management, in order to understand the rigors of the business world, must proceed in a sporadic and opportunistic way. Finally, professionals, although not necessarily interested in rising to the top, desire some form of reward for technical competence, for instance, resources and time to develop a paper on their research. Yet, in many industrial organizations, this professional type of reward is not well understood by management. Even if it could be communicated to management, technical people often lack the interpersonal skills to successfully negotiate their needs.

It is clear, then, that although management must have a sense of the personality styles descriptive of their work force, individual professionals must also understand their career anchors and be able to detect the fit between these and their present work environment. Let's suppose, as a final example, that a professional is aware of her pure interest in technical competence. Equipped with this insight, she might be in a better position to understand her urge to turn down promotional offers by her organization. Through self-assessment, then, one can make more informed career choices. Exercise 2-8 is designed to assist in identifying and understanding the implications of one's career anchors.

EXERCISE 2-8

CAREER ANCHOR IDENTIFICATION AND IMPLICATIONS. The following list reproduces Schein's five career anchors and DeLong's three career orientations, each accompanied by two descriptive statements used in DeLong's research.[32] Which of the eight most describes you? Do you have any combinations?

1. *Technical/Functional* — I would leave my company rather than be promoted out of my area of expertise.

I will accept a management position only if it is in my area of expertise.

2. *Managerial* — To be in a position in general management is important to me.

   The process of supervising, influencing, leading, and controlling people at all levels is important to me.

3. *Security* — An organization that will provide security through guaranteed work, benefits, a good retirement, and so forth, is important to me.

   Remaining in my present geographical location rather than moving because of a promotion is important to me.

4. *Autonomy* — The chance to pursue my own life-style and not be constrained by the rules of an organization is important to me.

   A career that is free from organizational restriction is important to me.

5. *Creativity* — I have been motivated throughout my career by the number of products or ideas that I have been directly involved in creating.

   To be able to create or build something that is entirely my own product or idea is important to me.

6. *Service* — I have sought a career that allows me to meet my basic needs through helping others.

   Being able to use my skills and talents in the service of an important cause is important to me.

7. *Identity* — I want others to identify me by my organization and my job title.

   To be recognized by my title and status is important to me.

8. *Variety* — An endless variety of challenges is what I really want from my career.

   A career that provides a maximum variety of types of assignments and work projects is important to me.

Next consider the following questions:

1. Why is this career anchor(s) representative? Think back first to your life before working, then to your early career. (Consult your work autobiography.) Can you identify four or five occurrences during these two periods which may have oriented you to this anchor?

2. Has your anchor(s) been stable over time? Were you ever dissatisfied in a job because your anchor wasn't matched by the job environment?

3. Is your anchor(s) consistent with your present work environment? In what ways is it consistent or inconsistent?

LIFE SPACE CONCERNS

Most of the treatment up to now in the self-assessment has focused on work-related components of your career. However, part of our value system that shapes our career choices consists of non-work-related experiences and attitudes. The purpose of this last section of the chapter is to explicitly examine the relationship between the work components of our life and those other aspects of our total life space.

The concept of life space refers to all those activities, thoughts, and feelings which together shape who we are as a person. Donald Miller, preferring the terms "personal space" refers to it as that "piece of the world which contains all of our relationships, our desires, our goals, and our understanding of our place and role."[33] Clearly, for most professionals work tends to be a key component of their life space. By virtual definition, *commitment to* and *identification* with work constitute discerning ingredients of professionalism itself. However, at least three major factors further discriminate the relative involvement of professionals in their work: (1) involvement is certainly a function of one's basic personality and early history, (2) it will be affected by the degree to which the work setting absorbs the professional in the work at hand,[34] and (3) it will vary depending upon the need orientation of the professional himself. Bailyn, for example, found that engineers with a cosmopolitan orientation were more involved in their work than locals.[35]

Beyond the three factors cited above, relative involvement in the job will depend upon the activity of the other components of one's life space. The other elements which I shall address include family, self, community, and a general category called outside activities.

Given sociologist Talcott Parsons' influential precept of 40 years ago that the traditional nuclear family was a requirement of modern industrialization,[36] it is at least curious that the family today is a controversial subject. Without going into detail on this matter, suffice it to say that given the growing numbers of single individuals or married couples without children in our country, the traditional nuclear family is no longer the absolute norm of adult lifestyle. Nevertheless, considering that one typically has some involvement with at least his or her own parents, it is unlikely that family activities will escape attention in one's life space.

Schein has developed a life cycle theory applied to the family, as opposed to the individual or the organizational career (both of which shall be taken up at length in the next chapter).[37] His work suggests that people go through stages when choosing the traditional family lifestyle, and the issues to be confronted and tasks to be accomplished vary depending upon the stage of development. The stages are:

Dependent child
Transition to adulthood
Single adult
Married adult
Parent of young child
Parent of adolescent
Parent of grown children
Grandparent

Whether one in fact goes through each of these stages or not, there are serious decisions to be made concerning the trade-off between home life and work life. You need to carefully review the time distributed to each of these two major components to determine whether the distribution provides the maximum possible satisfaction. There are certain features of the work environment which we know will affect the ultimate distribution:

1. The type of work itself – how much time is spent writing, reflecting, interacting, working physically, etc. These activities may affect how one behaves at home. For example, if you have to interact daily with customers on very technical subjects, you may not wish to get involved in "heady" subjects at home.
2. The intensity or emotionality of the work – how much of a commitment is involved. In starting a new business, for

example, outside involvements must be excluded in order to devote one's extra time to the business.

3. The success one has at work — there is an established association between fulfillment at work and satisfaction in life.
4. Income — the educational pursuits of one's children, leisure activities, etc., are affected by the standard of living brought to the family from one's earnings.
5. Travel and relocation — the amount of time spent away from the family on work-related activities or the frequency of job-related moves affect family stability. Given the relative coping ability of a family plus consideration as to the children's age, mobility is not necessarily a negative experience.
6. Time — the sheer number of hours at work as well as the ability to arrange one's schedule.

The next component of the life space to consider is the self. Practically speaking, this could refer to spending time alone, engaging in a personal hobby, or even attending to personal business. However, the crux of this component is the spirit of selfishness in the Ayn Rand tradition — that part of the life space which is strictly reserved for yourself. What you do with your time is not as material as the fact that you are willing to allocate some portion of your space to your own personal pursuits — whether it be for growth or educational purposes, enjoyment, or relaxation.

Community activities include religious, social, and political affairs of interest and for which one is willing to make a commitment of time and energy. A good deal of your efforts in this component could be termed volunteer work, in the sense that you may not receive any outright remuneration for your efforts. Nevertheless, you may be driven to participate due to a sense of social consciousness, out of a need to belong, or maybe strictly for purposes of enjoyment.

Finally, the last component, referred to as outside activities, is a catch-all category which includes time spent in affairs outside one's immediate work, family, self, or community. It includes: time with friends, educational pursuits, sports, vacation or travel, and other forms of social entertainment.

Turning to the implications of life space concerns for professionals, as perhaps expected, most of the attention in the literature has gone to issues of family and work. The most researched group of professionals has been the engineers. By discussing some of this research, general implications may be drawn for other components of the life space and for other professionals groups.

One concept which has been recently used to describe the conflict between career and family is that of accommodation. It defines the extent to which one is willing to subordinate the demands of the career to that of the family. A position of nonaccommodation would represent an attitude of extreme achievement orientation, with all components of the life space completely subordinated to the career. Bailyn's research,[38] cited earlier, has found many positive family consequences as a result of a position of accommodation. For example, wives of family-oriented men are more satisfied, whether they choose housework or career work. Yet, Perrucci and Gerstl[39] have suggested that the family orientation of engineers may occur as an adaptation or ego-maintaining alternative to a stalled career development. Bailyn also found accommodators to be more passive in their professional role (for example, they may publish less), to be less likely to see themselves as good leaders or to use leadership on the job, to be less likely to feel that they possess the ability to learn new things, and to be less concerned about advancement, high earnings, organizational power, and even about the intrinsic character of their work.

These findings point out the true dilemma a professional faces when having to make a choice between family and career. Those professionals who decide to extend a good deal of time to their family may be at risk in their career, at least in terms of advancement. However, not all is lost. Professionals who are family oriented can still perform important, if not the most spectacular or challenging, work for their organization. Further, from an organizational perspective, accommodative employees have been found to be quite loyal to their employing organization.[40] Finally, any erosion in the performance of accommodators as compared to nonaccommodators has been found to be mitigated where the accommodator is deemed to be self-confident.[41]

The conflict between career and family among professionals is to some extent replicated between career and one other researched life space component – community. Studies by Whyte[42] and Sarason[43] have suggested that "organization men" or professionals locked into vast impersonal bureaucracies can be characterized as rootless and bored people who have lost their ties with families and communities. Long-distance moves, new positions, new employees, and the blind pursuit of a career have only exacerbated their sense of not belonging. Perrucci and Gerstl[44] found such factors as these to be partly responsible for the general "apolitical" nature of the engineers in their sample. However, those engineers who held high technical or supervisory positions or who spent more time at home were more prone to participate in community efforts. They also suggested that community participation may be a function of one's age. Demands from family or career may lessen during the middle or later years as compared to the early years, allowing more time for community participation.

Although less has been written about the elements of self and outside activities in terms of professional career development, these life space components merit equal time at some point in your career. Indeed, your taking the time to read and work with this book suggests that you have decided to reserve some time to the development of self.

The next and final exercise of this chapter will assist you in organizing the distribution of your life space components. It is called the Life Space Sociogram.

EXERCISE 2-9

LIFE SPACE SOCIOGRAM. From the previous discussion, you should now have a reasonably good grasp of the five principal components of your life space. It is unlikely that each of these components will be of equivalent importance to you across the many stages of your life. It is not even particularly desirable that such a state exists for we all have our preferences as to how we control our life space. Certainly, too, some of the components may demand attention outside of our immediate control, for example, attending to an ill family member. It is, therefore, not critical that your life space look like the pentagon depicted in Figure 2-6, which displays the five components as being perfectly balanced (that is, symmetrically drawn). Rather, whatever your distribution of components, you should have a sense that there is a fair amount of choice in the distribution and that each component is receiving appropriate consideration given your age, your particular state of development, and/or societal norms.

Figure 2-7 depicts a hypothetical life space pentagon of a young professional worker at the ealy stage of his or her career. It is plain that work is the

FIGURE 2-6
Life Space Pentagon with Perfectly Balanced
Components

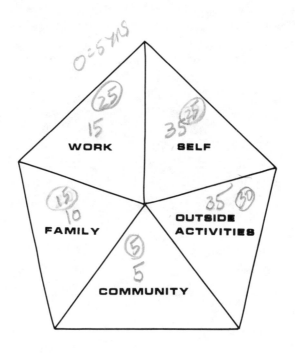

predominant concern of this young individual as he or she embarks on a fresh career. This is followed by outside activities. There is relatively little time devoted to the family, since the young person is probably unmarried, and to community activities, the latter being clearly subordinate to the overarching concern with work. The pattern depicted is again not necessarily unhealthy even though the components are unbalanced. What would tend to make the distribution unhealthy would be a persistence of this pattern even after external conditions in the young professional's life change. For example, continuing to overweigh work and underweigh family activities even after marrying and having children might place an inordinate strain on a spouse, resulting in some possible tension in a marriage. It is not always possible to have a completely desirable or ideal life space sociogram, but one should attempt to work toward that ideal. Most people do have a sense of the ideal sociogram for their particular life situation.

FIGURE 2-7
Life Space Pentagon with Unbalanced Components

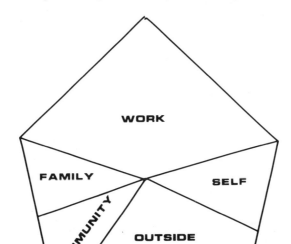

INSTRUCTIONS:

In the first blank pentagon in Figure 2-8, complete your life space sociogram by drawing five components of your life space according to the distribution as you see it right now. The five components are again (1) work, (2) family, (3) self, (4) community, and (5) outside activities. Consider the following questions once you have drawn your sociogram and labelled the components.

1. How close would you say your sociogram is to what would be considered ideal for your age group? In other words, do you think people at your age should be spending more time devoted to family activities than you have depicted, more time to self, etc.?

2. What prevents you from reaching your ideal? Are there circumstances that you must confront which are simply beyond your control, for example, an ailing parent, the need to get your family off the ground, buying a new car, a divorce? Are these circumstances really critical?

3. What steps will you take to reach your ideal? Will you make specific attempts to improve your time management, will you enroll in a course, will you run for office, will you resolve to spend more time with your daughter, etc?

4. What component(s) are you emphasizing right now? Why?

5. What component(s) are you deemphasizing right now? Why?

FIGURE 2-8
Life Space Pentagon Worksheet

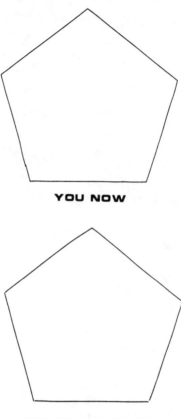

YOU NOW

YOU IN FIVE YEARS

6. Although this cannot be easily visualized, are there areas of overlap between some of your components? For example, will devoting more time to self-development through an assertiveness training program potentially lead to improved relations with your colleagues at work, which, in turn, may also allow you to augment the quality of your family life?

Now, in the second blank pentagon, draw your life space sociogram as you would like it to be five years hence. What changes, if any, have you made? What reasons do you attribute for possible rearrangement of some of the components? For example, do you expect your work career to have plateaued by then? Will your children have grown up? Do you expect your hobby to have blossomed into a full-time business?

The life space concerns which you have just mapped as well as the other career dimensions introduced in the chapter are very dependent upon the concept of stage of development — a concept which has only been alluded to up to now. It is sufficiently important, however, that I shall devote the entire next chapter to a discussion of career stages.

THREE: Career Stages

INTRODUCTION

It would be limiting to attempt to complete your self-assessment without a sense of your particular career stage of development. There is substantial agreement among career development practitioners that individuals are aided in their self-assessment by being able to compare their concerns regarding their career with others who seem to be going through similar problems or at least facing similar issues. One basis of comparison among individuals' career problems can certainly be age. However, many career researchers, especially psychologists have gone beyond the notion of age in an effort to discover development themes among people; that is, whether there are stages that all of us must inexorably go through as we make our way in life. However, empirical support is lacking in confirming any particular development theory; rather, stage theories are normally built through persistent observation by the theorist. Although the theories that abound have become popularly accepted, they should be viewed as patterns of average behavior and not as requisite norms of acceptable behavior. Certainly the patterns revealed by the developmental theories are affected greatly by age, but also by other cultural, historical, and structural factors, such as socioeconomic status, sex, and ethnicity. Moreover, as has been presented by the so-called "interactionists,"[1] the career patterns of individuals are largely affected by the environment. For example, career stages may be accounted for by economic factors. Firms during peak economic periods might favor youth not only in their hiring practices but by the opportunities they provide for growth and experimentation. During downturns, as the younger workers face inevitable layoffs, the older workers might experience a greater sense of self-worth or respect. Career stages, then, can be valuable in presenting a set of issues for self-examination and as a basis for understanding one's work role in comparison to others.

In this chapter, I shall present three different career stage theories. The first is a classic life cycle theory which presents stages of development which you as an individual might go through during your entire working career. As part of this theory, I shall also elaborate on three other subjects. The first is of predictable interest to the readers of this book — the threat of the so-called "mid-life crisis." Second, I shall explore the notion of psychological success as the driving force of the career stage movement. Third, I shall present a short digression on some alternatives which have been proposed to offset the classic "linear" life cycle approach. Then, I shall discuss two organizational career stage theories. The first is a theory of socialization which addresses how any newcomer gradually adapts to an organizational environment, from the point of entry to tenure. The second is a normative (as opposed to descriptive) theory which is concerned especially with professional development, in particular, the tasks which professionals typically accomplish on their way to successful and productive careers.

Although the discussion in this chapter will be more theoretical than in the preceding chapter, your careful attention to it will provide many insights into your particular career situation. Not only should the material lead to greater awareness on your part of your current career themes, but it should also provide comfort that you are not alone in confronting these themes. Furthermore, the developmental nature of the theories will suggest many avenues for work to be done as you make your way in your professional career. Finally, the text will be accompanied by some exercises which are designed to help you apply the theoretical discussion to your personal situation.

LIFE CYCLE THEORY

The initial framework examining career stages is the familiar life cycle theory. It is presented here as a compilation of the work of Erik

Erikson,[2] Roger Gould,[3] and Daniel Levinson.[4] Although these authors have incorporated childhood themes in their theories, I shall concentrate on applications which concern adults and their work experiences. The basis for combining the work of these authors is their general agreement that adults pass through recognized milestones in their careers, that is, there are developmental tasks which must be mastered if the adult is to pass into the next stage. In addition, the authors believe that these stages are relatively age-specific. This is not to suggest that one cannot hurdle over some of the stages, regress to earlier ones, or remain "stuck" in one constant stage. Variations do occur and provide exceptions to the theory. Nevertheless, the stages appear to describe the behavior of most people at definitive points in their career. Since by the time of adulthood there are fewer institutional situations, such as family composition or school, which stabilize our development, there is a benefit to describing developmental milestones as a basis of comparing our career to a set of societal norms. Regardless of occupation or industry, marital status, personality, and other cultural traits, the following adult stages have been shown to predict career patterns reasonably well. The titles of the stages are mine and are designed to reflect the principal tasks at the respective stage. The ages indicated for each stage are approximate. As indicated above, they will vary widely depending upon a number of situations. You will have an opportunity to determine your own stage of development in a subsequent exercise.

Taking a Stab (Ages 22-29) — During this first stage of adulthood, the individual explores a number of real world decisions, such as embarking on a definite career, marriage, lifestyle, etc. It is also a time when these decisions convert to a sense of responsibility and commitment, work and family being principal among the list of responsibilities. However, there is an equal impulse to continue exploration and experimentation during this period. The impulses of stability versus experimentation obviously need to be balanced if one is to successfully pass through this provisional stage.

Taking a Stand (Ages 29-32) — This is a period of reassessment of earlier choices. Career, marriage, and lifestyle decisions are exposed to intense scrutiny and sometimes disruptions occur. In other cases, the individual reaffirms earlier choices and enters the next stage with renewed commitment.

Getting Going (Ages 32-39) — After the intense questioning of the prior stage, this stage requires less shifting of interests and a desire to settle down in life and settle into one's chosen work environment. Career-wise, it is a time to seek out a mentor or someone who can "show you the ropes," partially as a means to becoming recognized in your line of work or profession. This stage is also characterized by time pressure, the need to recognize what one's true role is. This pressure is augmented by a realization near the end of the stage that life is half over and that one is no longer "growing up," but rather "growing old."

Backing Up a Little (Ages 39-43) — Also referred to as the "mid-life crisis," during this stage one becomes undeniably aware of the gap between what one wanted to become and what one has accomplished. It can be a painful time as grown-up children and parents make demands on one's resources. One wonders if the right road has been traveled, and in the search of that road, career changes are quite possible as are marriage disruptions. This period can be characterized as the "one last chance to make it big."

Coming Into Full Bloom (Ages 43-50) — This period is characterized by a new stability which arises out of the intense search of *backing up a little*. There may be a return to old values, and old friends are cherished. There is general acceptance of self and of mortality. The stable patterns of this period can be interrupted by the loss of loved ones.

Letting It Be (Ages 50-65+) — During this period one begins to mellow as he or she comes to accept the present. However, plans must also be made for separation from work and ultimate retirement. Health concerns become predominant as the individual realizes that he or she no longer can do things like the old days. Contributions to the world are reviewed, and the meaningfulness of life is questioned. There is less concern with emotion-laden topics and more focus on basic lifestyle concerns.

EXERCISE 3-1

DEVELOPMENTAL STAGE QUESTIONNAIRE. In order to obtain a better sense of your particular stage of development, a questionnaire is provided in this exercise. If there is stability in your life patterns at this time, it will be plotted using the scoring chart of Table 3-1.

INSTRUCTIONS:
Please fill out the questionnaire below by circling the letters a, b, c, d, e, f, or g for each question, describing your *current* behavior as you see it. In other words, your answer should reflect how things really are, rather than how you would like them to be.
In some cases, more than one answer may describe your current situation. However, you are to select the statement which is most characteristic of you.

1. My main concern is:
   a. becoming a contributing member of my chosen profession.
   b. financial security for retirement purposes.
   c. being able to fend for myself.
   d. accepting what I have not achieved with my life.
   e. taking advantage of my last chance to make it big.
   f. selecting the right career.
   g. finding out what I want out of life.

1. My interpersonal relationships are characterized by:
   a. turmoil and change often being caused by my wanting to find out more about myself.
   b. a desire for confirmation of my life choices.
   c. a lack of excitement but a need for support; achieving recognition in my career.
   d. stability and a sense of well-being.
   e. being less intense and less substantive.
   f. a need for support from my close friends.
   g. a reawakening of the old dependent-independent feelings.

3. One of my dominant goals is:
   a. maintaining my health.
   b. achieving independence from my parents.
   c. identifying what my life means to me and what I can do with the limited time I have left.
   d. deciding what to do with my life.
   e. making enough money to do what I want.
   f. discovering what is right for me.
   g. being active socially.

4. My primary value is:
   - ✓ a. security.
   - b. autonomy.
   - c. accomplishment/prestige.
   - d. independence.
   - e. self-identity.
   - f. commitment.
   - g. wisdom.

5. My life is:
   - a. full of an urgency to succeed.
   - ✓ b. not so rushed; it is a time for sharing human experiences.
   - c. unknown.
   - d. stable; what has been done, has been done.
   - e. for me to define and control.
   - f. passing too quickly; I have one last chance to make it.
   - g. uncertain and full of crucial decisions.

6. The future is:
   - ✓ a. uncertain and becoming increasingly important.
   - b. not as important as my being free from the external world of the present.
   - c. pressing in on me and I am running out of opportunities.
   - d. not as important as the present.
   - e. not important.
   - f. a time I fantasize about.
   - g. limited and I feel a time squeeze.

7. My career behavior is characterized by:
   - a. a developing taste for power.
   - b. a concern for power, politics, and influence.
   - ✓ c. learning about the world of work.
   - d. being a decision-maker.
   - e. being able to formulate and implement strategies for improving organizational performance.
   - f. a concern for being remembered when I retire.
   - g. identifying my competency and understanding elements of leadership.

8. My identity is:
   - a. defined by how well I perform in my job.
   - ✓ b. torn between what I am now and wanting to change.
   - c. well established with a feeling of relief.
   - d. questioned and related to the meaningfulness of my life.
   - e. closely related to my family.

TABLE 3-1 Developmental Stage Assessment Questionnaire Scoring Chart

INSTRUCTIONS:

Circle the letter on the chart corresponding to your circled answers on the questionnaire. When finished, notice the pattern. The column with the highest frequency of circled responses indicates the stage of development most characteristic of your behavior.

Stages of Adult Development

Question Number	1 Pulling-Up Roots	2 Taking a Stab	3 Taking a Stand	4 Getting Going	5 Backing Up a Little	6 Coming Into Full Bloom	7 Letting It Be
1	c	f	(g)	a	e	d	b
2	f	(b)	a	c	g	d	e
3	b	d	f	(e)	c	g	a
4	d	f	e	c	b	(a)	g
5	c	e	g	a	f	d	(b)
6	f	d	(a)	g	c	b	e
7	(c)	g	a	e	d	b	f
8	e	f	g	a	(b)	c	d
Column Totals	—	—	—	—	—	—	—

Source: Len Sperry, Douglas Mickelson, and Phillip Hunsaker. *You Can Make It Happen*, © 1977, Addison-Wesley Publishing Co., Reading, MA., pp. 85-88. Reprinted by permission.

100

f. well-defined even though I may not be completely satisfied with it.

g. something which I don't seem to have control of.

After plotting the lettered answers to the questionnaire, did you notice a significant pattern? Consider in particular any column with four or more circled letters. You may have identified a consistent stage representing appropriate tasks associated with this stage. If not, there may be particular environmental or cultural circumstances affecting your development. You may wish to reflect on these further questions as you examine your personal findings.

1. If you are at a consistent stage, what tasks are you concentrating on right now?
   a. What tasks do you need to accomplish? (Review the answers keyed to the next stage on the chart.)
   b. What characteristics of your current stage of development do you find the most enjoyable? frustrating?
   c. Do you feel this stage is representative of you right now?
   d. Is the stage appropriate for you? In other words, do you feel you should be further along in your development? Are there reasons for your current concentration in this stage?

2. If there is no consistency in your development, what circumstances might have led to this? For example, have you made a career change? Have you been laid off? Have you had a recent family disruption?
   a. Do you wish to achieve greater consistency?
   b. If yes, what stage would you think most appropriate for you right now?
   c. What tasks do you need to accomplish to get there? (Review the answers keyed to your conception of the ideal stage for you.)

Mid-Life Crisis

Of the various stages of development in life cycle theory, the *backing up a little* stage, otherwise known as the "mid-life crisis," has received an inordinate amount of attention in recent years. Since I suspect many of the readers of this book find this stage particularly challenging and since it is a stage which seems to have become quite consequential to many professional workers in general, I shall give it special consideration in this section.

Research by developmental psychologists indicates that mid-life crises tend to occur more often among males than females and that these crises are characterized by a substantial change in one's individual personality and/or a disruption in one's sense of identity.[5] The age range given for the mid-life crisis has also been much broader than what I have designated for *backing up a little*. Mid-life crises can in fact occur between the ages of 35 and 55. Regarding the personality change attributed to this stage, it can be expressed in a number of ways although the usual manifestation is a turning inward or introspection which often finds substantive value in culture and wisdom. For a variety of reasons, for most individuals at this stage, the striving for success characteristic of prior stages, including the possession of worldly or material goods, slows down or temporarily halts. Especially among professionals, concerns during this period may become more intrinsically oriented. In other words, individuals may express more interest in work that is meaningful, that carries with it a chance for greater responsibility and achievement, or which simply provides a better match with one's values.

Although the mid-life crisis has become part of our everyday language, with the exception of Levinson et al.'s mammoth study,[6] there is not yet a great deal of hard evidence on the mid-life phenomenon. In a review of the available literature, McGill,[7] however, found seven reasons or theories for individuals experiencing a rather dramatic personality change at mid-life.

1. *Achievement-Aspiration Gap* — According to this theory, the individual realizes that it is impossible to achieve all or a majority of aspirations. It may be precipitated by such events in organizational life as a passed-over promotion, a first-time neutral or negative performance review, conflict with one's boss, or realization of having reached a career plateau.
2. *The Dream* — The dream represents an idealized view of oneself, typically manifested by youthful zeal and opportunity, which becomes suppressed in order to meet career and family demands. In mid-life, many of these elements in the *dream* reemerge, and need to be reconciled. It may be characterized as a sudden or impetuous career move, or a "fling."
3. *Empty Nest* — This theory is age-specific in the sense that it coincides with changes in family life, for example, children moving away from the home or a spouse taking on a more active career role, also frequently occurring outside the home. The individual may consequently experience less support

or ego satisfaction from his or her family, precipitating an identity crisis.

4. *Limits to Life* — Also age-specific, an individual in one's forties, may confront his or her own mortality for the first time, especially as he or she realizes that life is half over, or as friends and family members pass away. Time, consequently, becomes a treasured resource as one realizes that there's only so much of it left in which to accomplish one's goals, whatever they may be.

5. *Physiological Changes* — By the forties, individuals begin to experience physical changes which may pose threats to vitality. Jung[8] pointed out that during this period men and women begin to look and act more like each other. Men become softer and flabbier and women's features tend to become coarser. Sexual performance is also affected as desire diminishes and ability wanes. These physiological changes in many cases lead to personality changes.

6. *Role-Status* — For many individuals during mid-life, there is an experiencing of a role change from external concerns to internal. Brought about perhaps by some of the previously discussed developments, individuals may reorient their interests in work, family, community affairs, or self. For example, a career-oriented individual who has achieved economic success may decide to change his focus and concentrate more on family affairs or on self-development. Under different circumstances, a woman may find time to relinquish her formerly treasured family duties and concentrate on building her career.

7. *Stagnation-Growth* — Another perception of mid-life by some may be that things are slowing down. This may occur in all walks of life, not only within one's career. In order to get things "moving again," an abrupt change in behavior may be made in order to regain the sense of challenge, excitement, and adventure that has been lost.

Although these above theories have each been supported by legitimate scholarship, not enough empirical research, as I indicated earlier, has been done to predict a mid-life crisis for particular individuals. The cause of such a crisis will vary for each individual. Further, the cause may as well be environmentally or situationally derived as by reasons associated with age or psychology. For example, Barbara Lawrence[9] has shown how the modern widespread use of effective contraceptives has largely accounted for the empty nest theory, how modern medical technology has made viable the limits to life theory, and how some expectations regarding female roles in our society have greatly affected the role-status theory. In the first two instances, the respective phenomena would not be prevalent in mid-life without these situational/historical changes. In the last instance, it is clear that a woman's assumption of a new career role following child-rearing and during mid-life is a relatively recent phenomenon brought about by both medical and socio-cultural advances.

Although the causes for a mid-life crisis are not predictable, there is nevertheless a fair amount of certainty that it *is* in fact a crisis period, that is, a time of instability. There has been concern that this instability could lead to some negative consequences, especially for professionals. Pelz and Andrews,[10] for example, found a drop in creativity among their sample of mid-career scientific researchers. Most observers of the mid-life crisis, however, have found that the majority of individuals who experience it report positive outcomes, such as increased feelings of job and life satisfaction, greater autonomy over their lives, and a rejuvenation in their outlooks.

Coping with the Mid-Life Crisis

In that the mid-life crisis may be an inevitable phenomenon for some of those reading this book, what suggestions can be made initially to make the most of it, that is, to turn it into a positive experience? Professionals, in particular those who face the crisis due to skill deficiencies, are vulnerable to obsolescence. According to Kaufman,[11] overcoming the mid-life crisis can keep one productive in one's company. Failing to overcome the crisis, on the other hand, can lead to frustration or to some of the deviant/adaptive behaviors referred to in Chapter One. For example, one might become solely interested in money or security rather than in the opportunity for growth on the job. Kaufman believes that continuing education programs can do much to update technically deficient professionals and thereby help them to overcome a "technical" mid-life crisis. Other strategies include temporary work assignments, job restructuring, and sabbaticals.

Another way to handle crisis is to anticipate it. Some writers like Sarason[12] believe that the notion of crisis at mid-life may disappear as we learn to accept its inevitability. There has been in our culture a gradual weakening of the "one-life-one-career" imperative, allowing for an acceptance of cyclical as opposed to linear career paths. Although I shall discuss the conception of the cyclical career path in an upcoming section, suffice it to say for now that a cyclical career path allows for interruptions and permutations from one's originally conceived career track. For some, this might mean a transition to a new work style which incorporates, at middle age, interest in inner values and self-development rather than in bureaucratic life. Perhaps it might lead to a temporary or even permanent shift from one's organization. If economically secure, some professionals might find more fulfillment in private entrepreneurial activities or self-employment where the rewards might be smaller financially but potentially greater in terms of personal satisfaction and autonomy. A second career might allow time for greater personal and professional development as well as ego satisfaction derived from past experiences and expertise. If Sarason is right, career changes like the ones suggested here, may not seem out of line. In fact, managers are likely to go along with such occupational shifts as a way to provide opportunities for their younger more ambitious employees.

For the great majority of individuals who choose to stay in their organization, there are other recommendations which can be offered. Orth[13] identified four common traps which if constructively avoided can help cope with a mid-life crisis.

1. *The "frying pan into the fire" syndrome* – This trap results from taking the mid-life crisis too seriously or becoming overly anxious about it. It can result in making precipitous decisions and avoiding the need for self-assessment and development which is required to overcome this period of transition.
2. *The "my whole world flew apart at once" syndrome* – Similar to "frying pan into the fire," the individual in this trap is overcome by the crisis but in a more disastrous manner loses practically entire control over his or her life or assigns control to someone else. This trap does not allow one to develop what Orth calls "stability zones" – relationships which endure

despite the onset of great changes — which are critical in managing crises such as the mid-life transition.

3. *The "expression of individuality" syndrome* — Individuals in this trap mistakenly assume that their salvation from the mid-life crisis is by divorcing themselves from their organization and its political overtones and going it on their own. However, this choice of extreme individualism may lead to unanticipated and undesirable consequences.

4. *The "overchoice" syndrome* — This last trap simply puts the individual into a state of indecision where choices cannot be made among the number of available alternatives. Consequently, one is condemned to remain in transition until a viable personal career development plan can be formulated.

Relationship to Personal Career Development

The way out of all these traps, as suggested in "overchoice," is to develop a personal career development plan. As I have said all along, professional career development has to be a personal experience. Professionals cannot rely on their management to plan their careers for them. Since the individual and not the manager is the one going through a mid-life crisis, it is reasonable that the individual professional is in the best position to initiate meaningful change throughout the transition.

What is called for initially is a self-assessment, which would incorporate an inventory of your abilities and values, as you have done, followed by a careful analysis of your current work environment. The latter should incorporate a clear understanding of the opportunities for a career transition within your own organization, abetted or stalled, whatever the case may be, by the political culture, your peers, your superiors, and your mentor and/or sponsor. Once you have examined the choices offered by your own organization, then you should be in a better position to determine whether it can meet your needs. If not, the development of a personal career development plan would specify where and how your career needs can be more appropriately met. The process outlined briefly above is what this book is obviously intended to facilitate. To continue the career stages portion of the self-assessment, I turn next to the notion of psychological success.

Psychological Success as the Driving Force
of the Career Stage Movement

Continuing with the discussion of life cycle theory, as I had stated earlier, there is much popular acceptance of the idea of stages of development. However, there is surprisingly little information to suggest what induces people to move through the designated stages. Douglas T. Hall has perhaps provided the best answer to this question in his conception of psychological success. According to Hall, psychological success is defined as the "person's feelings of success as opposed to external measures of success."[14] In the career realm, psychological success occurs when a person achieves a sense of personal competence or self-esteem in a chosen career area and meets the expectations of that career. Of course, the state of psychological success may be temporary unless the individual can link success at one stage to an aspiration at another stage. The process of growth or development works somewhat like this:

1. You achieve psychological success at a given stage.
2. You set a challenging goal for yourself (one representing a higher level of aspiration).
3. You determine your own means of attaining the goal.
4. You value the goal; i.e., it is important to your self-esteem.
5. You attain the goal.
6. You achieve psychological success in this new area defined by the goal.

According to Lewin,[15] this process will reiterate as long as you achieve success at your current level, the reason being that such success will inevitably lead you to establish a new and higher level of aspiration.

Although the individual has a lot to do with this process of development, the organization also plays a strong role in psychological success. It is the organization's responsibility to detect the aspirations of "successful" employees and do what it can to insure that such individuals meet their goals while concurrently meeting the goals of the organization. Of course, this task is easier said than done. The job of management is sufficiently difficult that the goals and skills of some professional employees are overlooked.

Ritti's research of engineers,[16] for example, has revealed large-scale dissatisfaction as a result of underutilization and lack of influence. Later in this chapter, when I examine the organizational career theories, I shall point out why such conditions as underutilization and lack of influence can significantly deter an individual from not only achieving psychological success but also from advancing to higher stages of development.

Research undertaken by General Electric[17] many years ago essentially established the key conditions for psychological success, consistent with what I have reported: (1) setting one's own goals and (2) independent effort in attaining the goals. The psychological success concept, as described in these two conditions, can be applied at any stage of the career process. For example, let's say that you are stuck in the mid-life crisis. All your years of professional study, though leading to a successful job, have left you feeling that you have missed out on something. You're simply not sure who you really are. You determine to reevaluate your true identity by taking a two-week backpack expedition on your own, with just you and the elements left to "battle it out." This trip along with a variety of other self-assessment devices set you on your goal of self-discovery. Lo and behold, you determine that you are relatively fulfilled in your job, but that you haven't been sufficiently aggressive in pushing for some needed funds to really carry through on a critical project you are now heading up. With renewed resolve, you prepare to confront management.

The application of the psychological success notion as in this example can do much to alleviate worker apathy and alienation within our organizations. Before moving on to the topic of organizational careers, I shall take another detour to present a recent challenge to the life cyclists.

Alternatives to the Linear Career Path Model

The career stage theories for the most part assume linear patterns of behavior in the development of people. That is, even in spite of the adjustments and permutations which are recognized by the theorists, there is a definite bias for people to move straight and upwards toward the accomplishment of successive career goals. I have already indicated that the interactionists have taken exception to this pattern of career movement. Other researchers, Driver,[18] in particular, have pointed out that some individuals may choose to follow flat or cyclical paths as opposed to linear paths in their development. In fact, three options besides the familiar linear model have been proposed:

1. The steady-state path — This path would typify an individual who has made a lifelong commitment to a chosen job, organization, or field.
2. The spiral path — This path would reveal an individual who in the interest of pursuing different but advancing occupational opportunities makes infrequent but major shifts in his career.
3. The transitory path — This path would be taken by an individual who in the interest of trying out any number of new career experiences makes frequent moves between unrelated jobs.

EXERCISE 3-2

CAREER PATH PREFERENCE. Perhaps some of you may fit one of the three patterns listed above better than the linear path. Another way of reflecting on your path preference would be to consider Table 3-2[19] which relates the four path options to some of the psychological needs which were presented in the last chapter. Try to determine if you have a path preference.

TABLE 3-2   Relationship Between Career Path Type and Psychological Needs

Path Type . . . related to . . . Needs
Linear . . . . Achievement and Power
Steady-State . . . . Security
Spiral . . . . Growth
Transitory . . . . Identity and Challenge

Source: Adapted from Mary Ann Von Glinow, Michael J. Driver, Kenneth Brousseau, and T. Bruce Prince. "The Design of a Career-Oriented Human Resource System." *Academy of Management Review* 8:23-32, 1983.

If so: Is it consistent with your psychological needs? For example, have you decided to stay permanently with your company because "you can't beat the security?"

If not: Have you engaged in different career path types throughout your life? Are you in transition now between types?

ORGANIZATIONAL CAREER THEORIES

The discussion up to now has focused on career stage theories applied to one's entire working life. For many of us, however, a good part of our working lives is spent within one or more organizations. Our experience varies throughout our stay in any one particular organization. We certainly feel quite different when we enter the organization compared to how we might feel after becoming a ten-year veteran, for example. Are there commonalities among us in terms of how we experience our respective organizations across time? Are we likely to experience similar feelings each time we enter a new organization? These are the type of questions which are posed by theorists who have examined the idea of organizational careers — that is, careers which take their own shape during one's tenure in an organization.

Organizational career theory owes its origination to the well-known concept of rites of passage, first presented in 1908 by van Gennep, but translated a full 52 years later in 1960.[20] The rites of passage were initially proposed as a way to classify communal rites observed by widely dispersed societies. They refer to the passing of a person or group of persons from one social state to another. According to van Gennep, there are three related phases: (1) rites of separation, (2) rites of transition, and (3) rites of incorporation. In the rites of separation, the individual is for the first time cut off from earlier social attachments. A period of isolation is then experienced in the rites of transition. Finally, in the third stage, the individual is reintegrated into a new social world. These phases of the rites of passage have immediate parallels to career development in their reference to stages a job incumbent goes through once beginning and then adapting to a new position in an organization.

Socialization Theory

Socialization as an organizational career theory is mainly concerned with how newcomers come to appreciate the values, abilities, and behaviors expected in assuming an organizational role. In the career field, John Van Maanen and Edgar Schein[21] have been pioneers in developing the socialization theory, although Schein, as we shall see, takes a narrower view of the concept. Socialization theorists essentially see the process as repeating each and every time one enters a new organization or assumes a significantly different role in the same organization. In that salaried professionals are likely to experience a wide variety of organizational roles between the point of graduation from their professional schools and retirement, it is clear that socialization is a pervasive process throughout our adult professional lives.

Although socialization hasn't been addressed in the literature strictly as a stage theory, for our purposes, it is best expressed in this format. The only major limitation is that the stage approach is most appropriate for newcomers, and as I have noted, socialization occurs even to "insiders" who might assume a new role in the same organization. Nevertheless, except perhaps for the very first stage, the bulk of the discussion will be quite pertinent to job changers as well as newcomers.

I shall rely on Schein's work[22] for the presentation of the first three stages: (1) entry, (2) socialization, and (3) mutual acceptance. Entry includes the period of recruitment, selection, and orientation to the new job. Socialization, per se, refers to the period of mutual testing by both the individual and the organization as the job incumbent "learns the ropes." To avoid confusion with the broader concept of socialization theory, I shall use the term, "acclimation," to describe this second stage. Finally, mutual acceptance occurs when the individual is formally and informally granted membership in the organization, signifying a match between personal requirements and organizational needs. From mutual acceptance, the individual can go on to lead a productive, satisfying, and even permanent life in the organization, or can, on the other hand, leave the organization due to a variety of reasons, including a breakdown in the pact of mutual acceptance. Provided the individual stays, a fourth stage may be entered, which I shall refer to as tenure. Although personal productiveness is the expected outcome of the tenure stage, some job incumbents, especially professionals, may experience a gradual deterioration of their skills during this period, otherwise known as obsolescence. In the ensuing pages, I shall discuss each stage and pay particular attention in the final stage to the professional's nemesis: obsolescence.

Entry

Entry refers to that jittery experience of starting a new job. It's a time of testing between the newcomer and the organization as each party decides whether it can live with the other. Schein sees this early stage as a time when the new recruit and the organization's management work out a viable "psychological contract," defined as a "matching of what the individual will give with what the organization expects to receive, and what the organization will give relative to what the individual expects to receive."[23]

Entry properly begins prior to the assumption of job duties with an organization, as the individual develops a consciousness of the types of occupational roles that would be of interest. Attention then turns to the type of organization in which the individual would like to work. At this point, the prospective worker might experience so-called anticipatory socialization, trying to predict the attitudes and behaviors which would be considered appropriate in an organizational environment. Finally, the individual is ready to "meet" the organization. Following a search process, there may be an invitation to visit the new organization or (in the case of a job changer) a separate unit within the same organization. This introductory meeting or interview is perhaps the most critical element of the entry process, for it is here that both parties "feel each other out." Somehow at this early meeting or in subsequent meetings, the parties must decide whether there is a fit between the aspirations and qualifications of the candidate and the needs of the organization.

Unfortunately, there is much room for error at the entry stage. Meyer finds the interview process to be most responsible for motivational problems encountered by an employee subsequent to entry. She claims that during most entry interviews, neither the interviewer nor the interviewee really discuss their true concerns primarily because the "present system does not espouse open dialogue."[24] She finds that the parties typically look for predefined answers to predetermined questions, which has the ultimate effect of distorting information. As a result, the psychological contract is based upon false perceptions and inadequate information. Each party is trying to outmaneuver the other to find out what "they're really like."

The main problem at entry, then, especially for the candidate, is the development of unrealistic expectations. This especially occurs once the organization's representatives show interest in the candidate and resultingly build up their expectations about the important contributions to be made. In fact, the initial work of the newcomer may turn out to be rather routine and uninspiring, causing this individual to "cool it," or face incredible frustration. Unrealistic expectations are particularly problematic for college graduates or professional school graduates who have had limited experience in the working world. The values inculcated in professional education address the intrinsic properties of work, namely, worthwhileness, growth, individuality, expression of new ideas. Graduates also tend to be taught overviews of organizational decision making under an ethic of pure rationality.[25] Professional schools are further distinguished by small classes, seminars in place of lectures, high personal contact between students and professor, school and class solidarity, fraternal associations, and even distinctive titles and dress.[26] The overall effect is the creation of an image or stereotype of professional practice. These young graduates then enter the organization with this stereotyped image of their discipline. However, they quickly find that adherence to a set of ideal norms characteristic of the profession places them at odds with the demands of the organization. Young recruits are told to forget their global ideas, be obedient, not be too pushy or overambitious, prove their loyalty, and accept their career paths gracefully.[27] These professional recruits, meanwhile, are loathe to give up commitment to their ideals due to three powerful professional attributes learned in school: (1) identification with legendary figures whose lives embodied ideal professional norms, (2) commitment to a professional code of ethics, and (3) identification with idealized professors.[28]

The problems of unrealistic expectations among seasoned veterans choosing to take on a new assignment are typically not as severe as the extreme case portrayed above for new recruits. Nevertheless, without accurately scoping out the climate of the new placement, even the "old pro can get burned."

The entry stage was described in some detail by Meryl Louis[29] particularly in her reference to the concept of surprise. Surprise is viewed as the difference between what newcomers anticipate versus what they actually experience once entering a new organization. However, building upon prior research into the unrealistic expectations of newcomers, Louis found that anticipations regarding entry experiences can be formed after as well as before entering an organization. For example, you might develop a whole new set of expectations about your worksite after inspecting all the equipment available to you, equipment which you may not have been allowed to fully inspect during the recruitment process. Anticipations can also be unconscious as well as conscious. After you begin work, for example, you might become anxious about relations with your new boss, a condition which you may not become aware of until several weeks into the job.

In order to successfully make the transition into a new organization, newcomers need to make sense out of these so-called surprise experiences. Louis advises newcomers to rely upon insiders to give them local interpretations or ways to sense out the culture of any new work station. Of course, inside information is only useful to the extent the newcomer knows what to look for. Hence, there is also no substitute for self-insight in managing the entry process, as was discussed in the last chapter. This goes for both the newcomer and management. Newcomers must understand their values and abilities, but management should have a clear understanding of the job in question and, in particular, the requirements for successful job performance. Then, the two parties need to move to the most critical task of all — communication. Newcomers need to communicate their capabilities as accurately as possible. Management must communicate the job's requirements and opportunities for growth in the company. I cannot minimize the difficulty of this communication process since a climate of openness is unlikely to occur at the first interview. Nevertheless, it is in your interest to provide accurate information about yourself without jeopardizing your position. You should likewise seek out managers who seem forthright in their commitment to providing accurate information on their organization. Getting them to introduce you to insiders (potential colleagues and supervisors) with whom you can interact might well convince you of their commitment to providing you with the information needed to make a successful entry.

Although I am directing the discussion to the individual professional in this book, a word is in order here regarding the role institutions, particularly schools, might play in facilitating the entry process. Professional schools can improve the transition from school to work by exposing the student to actual work situations, easing entry shock. Of course, many do this through apprenticeships or internship programs. However, the emphasis in these apprenticeship programs is typically on learning the practical applications of the profession rather than in learning how to adapt to the norms of an organization. In fact, sponsoring professionals typically try to avoid exposing their apprentices to organizational problems so as not to interfere with their professional training. Allowing the student greater contact with live organizational experiences will do much to relieve some of the frustration arising from entry problems.[30]

Acclimation

Although the entry process is common to most job candidates, regardless of occupational category, the acclimation stage presents some unique problems to professionals. Now admitted into the organization, they must learn to adapt to the organizational culture, learn how to make their way, and make their personal imprint without jeopardizing the essential norms of the organization. As I demonstrated at length in the first chapter, professionals by definition tend to resist acclimation. What this means is that they will tend to resist bureaucratic rules, will tend to reject bureaucratic standards, resist supervision, and maintain only conditional loyalty to the organization.[31] Of course, not all professionals will act in the same way, but research seems to indicate that the more cosmopolitan the professional, the greater the desire to engage in basic research, and the more advanced the academic training, then the more difficult the acclimation.[32] However, a local orientation is not without adjustment problems. Systems engineers, for example, do place emphasis on career advancement in the organization, a characteristic local trait. However, their academic training and professional orientation still tends to thwart their successful acclimation since their interest in organizational advancement is not so much a desire to manage people as to achieve sufficient organizational status to permit them a wider latitude of technical involvement.[33]

Regardless of the adequacy of the preparation of professionals for organizational life, they must eventually, if they are to remain with the organization, reconcile internal standards with the reality of bureaucratic life. A number of tasks need to be accomplished during this acclimation stage. First is the need for them to develop a working relationship with their supervisors and administrators. As stated above, professionals are typically poorly prepared on this account. Nevertheless, they must learn to accept this human aspect of organizational life, including the need to "politick" and compromise to get their ideas across. Besides the bosses, they also need to establish positive relationships with colleagues to whom they might be able to turn for support and advice. They also need to learn the technical aspects of their new job as well as the bureaucratic procedures associated with its successful performance. This might entail learning how to cope with ambiguity and uncertainty as well as outright resistance to their ideas. The ambiguity may even surround the nature of the new position. Feedback on performance, for example, may not be immediately available; consequently, professionals have to learn how to become a judge of their own performance.[34] Finally, they will need to establish an organizational identity which will encompass the process not only of gaining acceptance from management but also from their peer group. This process will be contingent on learning the reward system in the organization, that is, how to get ahead, whom to associate with, whom to trust. According to Feldman,[35] there are four indicators that the acclimation process is running smoothly: (1) feeling accepted, (2) believing oneself competent, (3) having a clear role definition, and (4) obtaining general agreement that one is on the right track.

For job changers, as opposed to newcomers, coping with acclimation may include three other tasks:

1. delegating responsibilities to others in order to decrease inordinate work demands,
2. trying new ways of tackling the new job that were not used on the old job (for example, using dictation instead of writing longhand), and
3. trying to increase the portion of the new job which is enjoyable and interesting and which falls within one's specific skill inventory.[36]

These tasks will be elaborated upon in the next chapter.

There is no question that the organization is a strong cultural force which exerts considerable pressure in obliging the individual to conform to its lifestyle. At the beginning of the acclimation stage, the pressure is likely to be strongest as the organization attempts to thwart the demands for autonomy on the part of the young professional. The organization's representatives want to be sure that these individuals fit in, that they will make a contribution, and that they will take on increasing responsibility.[37] It is likely that after proving themselves, the organization will in fact allow them that treasured autonomy, but only after it is convinced that they are devoted to organizational and not just professional goals.[38] Obviously, some professionals will resist early acclimation, and yet their technical contribution might be sufficiently vital that the organization might attempt to accommodate them. One way to do this, as I pointed out in the Chapter One, is by creating specialized roles for them in partially segregated substructures of the organization. For example, Barber points out that in the federal government bureaucracy, there are separate departments or suborganizations for basic medical research, for the development of medical technology, and for day-to-day medical care.[39] In addition to differentiated roles, organizations can also create accommodative authority structures, for example, in the creation of the role of professional-administrator. Barber defines this person as a "professional who can judge and direct another professional but who can also exercise superordinate control when necessary." Finally, organizations can also create opportunities for professionals to achieve professional rewards while concurrently serving the organization, for example, by allowing them to attend professional association meetings, to present and publish papers, to continue professional training through subsidies and leaves, to be allowed to advance in salary and prestige on a professional track, and so on.

In general, however, accommodation between the professional and the organization during acclimation is best achieved without having to resort to the creation of specialized roles and organizational structures since these risk alienating the individual even further from the mainstream of the organization. From the individual's point of view, there has to be an attempt to work within the constraints of the bureaucracy. This might mean initiating certain ideas and practices at times while also showing willingness to learn at others. It is critical at this stage that one be aware of the human and political side of the organization so that appreciation is given to what *can* be done as much as what *should* be done.

The organization and its management have perhaps the critical responsibility in "breaking in" young professionals during the acclimation stage. Schein[40] continually looks to the boss as the key linchpin, whose behavior towards newcomers can really predetermine their career development within the company. The boss may often feel threatened by the newcomers' state-of-the-art education and may even try to thwart their progress. However, acknowledging the need to tone down the theoretical idealism of their young professionals, the boss should still allow them an opportunity to do challenging work right off and to provide them with feedback on whatever they do. Newcomers also need to learn through the feedback process the areas in which they are sufficiently skilled and those for which they need additional training. Finally, newcomers also need to know the values and norms of the organization, namely, the kinds of activities and practices which are really cherished. For example, should a young engineer stress technical competence or general product responsibility?[41] Here again, the boss as well as the individual's peer group can be helpful in transmitting reliable information. I shall analyze the role and importance of one's boss in detail in Chapter Five.

Mutual Acceptance

In this third stage of socialization, the individual and the organization begin to firm up the psychological contract, which I spoke about as being first established at entry. Whereas during that stage, the process of mutual adjustment characterizing the psychological contract was merely surfaced, during mutual acceptance, both parties agree on the general terms of employment, both formal and informal, to last throughout the duration of the job. Schein describes this stage as follows:

> The new employee decides that she or he can perform, that the work is challenging and satisfying enough, and that the culture is compatible enough with his or her own personality and value system to continue to invest in the organization; the organization decides that the new employee has enough talent to make a contribution and the right kind of personality and values to fit in.[42]

During this stage, which might come after a few years on the job for a novice, but possibly in much less time for an experienced worker, the pact made between job incumbent and organization is not necessarily ironclad. It is, on the contrary, fluid and at times even ambiguous. Given changes in management, strategic position, or even wider environmental changes, such as political or economic disruptions, the psychological contract at times has to be renegotiated. Nevertheless, there are definite steps which the parties can take to affirm mutual acceptance.[43] Individuals can manifest their acceptance in three ways: (1) by indicating explicitly that they intend to remain in the organization, (2) by displaying a high level of motivation and commitment, and (3) by accepting from time to time undesirable work conditions to help the organization pass through a difficult situation, such as economic hardship.

The organization for its part can manifest its acceptance in five ways. It can:

1. continue to provide positive feedback on the employee's performance,
2. provide salary increases based upon merit,
3. increase the job incumbent's level of responsibility on the current job or make a promotion to a new job which is inherently more challenging than the original one,
4. share organizational secrets such as work-related information, personal feedback from others, politically sensitive information, or important anecdotes on the organization's history, or
5. give a party, a hazing, a private office, or some other initiation rite.

Feldman[44] discusses two other issues which are inherent to this period and which require resolution. First, as the demands of the job may increase during this period, individuals may need to resolve schedule conflicts between work life and home life. The organization needs to be aware of such conflicts and help these accepted employees to the extent possible through flexible work assignments. The second issue, and this arises especially among engineering, research and development (R&D), and hospital personnel, individuals need to deal with conflicts between their work group and other groups or departments or divisions within the organization. Although accepted within their work group, other individuals perhaps higher up in the organization may have very different expectations about how they have interpreted their work assignment. As examples, there may be disagreement on the use of a particular vendor, a conflict may arise on the true role of a nurse's aide, or the use of a given technology may be challenged. In the event of such intergroup conflicts, individuals will need the support of their work group and boss as well as other third parties to resolve the dispute.

Tenure and Obsolescence

The last stage of socialization is tenure. By this point, the job incumbent and the organization have reached agreement on the psychological contract governing their work relationship. The individual is assured of a job, except perhaps in cases of extreme economic emergency, and is essentially released by the company to perform his or her tasks under an increasing amount of independence and self-direction. Tenure virtually signals the rite or conferral of job independence within the constraints of acceptable organizational behavior. It is typically not formally conferred except within academic institutions, and may in some instances be quite implicit. Nevertheless, whether it be through a handshake, an invitation to the company club, or a promotion, one gets the message that one has finally "made it."

With tenure comes the expectation that one will take increasing responsibility for work performance. This will typically involve receiving less and less supervision but assuming a stronger role in supervising the work of others. Tenure on the job is often associated with the initiation of the mentor role, a function which I shall discuss in some detail in Chapter Five and as part of the next organizational career theory to be presented shortly. It can also be associated with the status of being a "company man," at least in the sense that the bond established with the organization presupposes diligence in working to accomplish organizational goals. Finally, although not a sole by-product of tenure, the individual's ability to influence organizational effectiveness is more likely to occur during and after this stage of development than during earlier stages.[45]

Although the conferral of tenure may constitute the impetus for a flurry of creative work for many, some individuals may find that the responsibilities of tenure may result in a gradual obsolescence of their skills. Tenure is by no means a cause of obsolescence; it can at most be said that tenure is associated with obsolescence. Further, the demands of a job do not perforce lead to obsolescence of the skills necessary to perform similar jobs. It is when the job changes dramatically, requiring new abilities on the part of its incumbent, that job obsolescence may occur. Professionals may also be subject to another kind of obsolescence which may occur paradoxically due to too much concentration on the job itself. This would be when they do not keep up with developments in their particular profession. The mass layoffs in the aerospace industry during the 1970s of technical professionals, most of whom had difficulty finding new employment due to a lack of professional versatility, is a good example of this kind of *professional* obsolescence.[46] H. G. Kaufman's definition of obsolescence combines both conceptions of obsolescence presented above:

> The degree to which organizational professionals lack the up-to-date knowledge or skills necessary to maintain effective performance in either their current or future work roles.[47]

Besides being associated with job and professional components, obsolescence can be looked at from the point of view of the source of its development. The literature seems to agree that the job incumbent is not solely responsible for its occurrence. The immediate work and organizational climate and even the wider knowledge environment surrounding the organization share in the blame for obsolescence. By the wider knowledge environment, I refer to the knowledge and information explosion popularized by Alvin Toffler and others.[48] Back in the 1960s, for instance, a familiar observation among so-called futurists was that 80 to 90 percent of all scientists who had ever lived were then alive! Clearly the pace of technology and the creation of new knowledge continues to accelerate on a scale which far outstrips the intellectual capabilities of most humans.

In order to keep pace with the amount of new knowledge in one's field, professionals need to have time to at least read the published literature in their field, let along gain experience in implementing new technologies. It has been estimated that about 20 percent of a professional's working time should be allotted to reading in his or her field.[49] Yet, few organizations are willing to sacrifice the contributions of their professional staff for this amount of time.

Other practices of management within organizations aggravate the problem of obsolescence. First of all, attitudes which associate age or experience with obsolescence essentially preordain senior persons to secondary roles within the organization and build in a bias for youth.[50] This is further compounded when management assigns its senior professionals to routine work or work which lacks intellectual demands, time pressure, and/or variety.[51] The way management structures the work environment can also have a significant bearing on updating. Work groups should be formed which include specialists with a diversity of backgrounds and skills and whose composition changes periodically to assure exposure to new knowledge. Management should also allow professional staff a fair amount of independence in their work, frequent feedback on their performance, and access to organizational decision making. Relatively flexible structures are preferred, then, to hierarchical systems which tend to stifle professional influence and participation.[52]

The individual is by no means a silent partner in obsolescence. Although the myth of the inexorable relationship between age and obsolescence has been dispelled, there are some personal characteristics which predispose certain individuals to obsolescence. These include:

1. A limited capacity for knowledge acquisition on the basis of the individual's intellectual capacity;
2. A lack of motivation to stay up-to-date based upon the individual's separate interests, needs, or energy; and
3. Personality traits which reveal a weak self-concept, high need for security, and poor adaptability to change.[53]

On the basis of the foregoing identification of the ingredients of obsolescence, what changes in job and organizational life can be suggested to mitigate its ill effects? Kaufman, on the basis of his estimable work on the subject as it relates to professional career development, offered eleven recommendations:[54]

1. Monitor the degree of obsolescence in the organization and establish controls for its detection among individual professionals.
2. Improve techniques of selection and placement to avoid a mismatch of professionals and position requirements.

3. Provide for periodic objective appraisals of future potential and career development.
4. Establish a flexible retirement policy and provide for portable pensions.
5. Redesign professional jobs to make them more challenging.
6. Provide for changes in job assignments to avoid narrow specialization.
7. Allow professionals who have become obsolescent the possibility of a career change.
8. Encourage development through colleague interaction by organizing work groups composed of professionals with diverse backgrounds.
9. Select supervisors of professionals primarily on the basis of knowledge and skills that are relevant to the type of work carried out by their subordinates.
10. Create an organizational climate through management policies that encourages and rewards growth and development.
11. Carefully plan and evaluate continuing education programs to help increase their effectiveness in updating professionals.

Professionals may have only limited control over these policy recommendations. Some of the specific steps they can take to overcome obsolescent conditions will be discussed in Chapter Six. For now, it is essential that the individual recognize the symptoms of obsolescence so that he or she can take action either to overcome it or strategically accept its inevitability. By the latter, I mean acknowledging its occurrence in conjunction with decelerating interest in work for work's sake. For example, one might choose to devote more time to family and community activities or other life space concerns.

The exercise below is designed to produce a greater awareness of your potential obsolescence.

EXERCISE 3-3

OBSOLESCENCE SELF-ASSESSMENT QUESTIONNAIRE.

INSTRUCTIONS:
Consider each of the questions and circle the appropriate answer using the following scale:

1	2	3	4
not at all true	slightly true	moderately true	very true

1. My skill level on my job has begun to deteriorate.　1　2　3　4
2. I don't find I have the energy to keep up with my work these days.　1　2　3　4
3. I am more interested in personal fulfillment than in becoming a success either in my organization or profession.　1　2　3　4
4. My knowledge of the latest developments in my field has decreased in recent years.　1　2　3　4
5. I am more interested in my home life or community than in my job.　1　2　3　4
6. Trying to keep up in my field is becoming impossible.　1　2　3　4
7. The reason I am unlikely to make a job or career change is that I have become too specialized in my work.　1　2　3　4
8. I have reached an age when it would be foolish to work like a dog again.　1　2　3　4
9. I no longer have the time to keep up with my professional reading.　1　2　3　4
10. I'd say it's time for the younger people in this organization to produce some new ideas or innovations.　1　2　3　4

Although this questionnaire has not been validated, it may produce some useful insights. Obviously the questions are derived from variables associated with obsolescence. You may wish to first get a sense of your total obsolescence potential. Simply add up all the circled responses. If your score is greater than 25, then there is some chance that you are falling into obsolescence. This does not portend disaster by any means. As I indicated previously, some obsolescence is virtually out of our control. Furthermore, some obsolescence may be desirable.

Your next task is to examine each question to which you gave a three or four. Does your answer reflect a growing obsolescence? If not, formulate why the question may have been misinterpreted. If the question does indeed reflect obsolescence, consider whether you wish to change the condition cited. For example, if you haven't been keeping up with your professional reading, how might you carve out the necessary minutes in your schedule to accommodate this activity? Perhaps, on the other hand, if the question reflects obsolescence, you may choose not to change the condition. Why might that be so? For example, if you are less interested in becoming successful in your profession, is it because you have developed some outside interests which have become more fulfilling to you?

Having completed this exercise, you should find the next and final section of the chapter quite relevant.

Professional Organizational Career Theory

As I had indicated at the outset of the chapter, the second organizational career theory to be presented is one which has been geared especially to professional work concerns. It also has a normative bent; in other words, its architects, namely Dalton, Thompson, and Price[55] believe that the professional's performance within an organization will be sounder assuming the professional successfully moves through the requisite stages. The stages, as in most developmental theories, are distinguished by the types of relationships to be engaged in and by the psychological adjustments to be made. It should be noted that Dalton and his collaborators did not expect the professional to be solely responsible for successfully negotiating the stages. In fact, in most of their writing, they suggested ways in which management could insure successful individual accomplishment. Nevertheless, awareness of these stages by the individual professional can provide the knowledge necessary to make adjustments in one's career that could lead to greater personal fulfillment as well as a better fit with one's own organization. Further, adherence to these stages can do much to prevent the negative consequences of obsolescence discussed in the prior section. The stages of this theory are as follows:

Stage One: Apprentice — This stage beings as soon as one joins an organization. During this early period, the young professional must learn to distinguish which tasks are critical to the organization and how to get them done, using both formal and informal means of communication. Although under rather close supervision and performing somewhat routine assignments, one is also expected to show some initiative and help the superior achieve his or her work goals. Critical during this stage is the need to have a good mentor who is capable of teaching the young professional "the ropes." Although the apprentice may feel constrained by the subordinate relationship, the ability to accept this early important role while showing signs of creativity will facilitate movement into the next stage.

Stage Two: Specialist — at Stage two, the professional gets the chance to strike out on his or her own and achieve independent technical competence. Given the complexity of skills required in today's organizational environment, the professional during this stage is advised to achieve some visibility by becoming temporarily competent in a chosen specialty. I say temporarily since it is important that the professional not become pigeonholed into one area, thereby closing off future opportunities. Although still under supervision at this stage, direction becomes more general as the specialist relies as much on colleagues and the profession as a whole for ideas and advice as his or her mentor. Although there is pressure to move quickly into supervisory responsibilities, the specialist should be certain to first gain sufficient technical competence.

Stage Three: Mentor — By this point, the more seasoned professionals should begin to take responsibility for guiding and developing young professionals who are typically in Stage one. This comes about as an outgrowth of success as a specialist. These individuals first broaden their area of expertise often as a benefit to the organization. Second, they develop contacts and clients outside the organization. In order to carry out their now more responsible work and to be of service to clients, they need the assistance of others who can help do the detail work and develop their ideas. Not only must professionals at this stage possess the interpersonal and managerial skills to bring on younger professionals, but they must also know how to collaborate effectively with their peers to get things done. At the same time, they must still understand and negotiate orders from the top. The key to being a successful mentor is the ability to develop the confidence of younger professionals, the restraint to let them move on, and the judgment to pull away from one's technical background in order to supervise, while not becoming stale.

Stage Four: Sponsor — Those professionals who make it into the fourth stage become a virtual force shaping the direction of their organization perhaps by interfacing with critical actors in the environment, by developing new ideas, products, or services, or by directing the resources of the organization. Although such individuals may be in formal line positions by this time, some are not. What characterizes them is the reliance others in the organization place upon them for innovative ideas and direction. Sponsors also tend to be recognized (through achievements and/or publications) outside the organization. Stage four professionals continue to develop people as in Stage three, but rather than focusing on teaching young professionals or bringing them along, their interest is in providing opportunities for promising individuals and then in assessing their performance. By this last stage, professionals clearly focus their energies outside the day-to-day operations of the organization and concentrate on long range concerns. They tend to influence others through ideas, through personnel selection, through resource allocation, through reorganization, or even through outright power.

As you peruse these stages, some questions might come to mind. For example, can one skip stages and still be successful? Can one be successful by staying in one stage? Must one be a manager to move into Stages three or four? Although there are no firm conclusions to be made in response to these questions, Dalton provides further detail on this framework on the basis of his ongoing research. First, although stages can be skipped, it normally occurs only when one can acquire the knowledge required in any particular stage through other means. For example, it is possible to learn the ropes without a mentor from a group of colleagues who perhaps joined the organization at the same time. However, such a pattern, which essentially bypasses Stage one, is usually not as effective as working with a mentor. Although skips are not advised, then, temporary reversions to earlier stages are acceptable. For example, a Stage three or Stage four professional might selectively revert to Stage two to pick up some additional technical skills. This might be particularly appropriate for someone who fears becoming obsolete.

As for staying put in one stage, although some individuals may find security and satisfaction, for example, in pursuing a chosen technical specialty, Dalton finds that to sustain effectiveness throughout one's career, one should seek to move to at least Stage three. Finally, as was mentioned in the discussion of Stage four, to reach the final stage or even to become a mentor, one need not become a manager. Many highly effective mentors and sponsors are "idea people" or entrepreneurs inside the organization who shun formal management responsibilities. Of course, Stage three or four nonmanager types cannot survive in a rigidly structured organization which closes off opportunities for informal guidance.

This concludes the discussion of career stage theories. As part of the self-assessment, these theories have been introduced to provide you with a general set of standards against which to compare your progress. Again, you should not consider yourself a failure if you skipped a stage or did not reach one or another stage. Rather, my presentation was designed to focus on the competencies expected to be achieved at a particular stage.

Now that you have some good insights into your personal abilities, values, and development, it is appropriate to shift the analysis from you to your job and organization.

FOUR: Job Analysis

INTRODUCTION

The self-assessment completed in the last two chapters was concerned with your personal career development from the viewpoint of yourself – those attributes about you (specifically your skills, attitudes, and development) which contribute to your identity as a person and as a professional. Before you can conduct a true diagnosis of the balance or fit between yourself and your work environment, you need to next analyze your current job and your organization. Then, you will be in a better position to assess the fit between your personal style and your organization's requirements. Subsequently, you will be able to implement your own personal career development plan.

In this relatively short chapter, I begin the diagnosis of your work environment with a job analysis. I shall save the organizational diagnosis for the following chapter. I focus on the job because it is really the basic building block of your career. So, if you are eventually going to move to other jobs and career opportunities, you will first need to analyze the skills and procedures attached to your current job. You will start with a job inventory and the preparation of a daily work balance sheet. You will also consider those aspects of work which produce personal satisfaction and then compare your results with other salaried professionals. Next, you will conduct what I refer to as a behavioral job analysis which critically examines the specific skills and activities which you perform on your job.

Once you have a firm understanding of the behavioral components of your job, that is, the things that you actually do and do well in your work, you will be invited to map out your potential career paths using a method which allows you to consider auspicious career moves inside your current organization. You will learn, for example, how to connect jobs which though not technically related may be functionally interdependent. Finally, the chapter will close with a discussion of some of the particular career path problems of professionals, to include an evaluation of the familiar "dual ladder" approach.

JOB INVENTORY

As was suggested in the introduction, the first place we must look in order to evaluate our current work environment is, of course, our job. Our job really tells us and others around us in the organization what we do. The job analysis must ultimately focus on the behaviors related to our work. By dissecting these behaviors, we can obtain a firm grasp of our skills and abilities and, in so doing, prepare for career growth.

Before analyzing the tasks entailed in the job, I would like to begin with a subjective assessment of the job which will elicit the feelings you have toward your work. Just as in the self-assessment, it is not sufficient to conduct a personal job analysis without considering your values and attitudes. How you conduct yourself on your job and how effective you are both are very much dependent on your attitudes. Once you have completed the subjective analysis, you will proceed to the objective behavioral analysis which together with the subjective data will provide a relatively complete personal job record.

The idea of a job inventory was developed by Edward Roseman.[1] It assumes that as workers we can catalog the satisfactory and unsatisfactory aspects of our job provided we take the time and are given an appropriate framework. Hence, it uses subjective analysis as the basis for evaluating your job. In Roseman's framework, the job is divided into four components, referred to as: (1) kicks, (2) bug, (3) show-off, and (4) under-the-carpet elements. A kicks element is one that provides a great deal of enjoyment. It might entail the nature of your work, its creative content, or its challenge.

It might involve the people you work with. A bug comprises things that annoy or worry you — the boring aspects of your job, your boss, a particularly unpleasant colleague, or poor fringes. A show-off element represents things which give a sense of pride, for example, being unmatched in technical skill, relating easily with people, developing a reputation of being able to perform under pressure. Finally, the under-the-carpet elements are obviously those which you would like to hide, for example, being messy, not being able to relate well to authority figures, or being terrible at spelling.

EXERCISE 4-1

THE PERSONAL JOB INVENTORY. Once you have a good understanding of Roseman's four job elements, you should consider this first exercise of the chapter in which using Table 4-1 you are asked to prepare a list of things which you do in your present job for each of the elements. You should also indicate next to each activity why that particular activity made you classify it as a kicks, bug, show-off, or under-the-carpet activity. For example, if you indicate a biweekly meeting with your staff in your kicks list, in the next column, you might say that you enjoy that activity because it gives you the sense of support you need in your current work environment. If you list making field visits as one of your bug activities, in the next column you might indicate that field visits cause you to deal with your inherent shyness, a condition you would like to avoid at this time.

TABLE 4-1   Job Inventory Lists

KICKS LIST

Things I do daily that are a source of   *Why these activities make me feel*
enjoyment   *good*

BUG LIST

Things I do daily that annoy and   *Why these activities make me feel*
worry me   *lousy*

Table 4-1, continued

SHOW-OFF LIST

Things I do daily that show off my   *Why these activities represent my*
skills   *strengths*

UNDER-THE-CARPET LIST

Things I do daily that I would like to   *Why these activities are embarrassing*
hide   *to me*

Once the four lists are completed, Roseman suggests preparing a daily work balance sheet. On the left side of the sheet, shown in Table 4-2, the daily activities which appeared on the kicks and show-off lists are recorded. How much time spent at these activities is also indicated. On the right side of the balance sheet, the bug and under-the-carpet activities are indicated with their respective durations. Assuming you work a minimal eight-hour day, the total time for all activities would obviously approach 480 minutes. (Any remainder would be considered taken up by nonclassified activities.) Roseman believes that the balance sheet as the culminating exercise of the personal job inventory helps people get a better perspective on their job. It helps them spot developing imbalances quickly. Of course, imbalances on the right side of the balance sheet are of more concern and need corrective action. Planning more kicks or show-off activities in place of the bug and under-the-carpet activities is one simple method of remediation, although it would be unrealistic to expect all of your bug and under-the-carpet activities to be eliminated. The idea behind the exercise is that once you take an inventory of your job, you will be in a position to take more control of your work day.

TABLE 4-2   Daily Work Balance Sheet

Kicks and show-off activities		Bug list and under – the – carpet activities	
ACTIVITY	DURATION	ACTIVITY	DURATION
Total minutes		**Total minutes**	

Source: Reprinted by permission of the publisher, from *Confronting Nonpromotability: How to Manage a Stalled Career,* by Edward Roseman © 1977 by AMACOM, a division of American Management Associations. All rights reserved.

133

JOB SATISFACTION

Literally thousands of studies have been mounted on the subject of job satisfaction, most of them seeking to find out its causes. Although there has been no agreement on a list of essential ingredients, social scientists have recently sought to explain the facets of job satisfaction rather than attempting to isolate the unique causes of general job satisfaction. The facets refer to specific aspects of the job which produce satisfaction or dissatisfaction. Hence, a neutral stance on general job satisfaction may merely represent an average of some very extreme attitudes on some of these job facets. As you shall explore in the next exercise, some of the familiar facets used in job satisfaction indexes include: satisfaction with pay, with working conditions, with the opportunity for growth, with the challenge provided on the job, with peer relationships, etc.

Generally speaking, professionals as a whole along with managers and executives tend to be more satisfied with their jobs, less often depressed by their work, and less likely to be trapped in their jobs as compared to semiskilled, unskilled, and clerical workers.[2] However, according to a survey of *Psychology Today* readers, they are more inclined to leave their organization if their demands are not met, and chief among the demands is the opportunity for personal growth.[3] This should come as no surprise to you. In Chapter Two, I reported that professionals as a whole lean towards the higher-order needs as a source of satisfaction. This conclusion is supported by Hall and Schneider[4] in their study of three types of professionals: (1) priests, (2) foresters, and (3) research scientists/engineers. All three types were found to be motivated most by job challenge. The researchers, however, were most inclined to leave their organization in search of greater self-fulfillment. Tenure was very important to the priests and foresters. Badawy[5] continued this line of research attempting to differentiate job satisfaction among professional types. He found that scientists wanted jobs entailing more opportunity to do meaningful scientific work, autonomy, and recognition, whereas engineers preferred jobs more attached to the organization involving such facets as advancement, pay, and influence. Generally speaking, salaried professionals are most satisfied with their work when it provides challenge, responsibility, and opportunity for achievement and recognition. Pure professionals might then differentiate from this general outlook by expressing satisfaction with their working conditions. This is because many of them work in very pleasant surroundings, perhaps even reminiscent of their graduate training. Quasi professionals, on the other hand, tend to express satisfaction with their peers (since they often need to rely upon them to perform effectively) and with opportunity for advancement. Recalling the discussion in Chapter One regarding the transition to management, many engineers as quasi professionals have virtually an ingrained sense that advancement to management is a normal progression from their technical work.

It is simply not possible to generalize across time, however, what professionals want from their jobs. There are too many environmental conditions, such as the economy, which change people's perceptions. Professionals themselves, as we know, differ greatly in their outlook toward work. Scholarship too has been indefinite on this subject. Argyris and Schön, for example, in their treatise on professional effectiveness believe that professionals want to become self-actualized in their jobs; they want "more of their total personality involved in their work."[6] These authors proposed a model of professional change wherein both the professional and his *clients* obtain greater freedom of choice and internal commitment. Katz[7] found that job satisfaction varied with the actual length of time one has spent on the job. Although the intrinsic factors may be important early on in the job, after about five years, the extrinsic factors — nature of supervision, pleasant peer relations, working conditions, pay, benefits — become more important.

Clearly, the facets of job satisfaction differ among professional groups and even among individuals based upon any number of unique personal, organizational, and environmental conditions. Nevertheless, there appears to be, at a minimum, agreement that job content matters. Perhaps the key question to ask, then, is whether the *quality* of your job meets your expectations; whether it fulfills you as a human being. With that in mind, you should proceed to Exercise 4-2.

EXERCISE 4-2

PERSONAL JOB SATISFACTION. As you have seen, there are many aspects of a job that account for satisfaction or dissatisfaction. A long list of some of the principal facets which social scientists have attributed to job satisfaction is provided in Table 4-3. Indicate in the first response column the importance

TABLE 4-3   Facets of Personal Job Satisfaction

	Importance	*Satisfaction*	*Difference Score*
Pay			
Peer relationships			
Job status and professional respectability			
Security			
Advancement opportunity			
Opportunity for growth and/or learning			
Pleasant working conditions			
Challenge			
Good variety in work tasks			
Opportunity to supervise others			
Good boss, adequate supervision			
Good feedback on performance			
Chance to make own decisions, level of responsibility and independence			
Closure — chance to complete the entire task			
Fair recognition and reward			
A feeling of belonging			
A sense of contribution to the overall purpose of the organization			
A sense of contribution to society			
Adequate power to accomplish my goals			
Opportunity to obtain professional recognition outside work			
Moral value of the work			
Opportunity to take risks and use creativity			

you attach to the respective facets on a scale of one through six, one being very unimportant, six being very important. In the second column, record, after you have completed your importance responses for *all* of the facets, your degree of satisfaction with the facet in your current job, again on a scale of one through six, one being very dissatisfied, six being very satisfied. Await further instructions on the third response column.

After recording all your rated responses for the first two columns, in the third response column, simply subtract the rating given for satisfaction from that given for importance for each facet. In other words, subtract column number two from column number one. Any positive number would indicate that for that facet, your current level of job satisfaction does not meet your requirements in terms of the importance of that particular facet. Examine that facet and others more carefully. Can you identify as precisely as possible why that facet of satisfaction is not being met on your job according to the degree of importance you attach to it? For example, if you have a positive difference score for "adequate power to accomplish my goals," it may be that your boss, in conformance with a corporate-wide restrictive personnel policy regarding job descriptions, simply cannot allow you to appropriate even minimal funds to start up some interesting pilot projects. Once you have critically explored the basis for your difference scores in this way, you will be able to contribute some important data in developing your personal career development plan later on in Chapter Six. As you will discover, in the plan for change section, a variety of options will be available to you to improve your job and career satisfaction. In the example cited, you might find that a vertical move in your technical classification or perhaps a lateral move into a related technical area might be appropriate for you. For now, it is useful to keep these facets in mind which have produced relative dissatisfaction in your job.

BEHAVIORAL JOB ANALYSIS

As stated earlier in the chapter, our job tells us and others in the organization what we do. Yet, most people very rarely document what they actually do on a particular job. Looking at the specific behaviors performed on a job is referred to as job analysis. The rationale for undertaking a job analysis is threefold: (1) There are many skills and activities which a job incumbent performs on any job. Without careful analysis, only a few of the key activities might come to mind, overlooking a number of secondary but critical tasks and skills. (2) Career mobility inside an organization can be thwarted if management doesn't know the critical activities associated with certain jobs. No one can really be prepared to take anyone's place since information on job behaviors is largely unavailable. (3) Performance on a job is more appropriately evaluated against the key behaviors of the job as opposed to some gross measures (for example, sales volume) of performance.

Each of these three points relates to personal career development. The first point, however, represents the special purpose I have in mind at this point in the chapter — how to diagnose the key tasks or behaviors you perform on your job so that you can ultimately determine whether it is meeting your career and personal needs. Accordingly, a comprehensive job analysis activity is presented below along with one optional exercise.

EXERCISE 4-3

A. PREPARING A JOB DESCRIPTION OF YOUR CURRENT JOB. In order to prepare a behavioral job analysis, you will need to develop a job description which entails an accounting of all the activities and procedures used in your current job. Beatty and Schneier[8] have devised a guide, shown in Table 4-4, to help in preparing a job description. Using the guide, prepare a current job description of your job. If you have a formal job description, you may use it to help you in this exercise, but be careful. Many formal job descriptions simply don't adequately describe what you actually do on your job. Think through each point on the guide very carefully. Once complete, share the job description with someone who also knows about your job — your boss, a colleague, a former job incumbent. Ask them if you were accurate in your description. What areas did *you* stress? Did you discover that your job had changed over time? In what ways?

TABLE 4-4   Job Description Guide

INSTRUCTIONS:
Consider the following points as you prepare your job description.

1. *Define your job.* State briefly what is done by the unit in which you work. Explain how your job fits in with others in the organization, and make clear the purpose of your position. This should be as brief and concise as possible.
2. *List your different kinds of duties.* Describe each briefly, but in enough detail to give a clear understanding of your work. Start with the primary duties of your position. Then estimate the percentage of time for each.

Table 4-4, continued

---

3. *If you have any responsibility for the work of others, explain the nature and extent of your supervision and guidance of their work.* This includes supervision over those who report to you and their subordinates, and it also includes indirect responsibility. State by kinds of jobs the employees for whom you are responsible and to what extent.

4. *Explain the scope and effect of your work.* State how and to what extent your actions, recommendations, and decisions affect your organization, your clients, or the public. Explain the consequences of possible mistakes or errors in judgment. Describe how you influence the quality of work produced by others. Explain the extent of your authority to speak or act for your organization. Describe the effects of your work on: (1) policy, procedure, and organization; and (2) use of people, material, equipment, and funds.

5. *Describe the supervision and guidance you receive.* State what supervision and help you receive before, during, and after performance of your assignments from your supervisor, others, written guides, or practices. Describe any other guides for doing your work, such as regulations, procedures, practices, manuals, and standards, and describe how directly they affect your work.

6. *State the nature and extent of the mental demands of your position.* They may include any or all of the following:
   a. *initiative* — taking action without specific instruction;
   b. *originality* — the creativeness or inventiveness demanded by the work;
   c. *judgment* — the selection of the best course of action; or
   d. *any other* significant mental demand.

7. *What are the knowledges, skills, and abilities required.* State any knowledges, skills and abilities actually required by the job. For instance, include special manual skills, physical abilities, and aptitudes required. Identify the tasks concerned in each case and describe how and why such requirements are necessary.

8. *State the nature and purpose of the contacts you have in your work with persons other than your supervisors or subordinates.* Tell whether your work contacts are to exchange information, to make explanations, to persuade others, or to take part in group action.

9. *List anything else that affects your position.* Specify any job conditions or other considerations not covered elsewhere in your position description which affect the responsibility or difficulty of your work.

Source: Richard W. Beatty and Craig Eric Schneier, *Personnel Administration: An Experiential Skill Building Approach*, © 1977, Addison-Wesley, Reading, MA. p. 65. Reprinted with permission.

Now that you have prepared your job description and determined its accuracy and particularity with the aid of a colleague, consider the following questions as you incorporate this objective data into your overall job diagnosis.

1. How does your job relate to other jobs in your organization which you are very much aware of and/or have interest in.
2. As you consider the duties of your job, which ones are you expert at? Which ones give you problems? Which ones would you consider essential in giving you job satisfaction?
3. If you supervise others, do you enjoy that responsibility? What appeals to you in supervision? Is it, for instance, the satisfaction derived from bringing others along? Is it the sense of power you get?
4. How responsible do you feel for representing your organization? What would you do if your organization asked you to do something on your job which might compromise your professional judgment?
5. How do you get along with your boss? Do you respond well to supervision?
6. Does your job give you sufficient opportunity to develop your professional skills? Do you feel like you're called upon in the capacity as a professional?
7. Are the skills which you utilize in your job consistent with the skills you indicated as "valued" in the skills assessment in Chapter Two, Exercise 2-4?
8. Overall, would you say that your job is in balance with your abilities and values?

Some of the above questions, the last one in particular, are posed for you to consider in a preliminary fashion. The data generated here as well as in the next chapter will become the basis for a balance-imbalance analysis to be initiated in the last chapter, wherein you will formally evaluate the relationship between yourself and your work situation.

B. THE JOB ANALYSIS QUESTIONNAIRE (Option). If there is not sufficient time to prepare a full job description of your current job, you might find it expeditious to use the questionnaire in Table 4-5 to get a sense of the job analysis process. Complete each question which applies. Once finished, you might also share your answers with someone else who knows about your job from experience or, minimally, from observation.

At the conclusion of this exercise, you should have a firm grasp on the components of your work. You should be able to identify the skills used, as well as the knowledge and abilities required. You should have a good understanding of the level of responsibility of your position and how it relates to other neighboring positions in the organization. In sum, you should recognize the behaviors you use in your daily activities. You can now combine the qualitative factors, identified earlier in the chapter, with this objective data to focus on the critical elements which make up your job. This attitudinal and behavioral diagnosis will be directed next to a career path analysis.

TABLE 4-5   Job Analysis Questionnaire

FOR CURRENT JOB

Name of employee

Department name   Position number (if applicable)

Organization name   Current position title

Information on this form will be used to help classify your job. Please be as clear and accurate as possible.

Describe below the work of the position, listing the different duties performed and time spent. (If more space is needed, please use additional sheets.)

Percent time spent: Duties or work performed:

Job definition:

Nature and extent of mental demands made:

Nature of contacts with others besides workers and supervisor:

Supervision exercised in this position (list names and job titles):

Name and title of immediate supervisor/superior:

Table 4-4, continued

Special requirements:	Indicate if incidental or important	Indicate percent of position's work time

Other relevant information:

I certify that I have read the above instructions and that entries are correct to the best of my ability.

Employee signature	Date

Source: Richard W. Beatty and Craig Eric Schneier, *Personnel Administration: An Experiential Skill Building Approach*, © 1977. Addison-Wesley, Reading, MA. pp. 67-68. Reprinted with permission.

CAREER PATHING

The subject of career pathing has become quite popular among human resource managers in recent years. Textual discussion of the topic, consequently, has typically focused on the development of career paths by management in behalf of organizational employees. In this section of the chapter, I shall focus exclusively on what the individual professional should know about career paths for the purpose of personal career development. I continue to employ the behavioral approach to careers in a similar way as was introduced in the last section on job analysis. In other words, the focus remains on what you actually do or could be doing in your organization. However, now that you have successfully analyzed your job, both subjectively and objectively, you are in a good position to realistically appraise the career opportunities that may exist within your own organization.

The concept of career path evolves nicely from the prior discussion concerning job analysis. A career path is nothing more than a patterned sequence of jobs within an organization. However, depending upon the attitudes and practices of management, career paths can run the gamut from a subjective feeling about a series of jobs to an objective description, from a prescribed lockstep pattern of the way to get ahead to a sequence of flexible position moves which can lead in many different directions — upward, downward, sideways, and diagonally. Walker[9] depicts the lockstep approach to career pathing as traditional, while describing the flexible approach as behavioral. Traditional paths come in two varieties: (1) historical and (2) organizational.

Historical career paths tend to be informal and are based upon the past patterns of the career movements of incumbents of now senior positions. Therefore, they represent the past practices of senior people who have perpetuated their own footsteps, so to speak. One can examine these historical paths by simply analyzing biographical histories. Walker points out, however, that although these paths may have worked well in the past, there is no assurance that they will be effective in the future. One has to question whether they have adjusted to the changing characteristics of today's employees and today's organizational circumstances.

Organizational career paths, as the second type of traditional career path, are reflected in the business plans and organizational structure of the company. They may be displayed, for example, in the organizational chart. They tend to be defined by management as meeting the present organizational needs for staffing the company.

In contrast, behavioral career paths are based upon "the logical and possible sequences of positions that could be held, based upon an analysis of what people actually do in an organization."[10] They describe, then, as much what is possible as opposed to what has been done. These three forms of career paths are depicted in Table 4-6.

Preparing for the adoption of the behavioral approach to career pathing entails a process similar to conducting a job analysis. The jobs in the organization must first be analyzed according to their specific content — what are the key skills, knowledges, and attributes

TABLE 4-6   The Three Kinds of Career Paths in Contrast

Historical	Organizational	Behavioral
Past patterns of career progression; how the incumbents got where they are.	Paths defined or dictated by management to meet operating needs; progression patterns that fit prevailing organizational need.	Paths that are logically possible based on analysis of what activities are actually performed on the jobs.
Actual paths created by the past movement of employees among jobs.	Paths determined by prevailing needs for staffing the organization.	Rational paths that could be followed, management willing.
Perpetuates the way careers have always been.	Reflects prevailing management values and attitudes regarding careers.	Calls for change; new career options.
Used as basis for promotions and transfers.	Usually consistent with job evaluation and pay practices.	Used as basis for career planning.
Basis is informal, traditional.	Basis is organizational need, management style, expediency.	Basis is formal analysis and definition of options.

Source: From *Human Resource Planning* by James W. Walker. Copyright © 1980. McGraw-Hill, Inc. Used with the permission of McGraw-Hill Book Company.

required. In this first step, again the focus is more on what people do rather than on the credentials they bring to the job. Then, the similarities among the jobs in the organization can be noted. It is important here that similarities be derived not only according to work-content or technical but also according to functional skills, as was discussed in Chapter Two. Once the common characteristics among a wide variety of jobs have been identified, then it is a simple matter to develop behavioral career paths or progression lines. It should be apparent that these lines do not have to be strictly vertical, but in fact can take many different shapes. The net result of behavioral career pathing should be a wide range of career options for individuals within the company. What the behavioral approach does more than anything else is bring together as similar jobs those which were previously considered totally different because they were technically different.

Given this introduction to behavioral career pathing, what can professionals do to augment their career opportunities in an organization? Few organizations have a complete career path digest incorporating all the jobs in the organization available in the form specified above. However, by working together with management, individuals can certainly develop career path information for their own career. Of course, targets have to be balanced by the needs of management and of the organization. One's boss and/or mentor, as I shall reveal in the next chapter, can be helpful in disclosing these needs. It is unlikely, furthermore, that management will oppose any individual's preparation of personal career path information flowing from one's job. In fact, there seems to be concurrence in the career development literature that individuals should take responsibility for assessing their own career ambitions and for taking the necessary steps to assure their own career mobility within the organization. It is management's responsibility to establish career information and to commit itself to administrative procedures, such as scheduling performance reviews and providing training, which assist individuals in their personal career development.[11] Professional employees are normally accorded wide latitude in determining the tasks and standards to be observed related to their work. It is the proper role of management to support this process by helping job incumbents perform more effectively and develop their capabilities.[12]

The key step in developing career path information from your job is to prepare a career path grid such as the one displayed in

TABLE 4-7   A Sample Career Path Grid

Operational Path (Plant Engineering)	Other Engineering Sub-Operational Opportunities	Other Related Technical Opportunities
plant engineer (large plant)	corporate engineering	technical director production superintendent corporate staff positions
senior project engineer	engineering superintendent senior project chemical engineer maintenance superintendent district engineer	technical supervisor quality control supervisor process control supervisor
project engineer	construction engineer safety engineer project chemical engineer	production foreman senior operations analyst
junior engineer	industrial engineer	field technician operations analyst

Source: From *Human Resource Planning* by James W. Walker. Copyright © 1980. McGraw-Hill, Inc. Used with the permission of McGraw-Hill Book Company.

146

Table 4-7. Exercise 4-4 is designed to take you through the steps to prepare the grid. Essentially, the grid starts with a plot of your current position in your traditional operational area. In Table 4-7, the traditional path is that of plant engineering and the job in question might be that of a junior engineer or a project engineer. Other columns are prepared showing opportunities in the same general operational area or in compatible suboperational areas. For example, in Table 4-7, related opportunities in construction, safety, and chemical engineering at comparable responsiblity levels or at higher levels are depicted. Finally, a column is reserved for opportunities which may exist in totally different operational areas but for which one may qualify given the individual's functional background. For example, the table lists a variety of opportunities in operations analysis, although they are not technically engineering positions.

Using the career path grid, one can project a wide array of positions which become potentially available to the job incumbent who uses the behavioral approach to career pathing. The listing of these positions is an essential activity in developing a personal career development plan. It displays opportunities for growth within the organization beyond the current job.

EXERCISE 4-4

PREPARING A PERSONAL CAREER PATH GRID.

INSTRUCTIONS:
Now that you completed subjective and objective analyses of your job and realize that career opportunities may be based upon behavioral as opposed to historical or organizational attributes, you can begin to define the career paths in your organization which surround your current work. In order to develop realistic career paths, complete the following steps:

1. Review your job analysis.

2. On a separate page, indicate how you may have revised your job analysis based upon what your superiors and colleagues said should be performed on your job.

3. Name up to five other positions in your organization (you need not recall formal titles) at about your level which: (1) are technically related but found in other operational or suboperational areas, and/or (2) are functionally, if not technically, related and found in different operational areas of the organization. Be creative. Seek out the assistance of others.
   a.
   b.
   c.
   d.
   e.

4. Develop a vertical progression line for your job within your technical area. Start by listing all jobs which naturally lead to your current position (these may be jobs you have formerly occupied or may not). Then list your immediate superior's position and any others above. Attempt to complete similar lists for the other positions named in step three by filling in the career path grid on the next page in Figure 4-1. Some of these positions may fall within your operational area or in parallel suboperations; others may be in entirely different organizational operations. You may need the assistance of your boss, your mentor, or the human resource department in order to fully complete the grid.

Career Path Problems of Professionals

The choice of a particular career path by a professional has very significant implications in terms of the development of knowledge in one's discipline. A given move, particularly during the early stages of the career, can either keep the professional in touch with the latest developments or at least in touch with colleagues who are familiar with such developments, or can create conditions which might induce obsolescence. In scientific careers, for example, one can choose paths which diverge on a number of dimensions, whether they be in applied or basic research, in research or administration, in a university or industrial setting, or in specialized or general practice.[13] Marcson[14] discussed four general career preferences typically followed by scientists:

1. They may remain devoted to research and their profession, although this choice will further break down by a decision whether to work in basic or applied settings.

FIGURE 4.1
Blank Career Path Grid for Personal Preparation

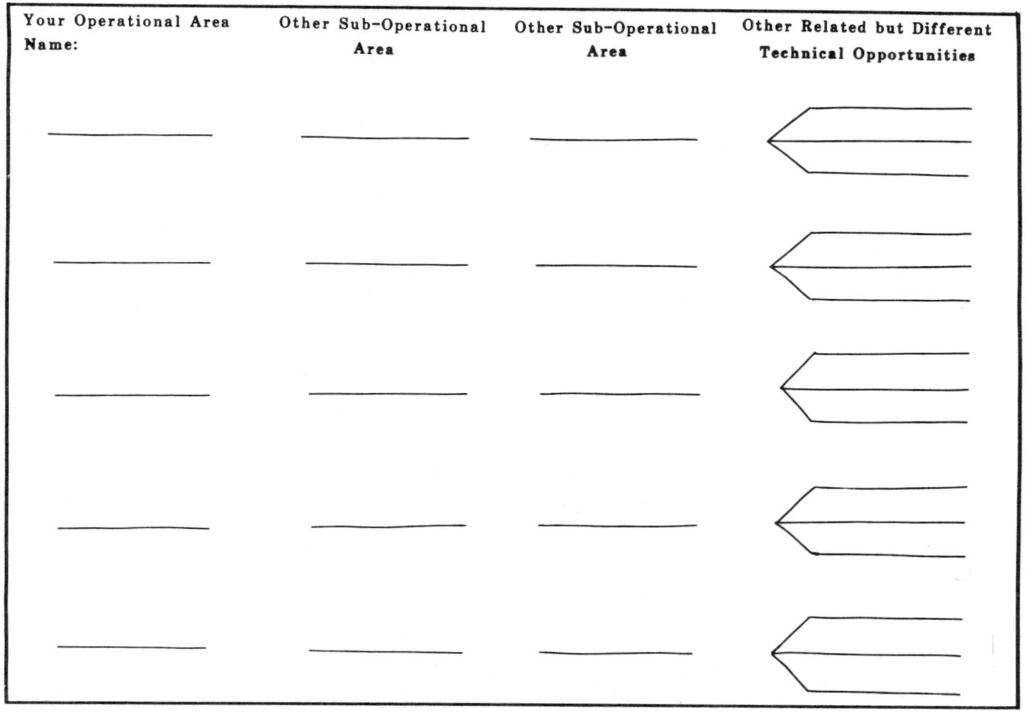

Your Operational Area Name:	Other Sub-Operational Area	Other Sub-Operational Area	Other Related but Different Technical Opportunities

Source: Based on the work of James W. Walker, *Human Resource Planning.* New York: McGraw-Hill, 1980, pp. 318-22.

2. They may become interested in administration and choose a managerial track.
3. They may be interested in research but choose a managerial track because of a perception of limited financial and status benefits in research.
4. They might turn to administration if they realize that they are becoming obsolete in their field.

Rothman and Perrucci[15] found that positions involving narrow technical activities, extensive administrative responsibilities, application rather than research, and organizational situations involving relatively stable technologies were most conducive to the obsolescence of professional skills. Consequently, salaried professionals have sought ways to negotiate the pursuit of important organizational activities while not compromising the need to remain updated in their particular disciplines.

Academic professionals face a dilemma regarding the organizational requirement of teaching. As depicted in Caplow and McGee's famous *Publish or Perish*,[16] the professor, although hired to teach, is ultimately evaluated almost exclusively on research and publication. Being that as it may, the professor may be torn by a desire to teach and to serve the institution against a need to pursue one's discipline and achieve professional prestige.

Similarly, career path choices are critical to lawyers who aspire to become partners in a law firm.[17] Besides such factors as sponsorship, social background, hard work, and personality, associates in about eight years time need to make "correct" career path decisions. For one, they can't be lured away from the firm by offers from competing firms or from corporations. Second, they must develop a specialty to show particular competence in one area of the law. Third, they have to know when to switch to a new technical area to gain broader visibility and demonstrate more general technical competence.

In sum, once plotting your career opportunities using the behavioral approach, as a professional, you still have to make some strategic decisions regarding the specific and accepted ways to advance in your profession and to gain allegiance within your own organization. In some cases, you can do both. For the most part, however, you will have to make some trade-offs, and these are likely to challenge some of the most fundamental assumptions regarding career development in your chosen discipline.

The "Dual Ladder" Approach

One familiar approach which has been proposed to resolve the dilemma of advancing in the organization while keeping professionally updated is the "dual ladder." Accordingly, professional accomplishment is rewarded on a comparable basis with managerial potential. The dual ladder approach was based on some evidence that young professionals, who were in organizations which placed less emphasis on the desire to manage, contributed more and were more loyal to their organizations than those who were in organizations which highly valued managerial aspirations.[18] The dual ladder, then, calls for the existence of the usual ladder of hierarchical positions which leads to managerial authority and another ladder of professional advancement which carries comparable prestige in terms of salary, status, and sometimes autonomy and responsiblity.

The way it works might be to establish career tracks using professional titles. For example, at Parsons Brinckerhoff[19] three broad titles are used: (1) professional associate, (2) senior professional associate, and (3) principal professional associate. Each title requires an increasing degree of recognized expertise and technical contribution. The last title, principal professional associate, is considered to be equivalent in status, authority, compensation, and benefits to that of vice-president. Selection and evaluations are conducted by professionals who hold higher ranks. To qualify for the more senior tracks, the employee must show increasing responsibility for internal company projects and must also be recognized as an authority by one's professional peers, for example, by publishing papers or attending and leading seminars.

The dual ladder approach, then, is designed expressly for professionals who make significant technical contributions to their organization but who disdain any interest in becoming a manager. Undertaken by such large technical companies as IBM, Polaroid, and Xerox, the dual ladder has gained popular support, even among professionals themselves.[20] It reportedly has significantly reduced conflicts between management and professional employees. For example, it tends to improve communication channels as professionals may no longer feel the need to hold back information as a means of creating power for themselves. It also establishes greater openness regarding promotion opportunities since individuals know what the requirements are if they or their colleagues are to attain a higher level position. Overall, advocates of the dual ladder believe it provides salaried professionals with the status and recognition they deserve while at the same time preserving their technical career opportunities.

Nevertheless, the dual ladder approach has not gained widespread use yet due to a number of pitfalls. First, climbing the professional ladder may not be desired by local professionals who really desire to enter the organizational mainstream but who may not be given the option of transferring to the managerial track. Further, the professional track, as pointed out by Goldner and Ritti,[21] simply does not provide the power to allocate resources and pursue alternative goals, and it is this assumption of power which is necessary to experience organizational autonomy. Another pitfall is that it simply hasn't worked; salaries and status in the professional track have not kept up with the managerial track. Finally, the availability of a managerially oriented professional track may in some cases still contribute to skill obsolescence since the senior professionals may have to divert time away from professional development to perform their administrative duties.

Having now considered both the job and the career, the discussion turns in the upcoming chapter to the organization. The diagnosis of your organization in combination with the analyses performed here on your job will allow you to consider whether your work setting is in balance with your personal attributes.

FIVE: Organizational Diagnosis

INTRODUCTION

Recalling a prior discussion and certainly a theme of this book, it is not unusual for professionals to concentrate much more thoroughly on their profession than on the organization which employs them. Organizations tend to be taken for granted by professionals once they enter them. By that I mean that professionals generally take their job and work surroundings as a given. If the job is simply not adequate in some way, they can always go elsewhere. This contention is based upon the fact that professionals spend little time studying organizations, and certainly even less time studying organizational careers. Those things take care of themselves. There is so little time as it is to become proficient in one's technical discipline.

What this chapter sets out to demonstrate is that there are points of access and flexibility in almost all organizations. One only has to develop the necessary sophistication to diagnose and then manage these points of access. This chapter will be devoted to the diagnostic aspect of organizational career behavior. To the extent resources inside an organization have been left untapped, I hope to demonstrate how to recognize some of these resources and opportunities available to you. From this point, the last chapter will take you to the final step — that of taking advantage of these resources and opportunities to develop a personal career development strategy.

There are four specific points of access which this chapter will focus on as key elements of your organizational diagnosis.

(1) I will begin with an analysis of your boss — perhaps the linchpin to your entire organizational career development. (2) The mentoring process will then be critically appraised especially given its acknowledged importance to professional development. (3) This will be followed by a process which I refer to as climate analysis which will encourage you to diagnose your organization's and organizational unit's style in order to appreciate the limits of personal development. At this point, we will come in contact again with the subject of strain or conflict between professional aspirations and organizational requirements. I shall also examine climate in terms of environmental uncertainty as you consider the effects on professional careers produced by economic, technological, political, and cultural changes. (4) I will close with an examination of the role of politics in personal career development. You will not be able to successfully negotiate your career ambitions within your organization without knowing how to manage these ambitions through the use of legitimate political tactics.

BOSS MANAGEMENT

One of the most underrated aspects of the work environment in terms of its ability to be managed is our boss. Perhaps because of Calvinist notions of authority inbred throughout our society, it is assumed that those who are assigned to supervise us cannot be managed. Yet, it is obvious that those in a position to guide our development in the organization are absolutely critical to our career growth. It is naive to expect that these individuals, who have many others to supervise besides ourselves and many other organizational obligations, will automatically do what is best for our career development. Consequently, we need to assist our bosses to better understand our needs and visions for our personal career development.

This section will address the topic of managing our bosses. The word "boss," considered synonymous with supervisor, is used very broadly here since there are many roles that an individual can play in carrying out the supervisory function in behalf of an employee's career development. Leibowitz and Schlossberg[1] identified nine supervisory roles in interviews with both employees and supervisors. Brief descriptions of each are provided in Table 5-1. The authors identified the appraiser role, for example, as being particularly

TABLE 5-1   The Roles of the Supervisory Function

Communicator
One who promotes a two-way exchange between oneself and the employee.

Counselor
One who helps the employee to clarify goals and identify steps to take in reaching these goals, whether or not they relate to the present organization.

Appraiser
One who evaluates an employee's performance, gives feedback to the employee and helps to work out a development plan so the employee can negotiate the goals and objectives specific to the current job.

Coach
One who gives instructions or skill training to enable employees to do their job more effectively.

Mentor
One who serves as a sponsor to facilitate an employee's career growth.

Advisor
One who gives information about career opportunities both within and outside the organization.

Broker
One who serves as an agent for employees and help them obtain information from the appropriate resources such as people and institutions.

Referral Agent
One who identifies resources to help an employee with specific problems.

Advocate
One who intervenes on behalf of an employee for benefits, promotions, etc., or who helps to eliminate obstacles.

Source: Adapted from Zandy B. Leibowitz and Nancy K. Schlossberg, "Training Managers for Their Role in a Career Development System." *Training and Development Journal*, July 1981.

important to employees who desire continuous informal feedback on their job performance. All of the roles are helpful to career development but not every supervisor can be expected to adequately perform each one of them. The supervisory function can indeed be carried out by a number of individuals, not just the supervisor. It is the job of the employee to identify others in the organization who can assist in the career development process through other than the traditional supervisory route.

The function of the boss formally occupies the first four of Leibowitz and Schlossberg's roles, with the remaining roles perhaps residing within the function of the mentor. However, a boss could indeed provide all of these roles. In fact, depending upon your organizational situation, one individual could perform both functions, as boss and as mentor. Typically, though, these roles are occupied by different people.

At the point of entry, your boss carries out merely the formal assignment of supervising the technical performance of your job. At least, this is what the organization's operational handbook or implicit code probably stipulates. However, we all know that our boss can ultimately be much more than just our technical supervisor. He or she can in fact be instrumental to our career growth on any number of accounts such as:

1. Being the recognized conduit to upper management.
2. Being your spokesman or representative at upper level meetings.
3. Knowing how to get things done in the organization; that is, "knowing the ropes."
4. Having access to information and resources to help you achieve your goals.
5. Knowing the "right" people who can help you achieve your career objectives.

It is therefore critical that you try to communicate your needs to your bosses so that once the technical work at hand is accomplished, they can direct some of their energies in behalf of your career objectives. Of course, the process must be a two-way street. Bosses have their own pressures to deal with as well as their interpretation of the organizational mission and their role in that mission. If you can learn about your bosses' perceptions of their own roles, you might be able to make a positive contribution to the resolution of their problems while at the same time, assuming their perceptions are accurate, work to accomplish the organization's goals. In this way, you join the boss in a united front to accomplish the organization's mission. For example, let's assume you are a product design engineer and learn that your boss is under pressure to move a product under development quickly into the marketplace due to a cash shortfall. Although you might prefer to concentrate your energies in making some final technical modifications, realizing the pressures the boss is under and believing the product is sufficiently developed to be safely launched, you convert your attention to product commercialization.

Of course there are times when bosses are inaccurate in their perception of organizational goals or when their decisions, perhaps due to inordinate pressures, are fallible. Once fully appreciating their position, it is then your task to try to work with them to make a better decision. There is a tendency to underestimate their ability to listen and to carefully reappraise a former decision. The idea being presented here is that you should endeavor to work with your boss to the fullest extent without compromising your own values and ethics.

Key to managing the relationship with your boss is an understanding of the boss' expectations and working style. If the boss is accustomed to reveal personal expectations, then few problems tend to emerge in this area. Formal mechanisms, such as performance appraisals, annual reviews, planning meetings, and most recently, quality circles, also exist in most organizations to make managerial expectations explicit. Nevertheless, some bosses are simply not prone to reveal their true expectations regarding, for instance, time-tables, strategic preferences, or even subjects about which they need to be kept informed. The subordinate in these cases must use some ingenuity to find out about these expectations so that he or she can be of most service to the boss and to the organization. Gabarro and Kotter[2] suggest a number of methods to infiltrate the boss' hidden agenda:

1. Draft a detailed memo covering key aspects of your work and send it to the boss for review.
2. Initiate a discussion with the boss regarding good management practices.
3. Obtain information through others who work for or under the boss.

4. Review the formal planning systems through which the boss makes commitments to his superiors.

With respect to the working style of the boss, there are many descriptions in the literature regarding style. I have already dealt with the notion of personality style in Chapter Two. The rather fixed nature of the personality might make it appear that there is little one can do to avoid personality clashes. However, even if personalities are stable, awareness of the boss' style as well as of one's own style can lead to a great deal of flexibility in establishing compatible working relationships even among formerly incompatible styles. The key then is to understand the boss' style, and given your own style, make the appropriate adjustment to ensure a compatible relationship.

Besides the personality, there are styles which depict patterns of goal accomplishment within the work setting. For example, the boss may simply be a listener or a reader.[3] In other words, he or she may prefer to be briefed on information either in person or in memo form.

Bosses can also be classified in their decision-making styles as involvement-types or delegation-types.[4] Involvement-types like to always be where the action is and want to be constantly informed about problems at hand. Delegation-types, on the contrary, prefer to concern themselves only with the most essential decisions and therefore delegate most of the day-to-day problem solving to subordinates.

Tables 5-2 and 5-3 depict two other classification schemes for determining not only your boss' working style but also your own. An individual may possess all the qualities of one type or may be a combination of a few different types. The first table is drawn from the work of Andrew Souerwine[5] and displays four basic types which are essentially based upon his pragmatic experience in working with managers. The second table depicts eight styles which are based more on personality and which represent Eugene Raudsepp's interpretation[6] of Carl Jung's personality theory. According to Jung, there are two basic types of personalities, introvert and extrovert. The introvert concentrates on the inner world of concepts and ideas whereas the extrovert focuses on the outer world of people and things. These two types can both perceive the world by sensing and intuition or by thinking and feeling.

TABLE 5-2   Souerwine's Boss Types

Action-Oriented Boss

    This boss is the person of action, he or she gets things done —
now. This boss is also a pragmatist, concerned with making
sure that whatever one does, with whomever one works, whatever idea one espouses, leads to something tangible. Finally,
this boss is a decision maker who likes results. These results are
based on tasks and projects, not on judgments or feelings.

People-Oriented Boss

    This boss emphasizes social relationships and sees the work set-
ting as a means for building team spirit. He or she is sensitive
to the feelings of others and tends to react more to the feelings
than to the content of messages. Finally, this boss tends not to
be very practical, but rather appreciates the personal or political
intrigues behind any situation. This boss is approachable and
cares about people's needs and feelings.

Idea-Oriented Boss

    This boss is a concept person, interested in exploring all the
possibilities. This boss is willing to dream, but may be accused
of being idealistic or intellectual. But he or she is an excellent
person for probing, for identifying the key issues, or for seeing
the complex interrelationships that are not readily apparent.
However, this boss tends to avoid getting involved in the nitty-
gritty.

Security-Oriented Boss

    This boss believes that people need comforts, good working
conditions, security first and responsibility only afterwards.
Therefore, this person may become preoccupied with matters
peripheral to the work itself. He or she is likely to spend time
working out standardized approaches, procedures, organization
charts, or job descriptions. This boss believes that one handles
new situations by consulting standard operating procedures,
not by constantly looking to new, risk-taking approaches.

Source: Adapted from Andrew H. Souerwine. "The Boss: Committing Power
to Help You Win," *Management Review*, February 1978.

TABLE 5-3   Jung's Supervisory Personality Types

Extroverted Thinking Type

This boss likes to take charge and run the show. A disciplined person who respects objectivity, well thought-out plans and orderly procedures, this boss likes to make decisions, organize plans and give orders. This boss is also naturally critical of others.

Introverted Thinking Type

This boss prefers to analyze rather than control. He or she can organize facts and ideas but not people and situations. This boss has the knack for working out the difficulties underlying a problem but allows others to do the implementing.

Extroverted Intuitive Type

This boss is an enthusiastic innovator. Confident in the worth of his or her ideas, he or she never tires of problem solving. This boss has an ability to animate, stimulate, and persuade others to accept his or her ideas. This boss, though, has an inability to do anything humdrum and routine, consequently, there may be a tendency to start too many projects and finish only a few.

Introverted Intuitive Type

This boss is stimulated by problems and completely trusts intuitive instincts. This boss is effective in situations where boldly ingenious ideas are needed but feels smothered in routine jobs. This boss has a tendency to ignore others because he or she needs little companionship and involvement.

Extroverted Sensing Type

This boss is an adaptable realist. Being very observant, he or she absorbs and remembers many facts about the world and about others. This boss is perceptive, open-minded, unprejudicial, and tolerant of others. This boss' major shortcoming is the inability to see the potential value of new ideas and concepts.

Introverted Sensing Type

This boss is very dependable. He or she respects facts, can absorb them many times, and also has an individualistic way of approaching problems. This boss is patient with details and has a persevering attitude that has a stabilizing effect on others. This boss can also cite cases to support evaluations of people, methods, and projects. The major shortcoming of this boss is

Table 5-3, continued

that he or she cannot understand the needs of others that diverge from what one perceives their needs should be; therefore, real problems are often dismissed.

The Extroverted Feeling Type
This boss radiates fellowship and is sensitive to the emotional atmosphere around one. He or she tends to be friendly, tactful, and sympathetic to others. This boss' forte is in jobs that deal with people. This boss, though, tends to be impatient with long slow jobs, especially when they require solitary absorption. This person also tends to jump to conclusions, to favor employees with similar traits, and be blind to conflict. He or she is loyal to the company and other supervisors.

Introverted Feeling Type
This boss is similar to the extroverted feeling type except that he or she cares more deeply about fewer things and works best at a job one believes in. This boss' major problem is tending to be overly sensitive and vulnerable to criticism. This boss believes true feelings should be hidden to a great extent and unpleasant situations should be avoided.

Source: Adapted from Eugene Raudsepp, "What 'Type' of Supervisor Are You?" *Supervision*, November 1980.

The authors of the various style classification schemes, particularly Souerwine, propose many adjustment or management strategies if there is incompatibility between the styles of the boss and subordinate. Of course, each situation demands a personalized response, but some general examples using Souerwine's scheme might be useful. If the boss is action-oriented and the subordinate people-oriented, the objective, pragmatic orientation of the boss may come into conflict with the subordinate's which places value on human relationships and the feelings of others. In this situation, the subordinate might either point out the advantage to be gained by being more sensitive to the needs of others, or might simply deal with the people aspects of the job by oneself. If the roles are reversed from the above, the subordinate, although typically in a prized position (having a boss who tends to listen and be patient), must try to objectify phenomena, thereby keeping the boss on track in dealing with important issues.

If the boss is idea-oriented and the subordinate action-oriented, the subordinate might work on proposals alone or with others while asking the boss for the long-range perspective that requires ingenuity for planning and strategy. This working situation can be ideal: the subordinate can do all the nitty-gritty details of implementation that the boss loathes doing. The boss might in turn see the subordinate as a valuable asset to his or her staff.

Obviously, other scenarios can be developed for each of the many combinations. The subordinate must simply use some creativity to devise ingenious ways to manage the relationship with the boss.

EXERCISE 5-1

BOSS ANALYSIS. If you are currently working, share with one or more of your colleagues whom you trust Souerwine's boss types. Approach colleagues who have the same boss that you have. See if you can agree on the type which he or she falls into. Describe in detail the attributes of this boss type. What aspects of the description of this type, found in Table 5-2, apply to your boss? What aspects don't? For example, if your boss is action-oriented, as a decision-maker, does he or she totally reject intuition or feeling? Or does he or she really just rely on the facts, namely, the results of tasks and projects? Is your boss perhaps a combination of some of Souerwine's types?

Discuss the best way(s) to relate to this boss type in order to reduce his or her defensiveness and to enlist his or her support in behalf of your career development. For example, if your boss is security-oriented, might you find it expedient in order to engender support to make sure that all requests are submitted in the proper form? (You may find it helpful in answering these points to use the Boss Analysis Sheet, Exhibit 5-1.)

Once you have attended to these considerations, you should draw up a plan for managing your boss in the future. In particular, consider the changes, if any, you would make from your current practice on the basis of the foregoing analysis. As you prepare your plan, keep the following five guidelines in mind.

1. Appreciate where your boss is coming from and try to help him or her accomplish goals within the context of personal values and ethics.

2. Above all else, demonstrate your integrity as well as dependability to the boss so that he or she feels secure placing trust in you.
3. Communicate your needs openly and directly to the boss but don't "go to the well" too often. Have a sense of priority about which things are most critical and which merit the boss' time. Provide the boss with options regarding ways to help you achieve your objectives.
4. Provide the boss with sufficient reliable information to help in making decisions and solving problems, whether they be the boss' or yours. Attempt to minimize the chance of failure.
5. Allow your boss to become personally involved with your plans if he or she so chooses. As long as the boss keeps on track, there's a good chance you'll gain a full commitment. Convince your boss that you're working on a common problem.

EXHIBIT 5-1   Boss Analysis Sheet

Boss Type _____

Consideration 1:
On the basis of discussion with your colleagues, write below some specific attributes describing your boss' "boss type."

Consideration 2:
Below jot down some notes, indicating how best to relate to your boss type in order to:
a)   reduce his or her defensiveness
b)   enlist his or her support in behalf of your career.

Consideration 3:
Now draw up a plan for managing your boss in the future.

MENTORING

The mentor role has already been discussed as a major stage of the organizational career theory proposed especially for professionals by Dalton and his colleagues (see Chapter Three).[7] In that theory, the mentor was depicted as an inspirational guide to the individual moving through the earlier stages of one's career. The mentor role proper was seen as evolving as an outgrowth of success one may have enjoyed as a technical specialist. The professional, entertaining the prospect of the mentor role, begins to look beyond the operational concerns of the organization to the external environment where support is found for what is now more responsible and recognized work in the organization.

In this section, I plan to reacquaint the reader with the role of the mentor, but also want to critically examine the role of the protégé. What are the risks and benefits to be had by successfully finding a mentor? Can one achieve career fulfillment without the services of a mentor? In some cases, a formal sponsor program may exist in one's organization to provide the young professional with accurate career planning information. For example, at the Jewel Tea Company each incoming trainee is assigned a sponsor during the initial training period.[8] Under the Civil Service Reform Act of 1978, the U.S. Office of Personnel Management explicitly calls for the assignment of senior executives as formal mentors to each new executive selected to participate in agency executive development programs.[9] In most cases, however, formal programs, such as those described above, will not exist, so the individual will be on his or her own to find a mentor. The evidence that I have collected from my own experience as well as from research associated with writing this book indicates that personal career development is likely to be ineffective when career information is obtained from peers, but tends to be effective when the information is obtained from successful individuals who are in the next readily accessible level above them or are of senior executive status. Moreover, a well-known survey of top executives conducted by Roche[10] indicated that nearly two-thirds of the respondents had at least one mentor during their career, that the number of such relationships was growing, and that those executives who themselves had a mentor earned more money at a younger age, were better educated, were likely to sponsor more protégés than their counterparts who did not have a mentor, and finally, were in general happier with their career progress. An earlier study by Jennings[11] bluntly stated that few executives make it to the top rapidly without a mentor. One conclusion you may draw from these findings is that you can still find career fulfillment in your organization without having a mentor, but it most likely will take longer.

Before searching for a mentor or protégé, whatever the case may be, one must be aware of the parameters of the mentor/protégé relationship and the organizational and personal implications of this relationship. In the Levinson study,[12] also referred to in Chapter Three, the researchers, based on interviews with 40 selected men, found that a mentor performs many functions; he can be a teacher, sponsor, host and guide, exemplar, and counselor. These words, as compared to the terms coach or senior advisor, imply an element of informality, whereas the coach, for example, is often expected to take on formal advisement as part of one's job function. The mentor is further characterized as having a personal relationship with the protégé for purposes of guiding the latter through the early stages of the career. Perhaps, the closest distinct role to the mentor is that of the sponsor. In fact, the two roles are often confounded. According to the Dalton et al. framework,[13] the sponsor, although a developer of people, is more interested in providing organizational opportunities rather than in teaching career-related knowledge and skills. Therefore, the sponsor is more of a power figure who can actually directly affect the career advancement of the young professional. Further, the sponsor's relationship to the protégé is rarely emotional or nurturant; indeed, the sponsor does not typically expect to learn anything from the relationship. The mentor, on the other hand, can be stimulated by the protégé and his or her ideas. The protégé, then, must distinguish the needs of those superiors who have taken an interest in him or her. A mentor is clearly interested in a closer personal and pedagogical relationship than the sponsor.

What, then, are the organizational and personal implications of serving as a mentor or protégé? Although the potential rewards are great, there are risks at stake. The greatest threat to the mentor is carrying out the mentor role beyond the bounds, formal or informal, established by the organization. One's reputation and effectiveness could be seriously tarnished if the mentor is seen to be meddling in affairs beyond the limits of legitimate authority in behalf of the protégé. Both parties are at risk if jealousy or resentment crops up among peers or superiors. If other employees see themselves at a disadvantage, they may, for example, form groups that would seek to destroy the effectiveness of the mentor/protégé relationship. If the mentor is a superior to the protégé's boss, the boss may feel that his or her authority is being challenged and might even attempt to thwart the progress of the protégé. A specific organizational implication for the protégé relates to both the timeliness and accuracy of the mentor's perceptions and advice. Has the mentor adjusted to modern conditions in the organization? Is he or she aware of the present outlook of management? As indicated above, does the mentor have the authority to affect certain decisions which may involve the protégé? In one's enthusiasm to support the protégé, the mentor may overstep one's bounds the net effect of which could thwart rather than promote the career progress of the protégé. For example, the mentor might attempt to advance the cause of his or her protégé at a succession meeting. However, if the norms of the organization prefer the boss to carry out this function, the mentor's role in this case may indeed be seen as meddling and could even damage the reputation of the protégé.

There are many personal risks to mentoring as well. The foremost is the emotional involvement demanded of both parties. This is in turn associated with substantial time demands both on the job and away from the job. Although the emotional attachment between protégé and mentor can be rewarding, it can also compete with other important relationships in one's life space, even with a spouse. Moreover, the protégé (and the mentor, too, in some limited cases) is susceptible to becoming overdependent and losing the confidence to act independently. The emotional involvement between the two parties may also lead to some blind spots when dealing with third parties, as objective, rational points of view are overlooked.

Women in particular are subject to substantial risks and benefits in the mentor relationship. Female protégés, like males, benefit greatly from having a mentor but typically require an even greater commitment from their mentors who have to spend considerable time "selling" their protégés.[14] A natural but particularly insidious offshoot of across-sex mentor/protégé relationships is the innuendo the parties must face regarding sexual entanglements. It is difficult enough to develop a mentor relationship without having to worry about this dimension. It is an equally explosive subject within the family circle. In some circumstances, the sexual involvement may become more real than rumored.

Other personal risks include dissimulation, which may occur on the part of either of the parties as they attempt to impress the other; blackmail, which may result from a disharmonious termination of the relationship; or embarrassment, which may befall one of the parties if the other fails in some way. Finally, an unexpected termination of the relationship may be emotionally difficult for either of the parties, but can be particularly demoralizing for the mentor who might have come to expect a degree of loyalty from the protégé. Unanticipated termination can create inhibitions about serving again in the mentor role.[15]

The risks and rewards of mentoring suggest three distinct steps the parties can take to ensure that the relationship works to their respective career advantage. First, regardless of who initiates the relationship, both parties should use their information resources to evaluate the other. The protégé wants to be sure that the mentor is respected organizationally and is personally compatible. The mentor wants to be sure that the protégé is a capable individual who has the personal qualities to achieve his or her career goals and who is willing to listen while not losing personal independence.

Second, the parties must be willing to share their mutual expectations. What does each hope to get out of the relationship? Is the protégé willing to go as far and in the same direction that the mentor hopes? Is each willing to invest the time and commitment demanded by the relationship? Will each be willing to accept criticism from the other? Although it may be awkward to surface some of these concerns in the beginning of the relationship, let alone at all, eventually they have to be aired to avoid the pitfalls, and in particular, to test the subjectivity of the relationship.

Finally, the parties need to analyze the relationship as it evolves to be sure that it continues to serve their mutual ends. The parties need to be particularly alert to the organizational environment to avoid losing sight of how others are viewing them. Not only must the parties see the relationship as constructive, but they want to be sure that others also see the relationship in the same way. Mentoring has become a very acceptable relationship in our professional environment, but petty jealousies do emerge and have to be managed. There are also boundaries established on the relationship very particular to each organization, and these must be correctly fathomed by the parties. Finally, there most certainly will be an organizational perception regarding the appropriate time for termination. The parties don't want to carry the relationship much beyond this acceptable threshold.

ORGANIZATIONAL CLIMATE

Now that you have carefully evaluated your job, the career opportunities potentially available in your organization, your boss, and the prospect of engaging in a mentor/protégé relationship, it would be timely to look out more broadly to the whole organization. In particular, in this section, I want to review with you the subject of organizational climate, the analysis of which could be essential in knowing how to develop your career within your organization. Your organizational climate sets bounds on how much flexibility you will have in initiating your personal career development plan. It may also predetermine how you might go about making your way in your organization, although there are some political tactics you might be able to use in any setting. The latter subject will be reserved for the next section of the chapter. Here, I shall focus exclusively on what you need to know about your organization and organizational unit in order to make the most of your career.

There has been no agreement on what climate really is other than a set of characteristics peculiar to a given organization. Some research has identified the components of climate, to wit, Gordon and Golberg's list of eight dimensions:[16]

1. organizational clarity
2. decision-making structure
3. organizational integration
4. management style
5. performance orientation
6. organizational vitality
7. compensation
8. human resource development

The last dimension is concerned with career development, per se. The authors describe it as the "extent to which individuals perceive opportunities within the organization that will allow people to develop to their full potential."

Although, as suggested above, research has been by no means definitive on the subject of organizational climate, it is apparent that organizations do in fact have distinctive climates which distinguish them from other organizations. Further, interorganizational climate differences are clearly more marked than intraorganizational (between departments within an organization) differences.[17] Hence, although climate differences exist between units within an organization, they are not expected to differ as much as what one would experience in moving to a totally different organization.

Although there has been concern about management's need to adjust its organizational climate, there has been little evidence that an organization's climate can be revamped. The issue of adjustment arises from research pointing to the effect climate has on both job satisfaction and performance, two constructs widely viewed as positive dimensions for any organization. Nevertheless, given the vast array of components making up an organization's climate, such as is depicted in Gordon and Golberg's list of eight dimensions, it is not surprising that Woodman and King in their review of the climate literature asserted that the concept "while certainly not unchanging, . . . has an air of permanence or at least some continuity over time."[18]

The reasoning posited above suggests that as a practical matter, after the stage of entry, individuals may be better off adjusting to their organization's climate than vice-versa. I had pointed out in Chapter Three that during entry, the individual and the organization work out a mutual psychological contract. Accordingly, an individual will attempt to choose an organization whose climate approximates the type of environment in which he or she wishes to work. Therefore, a person who has high needs for power will likely choose a power-oriented organization; a person with high achievement motivation will likely choose an achievement-oriented organization, etc.[19] However, the diagnosis of an organization with respect to climate is unlikely to be that carefully or accurately performed during entry, as I had pointed out. Most likely the diagnosis will be performed after the person has been a member of the organization for a period of time.

The subject of adjustment to an organizational climate is usually referred to as "fit" in the career development literature or what I shall refer to in the next chapter as "balance" or "imbalance." Now, adjustment is not construed as a strictly conservative notion which depicts the individual as conforming totally to organizational requirements. The psychological contract is a mutual process. Further, there are many avenues for career adjustment within the organization itself. I shall examine those avenues or options in the next chapter. Your task here is to consider some methods of climate analysis so that you can perhaps more accurately diagnose your organization's climate, and secondly to consider whether some climates are better than others for purposes of personal career development. I shall then devote attention to particular problems faced by salaried professionals in organizations and the types of climates and policies most conducive to their resolution.

Climate Analysis

The first task in doing a climate analysis is to determine how the organization handles its mission according to a predetermined set of dimensions. The dimensions vary from one author to another. Many authors have also developed questionnaires to assess these dimensions. As resported by Lafollette,[20] the Litvin and Stringer Organizational Climate Questionnaire focuses on six dimensions which are clearly people-oriented. These dimensions, and their definitions posed as questions, are shown in Table 5-4.

TABLE 5-4   Litwin and Stringer's Organizational Climate Dimensions

1. *A General Affect Tone Toward Other People in the Organization*: How does one perceive coworkers and other people in the organization?
2. *General Affect Tone Toward Management and/or the Organization*: How does one perceive management and the organization?
3. *Policy and Promotion Clarity*: How does one feel about the clarity of promotion policy and the opportunity for promotion within the organization?

Table 5-4, continued

---

4. *Job Pressure and Standards*: How does one feel about job pressures and standards within the organization?
5. *Openness of Upward Communication*: How is the communication between management and employees?
6. *Risk in Decision Making*: How much risk is involved in decision making within the organization?

Source: Adapted from William R. LaFollette, "How Is the Climate in Your Organization?" *Personnel Journal* 54:377-78, 1975.

A different set of dimensions are depicted in the House and Rizzo Organizational Practices Questionnaire.[21] These dimensions appear to be task- or structure-oriented, as opposed to people-oriented. They tend to reflect how an individual perceives the practices of management within an organization. These dimensions are displayed in Table 5-5.

TABLE 5-5   House and Rizzo's Organizational Climate Dimensions

---

1. *Timely Decision Making*: Are consistent guidelines for work communicated?
2. *Upward Informational Requirements*: How much detailed technical and administrative information is required by superiors in the organization?
3. *Top Management Receptiveness*: How much interest in and evaluation do top managers give to ideas from subordinates?
4. *Induction and/or Promotion of Those Outside the Organization*: How much does management fill positions from within and from outside the organization?
5. *Formalization*: Are job descriptions, performance standards, and appraisals established in writing and readily available?
6. *Selection Criteria Based on Ability*: Are promotions based on performance or "playing politics"?
7. *Job Pressure*: How much work is assigned and how much time is required to complete it?
8. *Subordinate Development*: What are the expectations of top management regarding subordinate instruction and career

Table 5-5, continued

development, and what are the rewards given for carrying out these expectations?

9. *Teamwork*: How does one's work group work together and accept changes?
10. *Intergroup Cooperation*: Is there cooperation among work groups in the performance of work?
11. *Chain of Command*: What is the degree to which direct orders come only from immediate supervisors?
12. *Information Distortion and Suppression*: To what degree is necessary information distorted?
13. *General Communication*: What is the general state of communication in the organization?
14. *Definition of Work*: To what degree is the job defined?

Source: Adapted from William R. LaFollette, "How Is the Climate in Your Organization?" *Personnel Journal* 54:378, 1975.

EXERCISE 5-2

PRELIMINARY ORGANIZATIONAL SURVEY. Using either the Litwin and Stringer or House and Rizzo dimensions, perform a personal survey of your own organization. In other words, try to answer in a couple of sentences each of the questions. For example, if you choose House and Rizzo, on teamwork you might say that your work group works very well together but is administered by a security-oriented boss who is slow to accept changes. This in turn makes the group slow to react. Once you have provided your answers, administer the survey to a coworker whom you can trust. Afterwards, share your answers. In which dimensions was there agreement? In which areas did you disagree? Can you put together a composite of your answers to describe the climate in your organization?

After completing Exercise 5-2, you should have a sense whether a composite of the dimensions of the climate questionnaire which you selected form a *type*. There are numerous classifications of climate or organization types. These each typically attempt to depict an organizational ideology or system of thought. Although only an abstraction, type classifications can be useful to individual employees as a preliminary step in better understanding their organization or organizational unit. For example, they may offer insight into the goals and objectives of their organization, its control mechanisms, its communication style, its relationships, or even the expectations of its management. Once the type has been derived, then the exceptions can be proposed to disconfirm the original type casting. Even if eventually discredited, the climate type represents not so much a substantive depiction but a rough classification scheme for better understanding your own organization or organizational unit.

EXERCISE 5-3

UNIT CLIMATE ANALYSIS.

INSTRUCTIONS:
Having completed the preliminary organizational survey for your organization, it might be useful to interpret this next exercise in terms of your organizational unit, department, or work group as opposed to your entire organization. Although, as was mentioned earlier, units will tend to reflect much of the overall organizational climate, they may each possess their own climate idiosyncracies. In this exercise, six climate types are defined (see Table 5-6).[22] Decide which one most aptly describes your organizational unit. Then, in conjunction with some of your colleagues, prepare a short list of strategies (you may wish to use the Climate Response Sheet, Exhibit 5-2) in answer to the following question:

How do you best make your way in this climate; that is, get ahead, keep your self-esteem, achieve personal satisfaction?

As an example, suppose your unit or department is characterized by the "rewards" climate type. In other words, if you do well and contribute to the department's efforts, you get sufficiently rewarded, usually in the form of a bonus. You may decide with your colleagues that although this type tends to reward individual accomplishment rather than group effort, by helping each other, together you can *beat the system*. You pledge to work together in the future and share all rewards equally. As a person with high needs for social interaction in the workplace, this arrangement will likely give you a great deal of satisfaction while at the same time help to meet your career goals.

Similar to the analysis of your boss, it is conceivable that a climate type may or may not be in conformity with your personality type. If there is conformity, then, other things being equal, an individual should thrive in this type of organization. If there is not conformity, this does not suggest that the individual must leave the organization. Beyond some of the career options I shall discuss in the next chapter, there are certainly some personal strategies one can use to overcome type incongruity.[23] For example, suppose as a professional, you consider yourself to be creative, that is, you are capable

TABLE 5-6   Climate Types

1. *Conformity:* People in organizational units that emphasize conformity might find that it's difficult to get their ideas accepted and that people are more interested in the rules and regulations than in getting the job done. On the other hand, such organizational units tend to be relatively easy to understand. Perceptive individuals who can detect organizational norms early in the game can become quickly accepted.
2. *Responsibility:* People in these organizational units feel that they have a lot of responsibility delegated to them and that they can do their job without having to constantly check with their boss. At the same time, such units might not provide sufficient direction to their employees, causing them to squander their time or to work in ways possibly inconsistent with the goals of the organization as a whole.
3. *Standards:* People in organizational units that emphasize standards might feel overwhelmed by what they may see as unrealistic norms of accomplishment. On the other hand, such units might be seen as simply maintaining high expectations for their employees and encouraging them to set challenging goals.
4. *Rewards:* People in organizational units that rely heavily on rewards to get things done feel that they get proper recognition for good performance. Yet, people in such organizational units might feel as if they're treated like children who are incapable of enjoying their work for its own sake.
5. *Clarity:* People in these organizational units can become stifled by the many rules and regulations which govern nearly every aspect of their work lives. On the other hand, some individuals may find that things are very well organized in these units and that they know what is expected of them.
6. *Team Spirit:* People in these organizational units find the work environment to be warm and trusting which leads not only to a sense of pride and identity but to good interpersonal relationships. On the other hand, such units can also be considered overly cliquish to the extent that independence of thought and action is suppressed.

EXHIBIT 5-2   Climate Response Sheet

Unit's Climate Type _____

Strategies for Making One's Way
(try to be as explicit as you can)

1:

2:

3:

4:

5:

6:

7:

of developing a lot of innovative ideas, but work in an organization which stresses conformity. In this climate, you have to convince someone in power to accept your idea(s). You must be persistent yet flexible, and must be certain that the idea centers on key tasks necessary to achieve organizational goals. Possibly, you could volunteer for new responsibilities and slowly gain power and recognition. Whatever strategy you ultimately choose, it is clear that in this type of organization, you must follow the rules and learn to work around them.

The type categories considered in the recent exercise were discrete; they had no underlying dimension. However, some diagnostic tools for assessing organizational climate do indeed presuppose an underlying dimension and are even prescriptive in nature. One such tool was developed by Rensis Likert.[24] Likert, focusing in particular on managerial concerns, arranged organization styles into four systems which are really points on a continuum. He also developed a questionnaire, some of the questions of which are used in the ensuing exercise, to measure the position of an organization on the continuum. In this exercise, then, you should refocus your analysis on your organization, not on your organizational unit.

EXERCISE 5-4

ORGANIZATION STYLE QUESTIONNAIRE.

INSTRUCTIONS:
Please fill out the questionnaire below by circling the letters a, b, c, or d for each question, describing the *actual* style of your organization. In other words, your answers are to reflect how things really are, rather than how you would like them to be. Select only one response for each question even though your perfect answer may fall between two of the choices.

After completing the questionnaire, plot your answers on the scoring chart shown in Table 5-7.

1. The amount of responsibility felt by organizational members toward achieving organizational goals can be described as:
   a. high managerial levels feel responsibility; lower levels feel less. Rank and file feel little and often behave in ways to defeat organizational goals.
   b. managerial personnel usually feel responsibility; rank and file usually feel little responsibility.

   c. substantial proportion of personnel feel responsibility and generally try to achieve organizational goals.

   d. personnel feel real responsibility and are genuinely motivated to achieve organizational goals.

2. Communication tends to be initiated:
   a. at all levels.
   b. primarily at the top.
   c. exclusively at the top.
   d. from the top but with some initiative from lower levels.

3. The amount of cooperative teamwork can be described as being:
   a. none.
   b. very substantial.
   c. a moderate amount.
   d. virtually none.

4. The amount of influence by subordinates tends to be:
   a. virtually none.
   b. a great deal.
   c. moderate amount.
   d. none.

5. The flow of information throughout the organization tends to be:
   a. almost entirely downward.
   b. largely downward but small to moderate capacity for upward and between peers.
   c. in all directions from all levels.
   d. downward only.

6. Decisions tend to be made:
   a. throughout the organization and integrated by linking processes.
   b. at the top for policy with some made at lower levels if within prescribed framework.
   c. mostly at the top.
   d. at the top for policy and general decisions, at lower levels for more specific decisions.

7. In terms of the control processes in the organization:
   a. very strong forces exist to distort; as a result, information is usually incomplete and often inaccurate.
   b. there is some pressure to protect self and colleagues, hence some distortion; information is moderately complete but contains some inaccuracies.
   c. there is strong pressure to guide own behavior and behavior of work group; hence, information tends to be complete and accurate.
   d. fairly strong forces exist to distort; hence, information is often incomplete and inaccurate.

8. In solving problems, management:
   a. usually gets ideas and opinions of subordinates and tries to make constructive use of them.
   b. always gets ideas and opinions of subordinates and always tries to make constructive use of them.
   c. seldom gets ideas and opinions of subordinates.
   d. sometimes gets ideas and opinions of subordinates.
9. In terms of training:
   a. I have received some training of the kind I desire.
   b. I have received a great deal of training of the kind I desire.
   c. I have received quite a bit of training of the kind I desire.
   d. I have received no training of the kind I desire.
10. In terms of organizational problems, particularly at lower levels, management:
   a. is generally quite well aware.
   b. is often unaware or only partially aware.
   c. is aware of some, unaware of others.
   d. is moderately aware.

Adapted from Rensis Likert, *New Patterns of Management*. New York: McGraw-Hill, 1961, pp. 223-33. By permission of McGraw-Hill Book Company and Rensis Likert Associates, Inc.

Analyzing the Organization Style Questionnaire – Is There a Best Climate Type?

As can be detected from the scoring chart on Table 5-7, compared to the prior climate classifications, Likert displayed a definite preference regarding the climate type which he felt to be superior in most management situations. The labels given to each style, referred to by Likert as "Systems One Through Four," are my own, but depict the points along Likert's continuum quite well.

At one extreme, in the tell organization, we find managers who have little confidence in their employees. Most organizational goals and decisions are determined at the top and transmitted down the chain of command. Coercive power is used as a motivation device. Having little control over their own destinies, employees react through the informal system of the organization, i.e., through gossip. Their reactions are often contrary to the goals of the formal

TABLE 5-7   Organization Style Questionnaire Scoring Chart

INSTRUCTIONS:
Circle the letter on the chart corresponding to your circled answers on the questionnaire. When finished, notice the pattern. Has one column received a disproportionate share of circled items? Pay particular attention to any column with five or more circled items.

ORGANIZATION STYLE

Question Number	Tell	Sell	Consult	Join
1.	a	b	c	d
2.	c	b	d	a
3.	a	d	c	b
4.	d	a	c	b
5.	d	a	b	c
6.	c	b	d	a
7.	a	d	b	c
8.	c	d	a	b
9.	d	a	c	b
10.	b	c	d	a
Column Totals				

Source: Adapted from Rensis Likert, *New Patterns of Management*. New York: McGraw-Hill, 1961, pp. 223-33. By permission of McGraw-Hill Book Company and Rensis Likert Associates, Inc.

organization. In the tell organization, there is no cooperative teamwork except on a very informal level.

At the other extreme of Likert's continuum, in the join organization, we find managers who have implicit trust and confidence in their subordinates. Decision making is widely dispersed throughout the organization, and information and communication flow occur freely both vertically and horizontally. Workers are self-motivated and participate openly in setting their own goals, improving methods, and evaluating their own progress. Informal and formal segments in the join type of organization become identical as all forces inside the organization work together to achieve organizational goals.

Likert's research seems to indicate a clear choice in determining which of his four types performs best in most management situations. He argues that his System Four, the join organization, is more productive (has higher output at less costs, less waste, and better labor relations) and inspires superior employee relations than the organizations learning towards the tell side of the continuum.

Management research in the last fifteen years has produced a good deal of conflicting evidence regarding "one-best" climate types. The gist of this research points to a contingency perspective of organizational behavior.[25] Accordingly, the appropriate climate type is dependent or contingent on any numbers of conditions in the organization's environment. Some of the contingencies cited have included:

1. Maturity of the organizational members, i.e., their time together, their achievement motivation, their professionalism
2. Technology of the product or service, i.e., mass production, continuous process, job shop
3. Nature of the wider product environment, i.e., stable vs. unstable
4. Organizational size
5. Leader characteristics

Of more direct importance for our purposes is the relationship of climate to opportunities for personal career development within organizations. Although there may not be a best climate type for all managerial functions inside an organization, it is my belief that opportunities for career development are greater as one moves to the join side of Likert's organization style continuum. I offer two broad reasons for this contention. First, information tends to be more available and shared in the join type of organization. Consequently, individuals get a better reading of where they stand and what career opportunities exist outside of their immediate work environment. In a tell organization, it would not be unusual for some individuals to be overlooked for positions outside their own department because of the simple reason that these individuals would most likely not be privy to career information outside of their department. A second reason for preferring the join organization over those types leaning toward the tell side of the continuum is that in the join organization, an individual has as much opportunity to affect his or her career development as the boss. This point, initially presented by Theodore Alfred,[26] suggests that individuals can take responsiblity for their own career development and do not and should not have to rely solely on their boss for spotting the good opportunities for them. Alfred indicates that in tell-type organizations, supervisors tend to hoard the *good* people resulting in imbalances in staffing among subunits within organizations. Some departments become overstaffed, while others remain understaffed, a predicament arising from misguided boss possessiveness as well as from incomplete, unshared career information within the organization.

Essentially, as Table 5-8 illustrates, the more join the climate type, the greater the opportunity for the use of the behavioral approach to job and career development. In the join organization it is plain that jobs get advertised more openly, there is greater freedom of movement, there is more responsive feedback, and better deployment of training and development. Of course, the other side of the coin is that efforts to develop an open career system,

TABLE 5-8   **Tell vs. Join Organizations and Career Development**

Tell	*Join*
Promotion along traditional lines, usually within department	Promotion via behavioral approach, widely interspersed throughout the company
Dependence on supervisor for career development	Dependent on self for own career development; can negotiate career plans with supervisor
Little information on jobs in other areas	Abundant information on all job openings
Little feedback on why turned down for any job	Open feedback regarding job applications
Need to play politics to get ahead	Role of politics in career development minimized
Little burden to company to develop open career systems	Time consuming efforts by company to develop open career systems

characterized in the join climate type, are expensive and time consuming. Not every organization can be a join organization. Individuals finding themselves in other organizational climates need not despair, however. Besides having to negotiate more traditional career development structures, individuals in these climates need to acknowledge the importance of managing their boss, as I discussed in the previous section. Further, and I shall have more to say about this in the next section, the more an organization approaches the tell side of the continuum, the greater the need to play politics to get ahead.

Problems in the Climate of the Professional Employee

Many of today's modern organizations provide an excellent climate for the professional to develop skills and interests while concurrently contributing to organizational goals. However, most professionals are far from satisfied with their organizational climates. In the first chapter of this book, I documented the growing evidence that salaried professionals have an inherent conflict with their organizations regarding, among other things, their need for autonomy. Faced with this conflict, professionals either work out some kind of accommodation with their management, resort to what I called deviant/adaptive behavior, or leave their organization. In Chapter Two, I also noted the disparity in need orientation between the professional and management. Having now introduced the concept of climate, I can extend the discussion of professional/management conflict to the structural arrangement in organizations in which professional employees find themselves.

First, to review the conflict argument, basically, it has been suggested that the need orientations and expectations of professional employees conflict with opportunities afforded them in most organizations.[27] The professional as we have seen, is interested in autonomy, self-control, and development of the generalized knowledge in which he or she alone is expert. Yet, it is the recognized role of the manager, in coordinating the functions considered essential in carrying out the goals of the organization, to maintain adequate control over the employees responsible for carrying out these goals. Whereas the professional, then, finds self-control or colleague-control to be the preferable pattern of authority in the organization, the manager insists on superordinate control. As a result of this difference in authority patterns, it is understandable that a natural conflict may exist when "professional roles confront organizational necessities."[28]

It is unclear from the literature whether the conflict in expectations between professionals and management results from the innate need orientation of the professional or as a reaction by the professional to the constraints of large bureaucratic organizations. Many researchers blame the bureaucracy.[29] In particular, four sources of conflict are cited: (1) misutilization, (2) underutilization, (3) microdivision of labor, and (4) overspecialization.

Misutilization results from work assignments which are sufficiently routine that they could be done by clerical personnel or by technicians. It is reported to be widespread among professionals.[30]

Underutilization is similar to misutilization in that it requires light intellectural demands but is perhaps even more burdensome since it tends to be accompanied by light time demands. It is frequently a complaint which professionals make about their work at the entry stage of their employment. As I noted in Chapter Three, if first job assignments do not contain challenging work content, professionals are likely, unfortunately, to become quickly discouraged, lose some of their aspirations, and even leave the organization.[31]

Microdivision of labor occurs when jobs are so narrowly drawn that the component tasks seem to have little relationship to the final end product. Professional employees, consequently, maintain little or no identification with the whole product since their role in relation to the product is barely perceptible. Microdivision of labor is usually accompanied by expressions of minimal responsibility, low initiative, and virtually no autonomy.[32]

Finally, overspecialization results from an assignment to specialized tasks which are largely governed by fixed procedures, standardized so as to eliminate ambiguity. Gmitter put it this way, "specialists tend to know more and more about less and less."[33] An implication of overspecialization is that professionals within the organization become increasingly compartmentalized as they become functionally and even geographically separated from others involved in different tasks.

Where these four above conditions exist in one form or another, it is likely, as I had earlier pointed out, that professional employees will react in some way, whether it be by physically removing themselves from the source of conflict, or by staying and either resisting or adjusting in some way. If they decide to stay, they might choose to resist the bureaucratic constraints imposed upon them. They might also choose to accommodate to these organizational conditions, but might unfortunately face a gradual obsolescence of their professional skills. Finally, they might resort to any of the deviant/adaptive behaviors which were listed in Figure 1-3 of Chapter One.

Looking at these professional reactions to the bureaucratic sources of conflict more closely, there is evidence that some professionals leave their organizations in relatively large numbers, according to one study, because of a need for "a change of career direction, more interesting work, and opportunity for advancement."[34] Kaufman, although finding personal characteristics, such as age, national origin, and educational level, to have a strong bearing on professional turnover, concurred that underutilization, especially on the first job, was a leading ingredient in termination.[35] However, professional forms of accommodation, such as society membership and professional licensing, certification, or registration, were found to enhance job security. It appears that professional activities buffer the individual's reactions to local organizational problems. Accordingly, scientists are reported to have lower turnover rates than engineers.[36] Engineers and other technologists, having a local orientation, are disposed toward accommodation with their organization. Consequently, they might prefer to stay with their organization even if their jobs are not satisfying.

Staying with an organization which provides little job challenge, however, can have negative career implications, especially, with respect to obsolescence, regardless whether the professional is a cosmopolitan or local. Ritti, in fact, cites the two principal causes of obsolescence as:

1. A work assignment which does not require knowledge of the latest developments (i.e., microdivision of labor, underutilization, and overspecialization), or
2. One in which the pressure of time demands leaves no time or energy for study (i.e., misutilization).[37]

As an ultimate reaction to conflicting expectations, the professional may resort to the deviant/adaptive behavior or psychological reaction of alienation, which, according to Pearlin, results when employees are prevented from realizing what is rightfully theirs.[38] The alienated worker responds to the organization by withdrawing from active participation in work assignments and, in some cases, by seeking extrinsic benefits, such as money or social status.[39] The professional is also likely to respond through the development of an informal organization of colleagues both inside and outside the organization. As was pointed out as a characteristic of tell organizations, this informal organization will most likely pursue goals and activities which are antithetical to those of the formal organization. Finally, it appears that alienation is somewhat differentiated by the cosmopolitan-local orientation dichotomy. Ties with professional colleagues, which cosmopolitans are likely to establish, may mitigate some alienation. Locals, on the other hand, who are thwarted in their drive to advance in the organization, even perhaps to make the transition to management, are quite susceptible to feelings of alienation.[40]

Toward a More Challenging Professional Climate

The creation of a challenging professional climate is clearly a management concern, but in the next section, I shall demonstrate how professionals can themselves take advantage of organizational opportunities regardless of climate type. In this subsection, I hope to characterize the organizational climates which have been found to be most opportune for professional development. This should give the professional a target to shoot for. Previously it was noted that the maturity of the work group was one contingency which preconditioned the effectiveness of any particular climate type. Professionalism is clearly an indicator of high group member maturity. In fact, professionals are among the most sophisticated of employees in organizations, particularly due to their well-noted interest in intrinsic needs such as responsibility, achievement, and, of course, challenge itself. I shall have more to say about the subject of job enrichment in the next chapter, but clearly climates which are join or participative in character, such that the professional is given increasing decisional authority over his or her own work, are very conducive to professional development and fulfillment in most cases. Naturally, professionals, like any other type of worker, have extrinsic needs, so for some, rewards such as greater salary, employee benefits, and job security are important. However, these extrinsic benefits are normally viewed as secondary to intrinsic interests. Besides job enrichment schemes, which attempt to redesign jobs by providing for greater opportunities for self-pacing, responsibility, and decisional authority, horizontal job enlargement procedures have also been used with some success to alleviate problems of overspecialization. These designs allow workers to engage in a wider variety of job tasks, even to the extent of working on the entire product, perhaps as part of a team.[41] Job rotation is another vehicle for enlarging work horizontally. Horizontal enlargement designs, however, will not adequately respond to the intrinsic needs of most professionals unless they are accompanied by the conferral of some decisional authority over the tasks at hand. Otherwise, they may be seen as just giving these individuals more things to do. Further, professionals skilled in one particular technical area may not wish to expand their repertoire to other technical areas but may prefer to simply add more depth to the skills they already have.

Given this backdrop, what specific climate options have been found to be most propitious for professional development? The following list represents a summary of the literature in this area.

1. *A participatory leadership style of management.* In this climate, the leader or manager consults with professionals before making a decision, provides them with freedom to explore new ideas and interests, and allows them considerable influence in shaping their own work. Yet, such a leader also challenges employees by giving them meaningful direction and feedback regarding their task accomplishments.[42] Accordingly, the leader is also technically competent and updated.

2. *A climate which encourages interaction among colleagues.* It is also important that work groups are composed of professionals with some diversity of background in order that they can be stimulated regarding new developments in their fields.[43]

3. *Open vertical and horizontal communication channels.* Professionals benefit intellectually and pragmatically not only by exchanging information with their immediate colleagues, but by having access to information from different departments and from other levels in the organizational hierarchy.

4. *Management policies which foster professional development.*
    Professionals not only appreciate organizational rewards — such
    as challenging work, promotions, or pay — but also opportuni-
    ties to take advantage of professional development activities,
    such as advanced degree work, refresher courses, and partici-
    pation in professional societies.[44] Although controversial, as
    we have seen, the "dual ladder" approach which rewards
    professional achievement comparably to managerial perfor-
    mance, contributes to professional skill development without
    the distraction of managerial work.
5. *Flexible but responsive organizational structure.* Professionals
    may need a differentiated role structure in large bureaucracies
    in order to carry out their technical specialities without the
    demands of constant and close supervision by management.
    In other words, they need some freedom from the constant
    pressures of line management. On the other hand, given the
    demands of fast-changing product and service markets, organi-
    zations need to respond quickly in their production goals.
    The matrix organization structure, and its many related forms,
    if installed in a carefully planned manner, provides an excel-
    lent vehicle for professionals to concentrate on their technical
    specialties and yet participate actively in wider organizational
    goal accomplishment.[45] In a matrix organization, professionals
    may report to a technical manager as well as to a functional
    manager since units of operation tend to be structured around
    projects instead of line functions. Reducing the number of
    levels of management authority, as in the so-called flat organi-
    zational structure, also tends to create the flexible type of
    control structure preferred by professionals.
6. *Career path opportunities.* As I pointed out in the last chapter,
    the provision of a variety of career opportunities can help some
    professionals, who find their skills becoming overspecialized
    or who simply want a change of pace, develop new or related
    technical skills. Open career pathing is also an effective vehicle
    for rejuvenating the *burned-out* professional.

Climate as Environmental Uncertainty

Besides carefully diagnosing your organizational climate, it would be helpful to project the effects on your career produced by the wider environment. For most professionals, the wider environment consists of uncertainties produced by impending economic, technological, political, and cultural changes. The response to environmental uncertainty will depend upon what is known about the future against the clarity of one's preferences. In the language of decision sciences, decisions wherein the future is accurately forecast and our preferences are clear can be approached by probabilities, whereas if the future is unknown, the decisions tend to be approached using judgment. If our preferences are unclear but our projections accurate, we tend to use compromise in order to accommodate our competing preferences. If our forecasts and preferences are unknown, we usually end up with no decision and our organizational and career position approaches paralysis.[46]

In order to improve your chances to make choices, you need to be clear on your preferences, a process hopefully initiated through the reading of Chapter Two. You will also want to insure that your forecasts are reasonably accurate.

What are some of the environmental forces with which professionals will have to contend in the future?

1. *Economic uncertainty.* This type of uncertainty has been a particular scourge among professional scientists and engineers given the large number of layoffs which occurred in conjunction with the recessions of the 1970s. However, during this same period, legal and accounting positions were relatively secure. The lesson taught here is that one should be alert to changes in our macroeconomy, especially in terms of potential dislocations in affected industries and occupations which might face demand shrinkage under constant or growing supply.

2. *Technological uncertainty.* We are now in a technological age characterized by the continuous creation of new products and processes. In particular, through the use of the computer and its incredible memory and storage properties, we are witnessing an information explosion. In addition, technology has contributed to a knowledge revolution, for example, in terms of the growth of R&D and education, which has virtually

transformed our society from a goods-producing to a knowledge economy.[47] One of the results of the forces of technological change has been a need for personnel within organizations who possess high levels of skills, and in particular, who are professionalized. Professionals need to stay updated on the many changes which their fields are experiencing. Technological influences could ultimately either upgrade or outdate their current occupational positions.

3. *Political uncertainty.* Although political behavior in the United States could be described as being relatively stable compared to other democracies, party changes can shift priorities in behalf of industries in which large numbers of professionals work. The Republican election of 1980 was followed by an increase in opportunities for most engineers and scientists, but a decrease in opportunities for many human service professionals. Worldwide political pressure can also have significant impacts on the home front which could affect certain professional cohorts, for example as might be experienced among nuclear engineers under a strategic arms reduction agreement. Finally, domestic legislation, such as tax policy changes (for example, the introduction of IRA's) can significantly influence career decision-making among professionals.

4. *Cultural uncertainty.* Given the increasing level of education experienced by most of our population, the continuation of a fair degree of wealth, and ready access to sources of information, people are less willing to accept patterns of authority based upon formal position, age, or seniority. People are more prone to demand that their individual rights be protected. Traditional norms, such as sex-role stereotypes in regard to both work and family life, are being openly questioned. Professionals are even less willing than in the past to conform to organizational constraints which might interfere with their self-development.

The description above of some of the sources of environmental uncertainty does little justice to the many idiosyncratic changes occurring among the specific professions. Nevertheless, the professional should be alert to these particular changes, attempt to make accurate forecasts, and in so doing, convert uncertainty into opportunity. It has been reported, for example, that many of the engineering professionals laid off in the recession of the early 1970s, were "lulled into complacency . . . under the assumption that the organization would take care of them."[48] Absorbed in overspecialized work, when the layoffs came, many were unprepared to enter new markets which demanded alterations and upgrading of their technical skills. A careful reading of the economic and technological climate of the period may have prevented some of the wide dislocations in technical human resources which occurred. The most difficult adjustments during times of uncertainty are faced by professionals in the more traditional industries. In the period cited, for example, this would include automobile manufacturing and aerospace. Yet, the fast changes which we are witnessing in all aspects of our lives defy any occupational group in almost any industry from becoming complacent out of a sense of stability and permanence.

While I am encouraging professionals to be alert to different job opportunities during times of environmental stress such as reduction-in-force (RIF), I would hope that mutual problem solving with management would prevent the need for conducting career planning exclusively outside the organization. Research on engineers and scientists during times of economic uncertainty points to the need to increase rather than decrease internal career planning. Bucher and Reece[49] found that the predominant psychological needs or motivators among engineers and scientists did not change during contrasting economic environments. Interesting and challenging work and feelings of recognition and accomplishment were cited in both periods as the paramount work motivators. The only motivator which received increased emphasis in the down period was security. Hall and Mansfield[50] reported similar results in their study except that although needs were relatively unchanged, expressions of satisfaction regarding various elements of the work environment were significantly altered. In particular, the engineers and scientists in their sample, when faced with a reduction-in-force, were less satisfied with opportunities for promotions, pay raises, security, self-esteem, and self-actualization in their work.

The implications suggested by the authors of these two studies are that management must involve their professional workers in any program to cope with environmental stress. The result of such a mutual problem-solving approach would be greater organizational identification by the affected employees. Professionals are especially capable of diagnosing and implementing the necessary adjustments in their occupations in response to environmental uncertainty. It is entirely reasonable that they should be involved in organizational strategies which attempt to address the instability caused by environmental stress. At times, they might even take the initiative, but after carefully analyzing their respective organizational climates and using the appropriate political channels and tactics. I turn to this latter and important issue next.

THE ROLE OF POLITICS IN PROFESSIONAL CAREER DEVELOPMENT

Although all forms of organizational analysis are important in developing your organizational career, even in the most cordial climates you will not be able to achieve career fulfillment if you neglect to observe the appropriate political tactics prevalent in your organization. It is critical that you "fit in" if you are to achieve the advanced stage of mutual acceptance (recall Chapter Three) in your organizational career. Politics is both a way of speeding up and ensuring that you attain the stage of mutual acceptance.

Using the word politics here probably conjures up in you the specter of an evil process which depicts people serving their own ends to the detriment of others. It is viewed no less favorably within the workplace. Employees tend to consider politics as detrimental to organizational effectiveness. Yet, perhaps as a reaction to the harsh reality of everyday organizational life or out of cynicism, employees tend to believe that one must be politically astute in order to get ahead.[51]

This certainly implies some confusion regarding the role of politics in professional career development. One might consider it an unethical process that must, however, be done. Yet, engaging in political behavior and detesting oneself for doing so are hardly ripe ingredients for personal career fulfillment. If politics indeed represents a fact of life for organizational survival and development, then perhaps the ambiguity around its practice can be clarified by viewing it in a different light. Weiler believes that politics does not have to connote unethical compromise or manipulation. He prefers defining it as

an astute awareness of human dimensions . . . and . . . a carefully, consciously developed set of interpersonal competencies [for using that awareness] to accomplish change or improvement.[52]

Politics, then, although very much a selfish process which does make use of power and influence, does not have to be carried out in opposition to what others want, but can be used in conjunction with what others need. In view of the fact that most people consider politics to be necessary to get ahead, it may be helpful to consider why political behavior may indeed be so important to career development. Earlier in this chapter when discussing organizational climate types, I suggested that the more "join" an organization, the less the need to play politics in order to get ahead. However, I also suggested that few organizations perceive themselves as capable of becoming pure join types. Therefore, politics and the games associated with it are probably a fact of life in many large, bureaucratic organizations. Many of us might herald the day when the openness characterized by join or participative organizations spreads across all organizations. But, perhaps out of a basic human need for predictability, most large organizations rely upon standards and norms which block such unstructured and threatening designs as completely open communication channels. Consequently, with the standards, rules, and regulations firmly in place, it is natural to expect that informal methods of behavior or customs will emerge as a means of getting things done. Politics in this setting is no more than learning about these customs and managing them for the betterment of oneself and one's organization. Weiler gives a good example of this in the context of hiring.[53] Although there are countless organizational and governmental standards with regard to selection, Weiler found that managers will still tend to follow a predictable sequence in seeking a so-called "fail-safe" candidate:

1. They first look for someone they know on a personal basis.
2. If such a person can't be found, they look for someone whom they have observed meeting lower-level but comparable responsibilities.
3. If neither of the above, personally known, types can be found, they ask for recommendations from close colleagues or friends.
4. They then use the more formal selection systems to augment their list with unknown candidates from inside or outside the organization.

Now perhaps the process indicated here represents political gamesmanship, but given the real pressures of management, it is understandable and may even produce desirable results. Likewise, politics in professional career development can be viewed as a legitimate process of influence that produces desirable results for the individual in the sense of providing the means to achieve fulfillment in one's organizational career.

There are obviously no preestablished guidelines for determining which tactics could or should be used by individuals in furthering their career, but based upon a review of the literature, six tactics are proposed here with accompanying explanations of their potential use.

1. *Managing Organizational Symbolism* — This first tactic arises out of the capacity to astutely observe an organization and to understand the symbols which are used in getting things done. For example, there may be a need to use appropriate speech, dress, or manner in certain circumstances, whether it be in dealing with customers or clients on the outside or colleagues or superiors on the inside. Although it may appear as rather shallow, "looking the part" won't perforce gain you entrance into the top circle unless it is associated with an understanding of the "way we do things here." Reacting to this symbolism by asserting independence, by refusing to be governed by any constraints of speech or dress, is another option to pursue, but it suggests that the individual is not interested in meeting the organization halfway. Appreciating that organizations are made up of fallible human beings who occasionally seek comfort in engaging in repetitive patterns of behavior demonstrates a willingness to merge personal interests with the organization's to accomplish mutual goals.
2. *Building a Good Image* — Beyond managing organizational symbols, the individual has to go to the next step of proving oneself worthy of accepting increased responsibility, even to the extent of being given the freedom to manage one's own career. Part of this responsibility arises out of the development of a positive image in the organization which tends to be more than just an impression. A good image is built as a reputation for doing good work, for being reliable and dependable, and perhaps above all else, for being honest. Image also emanates from political astuteness regarding strategic organizational goals. If you are clever enough to forecast where the organization

is going to be some years down the road, you will see to it that you become part of the important activities that are going on and, in particular, become associated with the successes rather than the failures along the way.

3. *Controlling Information* — There is probably no greater resource to obtain within an organization in developing a career than information. There are three types of information which could be considered useful for this. First, there is work-related, patented information, such as trade secrets. Second, there is inside information on the talents and weaknesses of fellow employees. Third, there is information that the individual really has to prove worthy of keeping — Schein refers to it as information concerning "how things really work."[54] It might include informal procedures which can short-circuit red tape, key people to watch out for, ways to deal with the boss or with other power figures, etc. All three kinds of information are critical but take time, patience, and skill to amass. Some of the information can be gained simply by experience in the organization. If the mutual acceptance or tenure stage of development has been reached, for example, or an otherwise positive image has been built, some information will simply be brought to one's attention in an unsolicited manner. Of course, the use of more common research methods should not be overlooked — for instance, consulting the literature on a subject — to gather important data on the organization and its competitors. Once having obtained the information, it is advisable to check its accuracy using a number of reliable sources. It would be foolish to waste a good reputation on the communication of inaccurate facts which could cause irreparable embarrassment. Finally, a judgment has to be made regarding what information should be shared with others and when. Timing can be considered a useful vehicle so one might wish to withhold the information until such point that it can be fully understood and appreciated.[55] In the meantime, as people in the organization perceive an individual to be a reservoir of reliable information, they will tend to rely on the individual more and more. Once in this position, one can build trusting relationships with others and work with them to accomplish mutual career goals.

4. *Controlling Decision Making* — Decisions regarding the disposition of an organization's assets and resources occur continuously. To the extent an employee can be a part of the important decisions as well as the decision-making process, personal
   credibility in the organization will be advanced. This tactic
   entails three separate steps. First, possible outcomes of decisions need to be analyzed before the decisions are made. This is
   suggested in order to appear more often on the winning circle
   than the losing circle. Further, doing homework on complicated
   decisions can reveal problems which can be turned into opportunities. A lawyer who might use some after-work hours to
   pursue research on a minuscule legal point which, however,
   might win an antitrust challenge is an example of making effective use of preoutcome decision analysis. A second step in
   controlling decisions is to simply understand where others
   are at. In this way and in conjunction with the first step, in
   supporting a particular decision, an attempt can be made
   to guarantee favorable outcomes to oneself *and* to others.[56]
   Finally, the last step entails being at the right place at the
   right time. After getting the necessary inside information, an
   attempt should be made to become associated with decisions
   considered major by the organization's management. In that
   way, one can gain personal recognition while concurrently
   working to help management accomplish its own ends.

5. *Developing a Base of Support* — The prior tactics, if heeded,
   would describe an involved organizational member who plays
   a role in many activities and decisions, especially the important
   ones. In this way, the individual becomes indispensable to many
   others throughout the organization. In turn, the individual can
   look to others for support. Support essentially can come from
   three different sources. First, commitment of subordinates is
   critical. Although it would take a textbook on supervision to
   describe the numerous methods to adopt, certainly one of the
   most auspicious is to let subordinates express their views on
   decisions which affect them. Subordinates can indeed be a
   powerful arm in supporting a position on critical organizational
   decisions. Besides subordinates, the support of both peers and
   superiors is also needed. With both groups, the individual has
   to take the risk of communicating ideas but releasing only as

much information, as I had pointed out above, as is needed to clarify one's position. Another technique is to facilitate problem solving, perhaps in conjunction with meetings where decisions are usually made. However, the astute political tactician understands that many important decisions occur *before* a meeting, so he or she will attempt to clear decisions before the meeting occurs. Some of the other techniques available in amassing support with peers and superiors were discussed in the prior section on boss analysis. Perhaps paramount as a basis for that section regarding managing relations with the boss or peers is again a facility to accurately perceive the needs of superiors and colleagues so that in furthering one's own career goals, one can be also attempting to meet their needs.

6. *Getting to Know the Right People* — Beyond obtaining information regarding who to "get to know" both inside and outside the organization, one also has to put this information to good use and actually begin to associate with these individuals. The establishment of a relationship with these people cannot be done on a strictly self-serving basis, for alert, powerful people usually have gotten to where they are through a careful sense of interpersonal behavior. Rather, contact must be initiated on the basis of mutual interest, whether it be strictly on technical matters or, although much more rarely, on personal considerations. As I also discussed in the section on mentoring, the role of protégé to a mentor or sponsor carries with it certain responsibilities. Protégés, in seeking out a mentor or sponsor, want to be sure that their information regarding the prestige of this important person is accurate. Further, they will need to be sure that they are personally compatible with their mentor, that they share expectations openly, and that they and their mentor agree to periodically evaluate their relationship as it evolves.

EXERCISE 5-5

ORGANIZATIONAL POLITICS. In this exercise, I present a short case, entitled, *Jack of All Trades*, depicting a political predicament which has befallen the central character. The case is used to further analyze your consideration of political tactics in developing your career within your organization. Please read the case and then consider the questions at the end.

JACK OF ALL TRADES

"Jonnie came to us with some of the best school credentials," Dave suggested to Paul Morin, personnel manager of Design Circuits. "I just can't understand how by now — what is it, four years he's been here with us — he hasn't made principal or at least become a project leader. But I guess he's happy enough. What I'm afraid of is that one day he'll just ask for a project and no one will give him one. I know I had to pass him up for a new low current project, even though he had relevant experience. He just hasn't proved himself yet. I had to give it to Ralph Brown, even though Brownie has been with us for only a year and a half."

I guess no one blamed Dave. As section head, he had to pick the best. He has tried to be a mentor to Jonnie, but Jonnie had his own ideas. Personnel just had to get it straight. Jonnie's so interested in trying new things; so afraid of becoming bored. Yet to make project leader, you've got to have not only technical competence, but display excellent organizing skills. Jonnie is certainly technically proficient. Professor Kilpatrick at Rensselaer said we could count on him as one of his brightest. But he just hasn't displayed that *umpf* that leaders have. Plus, he's gotten himself involved in so many projects that we wonder if he's building up to anything.

From what I hear, he was really quite attracted to this place when he first came on board. I mean we do have a good name, a great name really, in instrumentation, and a pretty wide product line from D.C. measurement instrumentation to computer controlled systems. Jonnie's first assignment I believe was on a digital interface scheme. It was a straightforward design job but he should have gotten some good experience working on the multiplexer and on such design basics as parts, prototype debugging, modification, and a good grasp of digital logic. As a first assignment, it would also be his chance to see how things get done around here, that things don't always work out as neatly as in the school labs. And he probably got a taste of some market pressure. As I remember, I think Candex Corp, whom we were designing this for primarily, was pushing real hard. Jonnie was probably asked to cut a few corners.

Then, as I recall, Jonnie went on to the low current measurement project. I guess we all thought that's where he was going to make his mark. I mean that project had all kinds of potential. It was state of the art. There were so many second-order effects that he could have studied and brought out. I remember us having so much trouble, for example, with low current measurement under different degrees of humidity. And then, there was the "cross-talk" problem. Well, anyway, this should have been Jonnie's jumping off point. He wouldn't be considered a kid anymore. He was one of us. Rensselaer was behind him.

I guess he did ok on low currents, but from what I understand, he didn't push it. He could have stayed with it but no real discoveries were coming out of that shop. He saw a better opportunity from what I remember him telling me, working with Nancy and the voltmeter crew. I mean that's not a bad project. It does have good interface with low current measurements and they're really doing some interesting things down there. Nancy runs a pretty tight ship, too.

But then I heard Jonnie wanted another transfer, this time to the EEROM[57] group. This one I really couldn't make out. I mean this didn't entail much. It's an elementary design job, far as I can make out. Jonnie thought he could really help out, he claimed, by applying EEROM technology to voltmeter development. Nothing much came of it, though.

He's now on digital signal processing, by the way. What can you expect Dave to do? Jonnie's really quite far away from low current measurement at this point. He has been a good utility player. He's done a lot of things. But can he really cut the mustard? Dave would let him go to our Test Circuits Division across the river to head up one of their voltage reference projects, but they don't like his record. Last I heard, Jonnie's bored again. He wants out of digital signal processing. Dave doesn't know what to do with him. He can't go around to each project leader and tell them to hold onto Jonnie.

Paul's right, though. Jonnie's career is imperiled with us. But Dave thinks he may yet come out of it. Look at Robert Duvall, the actor. Didn't he play about every kind of role before he made it big? A versatile guy, really. But this is business. It may not be the same. Jonnie's got to get his career straightened out before it's completely too late.

The case was prepared by the author with the assistance of Charles Kohn and Richard Dolin.

Questions to consider:

1. Does this case suggest that there are political tactics or "games," to be played in some organizations in order to get ahead?
   a. What game(s) did Jonnie not successfully play in this case?
   b. Are you a jack or jill of all trades?
2. Can you prepare a brief list of "games" that exist in your organization or organizational unit which are required in order to get ahead? (You may find it helpful to review the preceding text before answering.)
   a.
   b.
   c.
   d.

e.

f.

g.

Revise or add to your list by consulting with a colleague.

3. Which of the games you and your colleagues identified would you be willing to participate in? Why or why not?

4. What are the implications from this exercise that you should consider in developing a personal career development strategy within your organization? Include, as you reflect on your answer, your feelings now about using political tactics to develop your organizational career. After this, you will be moving on in the next chapter to the formal development of a plan for change.

SIX: Balance-Imbalance Analysis and Plan for Change

INTRODUCTION

Having completed thorough diagnoses of yourself — your personal abilities, values, and stage of career and organizational development — and of your work situation — your job and organizational climate — you should now see the logic of combining the two as a basis for personal career development. I consequently present in this culminating chapter the notion of balance-imbalance which describes the congruence between your personal style and your organization's style. It is expected that for most individuals there are going to be areas of balance and also some areas of imbalance with the organization. Once the critical points of balance or imbalance are identified, you can take the appropriate action to solidify your career position or to enhance your career potential in the organization.

I wish to emphasize at the outset that it is not necessary that your personal style, which incorporates your professional self, conform to managerial expectations. That would be contrary to everything I have said regarding the integrity of your professional identity. However, if you can make your career aims consistent with the values and goals of your organization, you should find ample opportunity within your organization for personal and professional career development. Now, if you are in imbalance, slight or major, with your organization, I shall introduce in the chapter numerous options for change which are available to you including, of course, removing yourself from the principal source of imbalance, namely, your organization. These options, besides removal, have the potential of rebalancing your career aims with your organization and include: vertical, lateral, downward, enrichment, adjustment, and exploratory. They are described in full detail in the chapter as part of the plan for change designed to operationalize your personal career development strategy. The plan for change section incorporates four steps: (1) reflecting, (2) planning, (3) doing, and (4) evaluating. You will be guided through these steps one at a time with the ultimate objective of preparing a document detailing your personal career development strategy. I emphasize throughout that career development is a process, not an end point, and demonstrate how it can become a lifelong activity which can allow professionals an opportunity to control their worklife rather than leave it to chance.

THE BALANCE-IMBALANCE DECISION-MAKING MODEL

The notion of balance between personal style and the style of the organization is a well-known concept in the career development literature. Some of the architects of the career development field, in fact, have built some of their original theories around this concept. Donald Super, for example, in presenting his developmental perspective about careers, defined the career as a synthesis of the individual's self-concept and the external realities of the work environment.[1] John Holland based his theory of personal orientation on the assumption that individuals will gravitate toward work environments congruent with their personal orientations.[2] For example, an investigative person, such as a scientist, will tend to choose an investigative organizational environment. Holland went on to suggest that incongruity between organizational and personal orientations would likely result in frustration and turnover among "unmatched" individuals.

There is also some evidence that balance between individual and organizational styles can affect career performance. In an early, well-known study, Argyris found that bank employees who were characterized as right types tended to be promoted, while nonright types tended to leave.[3] A right-type person was characterized by the bank as being quiet, polite, unaggressive, and interested in receiving orders, but disinterested in giving them. Storey asserted that personal career development is facilitated by balance between job demands and the individual dimensions of talent, interests, and personal values.[4]

In Exercise 6-1, I introduce a model for performing a balance-imbalance analysis. It represents an attempt to systematize the integration of personal and organizational styles and has been used successfully in my career motivation workshops. It also offers a decision-making framework for reducing imbalances between you and your organization regarding your career development. Once having completed the exercise, I shall discuss the decision-making process more thoroughly.

EXERCISE 6-1

A. BALANCE-IMBALANCE ANALYSIS

BACKGROUND. There are, of course, any number of factors which can be used to characterize "style" which I define here as a set of traits which represent the essence of either an individual or an organization. For performing this exercise, it is critical that the factor (and its dimension list) chosen to discriminate style be applicable to both the individual and the organization. It is also important that this factor represent a meaningful variable for the professional in that it be capable of capturing the critical differences between professional performance and organizational responsibility. I have spoken at length about the pervasive problem of conflicting expectations between professionals and management. However, I have also reported that there is discrepancy among professionals with regard to their resistance to managerial control. For example, the need orientations of cosmopolitanism and localism were found to differentiate professionals in terms of balance with organizational expectations.

There is, consequently, no completely acceptable factor which can be applied as an unchallenged descriptor of professional style since professionals differ so markedly and react so differently depending upon the climate in which they find themselves. The factor I have chosen in this exercise includes the six dimensions of the AVL Study of Values referred to in Chapter Two. These six values are thought to capture style differences well for both individuals and organizations or organizational units. To review the meanings of the six AVL values, read the list below:

1. *Theoretical* — displays interest in the discovery of truth, is concerned with reasoning of an empirical or rational nature.

2. *Economic* — is interested in what is useful or practical, may be concerned with accumulating a fair amount of wealth
3. *Aesthetic* — is interested in form, harmony, grace, or symmetry, appreciates artistic expression
4. *Social* — tends to be sympathetic and unselfish, maintains a love of people, may be philanthropic
5. *Political* — is interested in power but not necessarily politics, wants to gain influence or reknown
6. *Religious* — seeks unity with a higher reality, may or may not participate in organized religion, is more interested in understanding the cosmos

Another dimension list beside these AVL values which may also be successfully used in this exercise are the six Holland personality/occupation types. These were also reviewed in Chapter Two. Only their labels are shown here:

realistic
investigative
social
conventional
enterprising
artistic

INSTRUCTIONS — PART I
Once familiar with the meanings of the AVL values (or Holland types, if you prefer to use those), your first task is to rank order these six values for yourself. Using Table 6-1, in Column one, place a six next to the value which most characterizes you, a five next to the next most characteristic personal value, etc. Of course, you could also choose to actually complete the AVL questionnaire, which might be available to you from your career counselor or which you could order from Houghton Mifflin Company. If you complete the AVL Study

TABLE 6-1   AVL Rankings and Balance-Imbalance Index

AVL Values	*Column 1* *Your Ranking*	*Column 2* *Organization Ranking*	*Column 3* *Balance-Imbalance Index*
Theoretical	_____	_____	_____
Economic	_____	_____	_____
Aesthetic	_____	_____	_____
Social	_____	_____	_____
Political	_____	_____	_____
Religious	_____	_____	_____

of Values, you will obtain raw scores on these six values which you would then simply convert to rankings.

Next in Column two of Table 6-1, assign rankings to the 6 AVL values *for your organizational unit*. Finally in Column three, which represents the balance-imbalance index, take the absolute value of the difference between Column one and Column two (subtract the two values and avoid writing any minus signs). The balance-imbalance index represents the difference or disparity between your style and your organizational unit's style according to the six AVL values.

INSTRUCTIONS — PART II

Having completed your balance-imbalance index, you should now have a preliminary accounting, which might simply have formalized your intuitive sense, of the degree of balance or imbalance with your organizational unit. In Part II of the exercise, we move ahead to the consideration of options which hopefully will become part of your implementation plan for change. Of course, if you are essentially in balance with your organization, there may be little point to proceed with this part except to consider any adjustments to those small areas of imbalance. I suspect, however, that most of you will have some areas of significant imbalance. I shall also be exploring the seven options listed below in great detail later in this chapter. For now, however, I provide only brief explanations of the options for purposes of completing the exercise.

1. *Vertical* — moving to an available higher position in your line or job category
2. *Lateral* — moving to another position at equivalent status in another operational area
3. *Downward* — returning to a lesser position
4. *Enrichment* — staying with your current job but seeking and then performing ways to make it more interesting and challenging
5. *Adjustment* — staying with your current job but changing yourself so that the job becomes less onerous and more interesting
6. *Exploratory* — actively investigating other options
7. *Removal* — leaving the organization with which you have been affiliated in order to seek employment elsewhere or engage in other kinds of work or leisure activity

After studying these options, you should turn to Table 6-2, the Balance-Imbalance Analysis Worksheet, to finish the exercise. Your first step is to simply record again the balance-imbalance index in Column one. You will next note that the remaining cells of the table are created by a matrix with the balance-imbalance index scores on the vertical axis and the option steps on the horizontal

TABLE 6-2 Balance-Imbalance Analysis Worksheet

AVL VALUES \ BALANCE-IMBALANCE INDEX	Vertical	Lateral	Downward	Enrichment	Adjustment	Exploratory	Removal
		OPTION			STEPS		
Theoretical							
Economic							
Aesthetic							
Social							
Political							
Religious							
Totals							

205

axis. To fill in the cells, you will need to heed the following explanation and algorithm.

Study the seven options. Apply each option to each AVL value by multiplying the balance-imbalance index score by the *expected results* of the option (if it were to be implemented) using the following algorithm:

worsen a great deal	X 2
worsen moderately	X 1.5
make little difference	X 1
improve somewhat	X .5
remedy	X 0

In other words, you are to consider what would happen to each of the AVL value differences if you were to follow any one of the seven option steps.

Let's consider an example. Suppose your theoretical balance-imbalance index score was 3. This displays a moderate imbalance between you and your organizational unit on the theoretical value. Perhaps you like to approach problems with an air of inquiry whereas your manager insists on pragmatic problem solving. You then consider what would happen to this theoretical imbalance if you were to move to a position immediately above yours. Since everyone in management in your line of work takes virtually the same position regarding pragmatic results, you decide that little change in theoretical imbalance will result from such a move. Accordingly, your score remains a 3. A downward move might even moderately worsen the problem since there will still be pressures to conform to the unit's pragmatic style but you might even be in less of a position to occasionally insist on empirical analysis. Your score becomes a 4.5. A lateral move, however, could place you in a research department where your rational style would be welcomed. However, you fear becoming "locked in" in such a department since it is not considered a mainstream career unit in the company. Nevertheless, getting a responsible position in research could improve your overall position somewhat. Your score is now a 1.5. And so on.

Once you have filled in all the cells of the balance-imbalance matrix, add up the totals for each column. Consider the one or two columns with the *lowest* total score. The option step(s) identified could conceivably represent your most auspicious option for developing your personal career development strategy.

B. FORCE-FIELD ANALYSIS (Option). For those readers who were sufficiently in balance with their organizational unit that the balance-imbalance analysis did not afford a practicable solution to some of their most pressing career challenges, I offer a more general decision-making vehicle here. It may also be appropriate for those of you who wish to consider creative options beyond the six proposed in the balance-imbalance analysis. Known as the force-field analysis, it was developed by Kurt Lewin who saw decision making as a process of violating states of equilibrium inside us.[8] At any given point, forces may be acting on us to change our current decision. In force-field analysis, a method is proposed to bring to light these forces so that an inventory of the important influences on any given decision can be drawn.

Lewin talked about the sets of forces affecting our decisions. The facilitating forces, known also as deviation-amplifying forces, drive us ahead to make changes, to seek our ideal state. Of course, any dramatic change from our current state of equilibrium entails a good deal of risk. If we move too fast, we might not be able to cope with the new state due to lack of preparedness, resistance by others, emotional stress, etc. Fortunately, there are restraining or deviation-reducing forces in all of us to resist any headstrong, impulsive decisions. However, these forces bring out the conservative patterns in us, and if allowed to become too influential, can cause us to become hypervigilant and unwilling to take any chances for fear of failure.

Figure 6-1 depicts the force-field analysis. Note that the arrows or vectors representing the forces are drawn at varying lengths, representing the importance or influence of the respective force.

INSTRUCTIONS:
Consider any career dilemma which you are faced with right now. Maybe you need to terminate your mentor relationship but are unsure of the consequences. Maybe you want to move up but are unsure whether you wish to tolerate the additional responsibilities. Maybe you'd like to move down but are afraid of the embarrassment it might cause you.

With the help of someone who knows you quite well (or simply by yourself, if you prefer), brainstorm a list of all the facilitating forces which are inducing you to make the change. For example, in the mentor example above, one such force might be that you no longer need technical assistance. Another one might be that you have set your eyes on a potentially better mentor. Compose this list in order of priority. Then, list all the restraining forces which impede you from making the change. Again in the mentor example, you might acknowledge that other employees who have stayed with this mentor have done extremely well in the company. Moreover, you may be viewed as insensitive and unreliable if you terminate too quickly, and so forth. Compose this second list in order of priority, as well.

Lewin found that to move to your ideal state, you could either increase the strength of your driving forces or reduce the influence of your restraining forces. However, the second method was found to be preferable since it invited no counter reactions. Therefore, review your list of restraining forces. Can the influence of any of these factors be reduced in any way?

You may find after reducing the influence of some of the restraining forces that a feasible solution to your decision problem may emerge. To complete

FIGURE 6-1
Force-Field Analysis

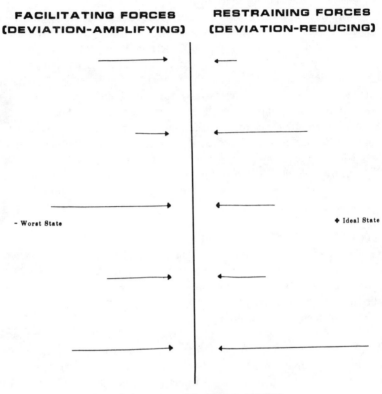

the example I've been using, let's suppose you discover that others in your company have changed mentors and in so doing, have not been labeled unreliable, as long as they have made the transition in a constructive and sensitive way, that is, by having ensured that all the parties had input into the decision. If you were to deploy this strategy, you would essentially be reducing the influence of one of your restraining forces while moving toward your desired change. See if this strategy works in your case.

The balance-imbalance analysis, as one would readily comprehend once going through the steps of the exercise, actually affords the individual an option which is likely to produce a greater sense of self-fulfillment and career satisfaction than might be afforded by one's current career situation. However, the exercise should be absorbed as much for the process of decision making which it attempts to instill as for the outcome produced. Some might view the model of balance-imbalance as no more than a gimmick which attempts to quantify the unquantifiable. Although I might be convinced that the numbers are symbolic rather than real in the balance-imbalance analysis, I believe that models such as this one can be helpful aids in the personal decision-making process to the extent that

1. they provide an opportunity to insert objective, unbiased data into a decision,
2. they temporarily suspend the impact of stress and social pressures on decision making, and
3. they provide the decision maker with a greater set of alternatives and contingencies with which to make the decision at hand.

The decision regarding career options can be an extremely important one for the professional. Further, a decision is, in fact, always prevalent since deciding to do nothing constitutes a decision — even if not consciously made. However, from time to time, opportunities for a change crop up. Janis and Wheeler[5] discuss four common coping patterns which people engage in during such occurrences.

1. *Complacency.* Some people react to any new decision by simply avoiding any challenging information connected to the decision. For example, they might immediately accept an offer for a vertical move without exploring the full ramifications of such a transfer.
2. *Defensive Avoidance.* In this pattern, people might have an understanding that there is important information to be garnered regarding the decision, but neglect to check it out for fear that they will not be able to find an acceptable solution. It's like the patient who refuses to check out a physical symptom because he or she is afraid of what the doctor might find out.

3. *Hypervigilance.* This is nearly the reverse of the defensive avoidance pattern as people become so aware of the criticalness of their decision that they become obsessed with it. They may complain that they don't have enough time to make an adequate choice. They also may display a great deal of emotional stress, leaving them helpless to mount an effective search in the limited time available for information regarding the decision.

4. *Vigilance.* In contrast to the above three patterns, the vigilant person when faced with an important career challenge will take the challenge seriously and will find the time to search for alternatives and to carefully evaluate these alternatives. In this way, the vigilant person believes one can find an effective solution and, in most cases, will be successful in doing so. Further, when one's original solution is thwarted, the vigilant individual has prepared contingency plans to cope with any new risks.

The vigilant decision maker, then, cannot really fail in decision making, for it is understood that decision making is a process which is constantly evolving. Setbacks are accepted as part of the game, but contingency plans are readied to move the individual into a more favorable position. The decision-making process is therefore accepted as a perpetual task. The individual periodically evaluates present circumstances and maps a plan for change in the event a new move might be made to contribute to career growth or in the event some external force outside of one's control (for example, an impending layoff) requires a change. The decision maker's plan cannot always be correct, in fact, there are two general sources of error. As Table 6-3 indicates, these occur when the decision maker rejects what would have been a good choice (the Type I error) or accepts a bad choice (the Type II error).

Neither error is preferable to the other; Type I tends to result from being overly conservative in making choices; Type II from being overly impulsive. What is critical is knowing which type of error is most likely made and how to recover from each. If you believe you constantly make Type I errors, you must attempt to take some more well-researched risks. If you believe you make too many Type II errors, you must try to hold back on making rash decisions and think through your decisions more carefully. As pointed out in the discussion of the vigilant decision maker, care in decision making entails producing a clear set of objective, unbiased alternatives and evaluating these alternatives by projecting their likely consequences.

TABLE 6-3   The Sources of Error in Decision Making

DECISION MAKER'S PLAN

		REJECT	ACCEPT
	GOOD	TYPE I ERROR	CORRECT
DECISION OUTCOME			
	BAD	CORRECT	TYPE II ERROR

In the area of career development, I see the challenge faced by the professional within the organization similar to Hall's conception[6] of achieving a better integration of personal, professional, and organizational goals. In balance-imbalance analysis, I focused specifically on a means to achieve a better fit among these three variables. Some readers might react that the process described implicitly advocates conforming to the organization's style. I do not want to create this impression. Balance does not imply conformity, but rather a state wherein one can become more fulfilled and satisfied in one's career within the context of one's organization and one's profession. Even if a conformist-oriented individual believes his values are being compromised within a particularly doctrinaire organizational unit, then one would hardly expect that situation to be characterized as being in balance. What I am suggesting is that opportunities for career growth are maximized to the extent personal values, interests, and aspirations are compatible with the style and practices of the organization and profession. Finally, I am also suggesting, consistent with the underlying philosophy of this book, that professionals as active contributors to their own organizational career can make effective decisions regarding their careers, especially those individuals who believe they have a fair degree of control over their lives.[7]

PLAN FOR CHANGE

It is now time to map out a plan for change. Literally all the material in this book preceding this point has prepared the reader to implement a personal career development strategy. The plan for change is the document which operationalizes this strategy for the professional.

The focus of the book has been to integrate the career needs and style of the professional with the goals and style of the organization. Change, then, is defined here as individual activity directed at addressing the imbalance between the individual and the organization. Change is also thought to represent personal activity in reaction to a problem. Therefore, I view the imbalance between the individual and the organization as the paramount problem to be resolved in the plan for change.

Other symptoms of the problem of imbalance have been discussed by Miller[9] and include:

vague uneasiness
boredom
repeated disappointments
crises
new information which doesn't fit

Miller also points out that change may be precipitated in the career domain by personal assessment, similar to what was depicted in Chapter Two, by the need to achieve a goal, and by an environment which permits, accepts, and even encourages the change. It is my hope that on the basis of the preceding material in this book, you will see the need to initiate a goal for change given any imbalance in your present career. Further, having completed an organizational analysis, including an understanding of the politics of personal career development, you will have identified "pockets" of acceptance and encouragement for personal change and growth within your organization.

The model for developing a personal plan for change which I introduce here is a simple one. It entails merely four steps organized as a continuous loop, and is depicted in Figure 6-2. The bulk of this section will concentrate on the Planning step, wherein the options identified in the Balance-Imbalance Analysis will be carefully developed. The other steps are expected to be quite familiar to the professional audience. I shall consequently describe each of these with greater conciseness.

FIGURE 6-2
Plan for Change Model

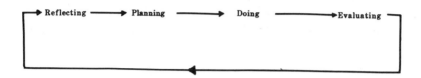

REFLECTING

The reflecting step of the plan for change is constituted of no more than the activities prescribed in the prior five chapters. It is of course accompanied by a willingness to look at yourself and your current situation honestly and openly in anticipation of a plan of action to improve your career position.

There are six diagnostic elements in the reflecting step:

1. Diagnosis of self
2. Diagnosis of self in relation to others
3. Diagnosis of job
4. Diagnosis of career path
5. Diagnosis of organization
6. Diagnosis of environment

Briefly, and in review of prior material, I describe these elements as follows. The diagnosis of self entails a full analysis of oneself in relation to one's work. Hence, perhaps through the use of the self-interview, the following should be conducted: an interest and skills analysis, a learning style inventory, a psychological needs assessment — including an understanding of professional need orientation, and a personality style assessment.

The diagnosis of self in relation to others emanates from a need to understand the role of career in the total life space. Therefore, one must appreciate how potential changes in one's career may affect important others in the family, in the organization in which one works, in the community, and in outside activities, which would include friends. One also benefits from comparing one's progress or stage of development as a growing human being, as an organizational constituent, or as a professional with others who are confronting issues at the same stage of development.

The diagnosis of the job should consider the level of satisfaction derived from one's work. It should also entail a behavioral understanding of the components — skills, knowledges, activities — one contributes to and derives from one's job, perhaps best captured through a personal job analysis.

The diagnosis of career path looks at the present work situation as a point along a sequence of opportunities which form a path representing one's career potential. The career path can be viewed solely in terms of the organization, or it can be considered a professional path which is uninhibited by organizational bounds.

The organizational diagnosis might begin with an analysis of one's boss and mentor or sponsor in order to determine the available support in meeting one's career needs. A climate analysis should then be conducted to determine the type of organization of which one is a part and its degree of receptiveness to personal career development. As a professional, the position of the organization vis-a-vis professional development must be anticipated. An acute awareness of the political climate in the organization is also required in order to consider the appropriate strategies to use in pursuing a professional career while simultaneously meeting organizational goals.

Finally, the environmental diagnosis entails a search for opportunities and pitfalls in pursuing particular career objectives on the basis of environmental uncertainty. One should be aware of the impact on career choices produced by such environmental forces as economic, technological, political, and cultural uncertainty.

PLANNING

The planning step incorporates two separate tasks which are required before being able to carry out a plan for change. In the first place, one must choose and make a commitment to an option which appears to satisfy one's present career needs given all the information heretofore brought to bear on this choice. The choice of an option is not irrevocable. After a thorough analysis of any one option, yet another option may be considered before ultimately making a firm career decision. Even a decision, which is expressed in the form of a set of behavioral objectives (to be described subsequently), is never really finite. Nevertheless, an option must be chosen to move into the next action step.

Option-setting, then, is the first task of the planning step to be followed by objective-setting. The options which might be considered are the same ones as I discussed in the balance-imbalance analysis. Beverly Kaye in her career consulting practice also considers six of the seven options presented.[10] They are again:

Vertical	Downward	Exploratory
Lateral	Enrichment	Removal
	Adjustment	

Below and throughout the major portion of this section, each option will be described in detail. You may choose to review only the option or options which apply to you right now. This option may be in fact the one proposed as the solution to your balance-imbalance analysis. It may have emerged from a force-field analysis of a personal career dilemma. Or, it may simply be an option that is intuitively attractive to you. In any case, exercises will also be presented to allow you an opportunity to experience as much as possible the consequences of selecting a particular option. Following the presentation of the options, I shall discuss the objective-setting task of the planning step and then consider the last two steps in the plan for change model. I begin with a discussion of the vertical option.

Vertical Option

Of the seven options available, perhaps no other compares to vertical promotion as a measure of organizational success. Even acknowledging currents for self-fulfillment among especially younger professional workers today, the drive for upward mobility by all standards still reigns supreme as the commonly accepted standard of personal accomplishment. Given its importance, researchers have for years attempted to isolate the ingredients for advancement. However, no clear set of factors have ever emerged which have been supported by empirical analysis. This is probably due to a number of reasons. For one, U.S. societal norms appear to be in constant flux, somewhat representing the nature of the population. Consequently, fixed lines of ascent are difficult to draw, especially across the wide variety of institutions in our society. Second, within each institution or organizational entity, individual and group interests are expressive enough to block the creation of fixed promotion paths. Finally, the cult of individualism in American society is still sufficient to allow personal idiosyncrasies to affect promotional decisions.

In spite of the above, there are some general guidelines that the literature has offered on the advancement process which can be of some service to aspirants. Although now over 30 years old, C. Wright Mills' *White Collar* placed the success pattern in the United States into a rather derogatory perspective.[11] Compared to the entrepreneurial pattern of the first part of the twentieth century, we are now witness to the so-called efficiency pattern. Accordingly, agility has replaced ability, getting along is more important than getting ahead, who you know is preferred over what you know, techniques of self-display and people management are preferable to moral integrity, substantive accomplishment, and solidity of person; and finally, loyalty to the firm can get one further ahead than entrepreneurial virtuosity. Although one may not be willing to go as far as Mills in his description of the success ethic, there are perhaps some sobering truths in his comparisons. Perhaps Dalton's piece from the same era[12] offers a more dispassionate analysis. He suggests that the first criterion for advancement is adequate skill or proven ability. Only after this has been satisfied do the more informal criteria come into play. In the terms I have been using in this book, the informal criteria constitute the self-management skills. Another way to refer to them is the ability to relate well to people. For the professional, the list of relevant self-management skills necessary to get ahead will vary by professional type. In the case of the lawyer working toward achieving partnership status in the law firm, some of these informal skills, according to Smigel,[13] entail seeking additional work and responsibility, taking on additional night work, displaying excessive drive, seeking out work for important partners, or taking risks.

Much of what has been written on the vertical option, then, leaves a lot of discretion to the jobholder to plan his or her own advancement. Clearly, one must start with the necessary technical (work-content) and functional skills. There are many ways to acquire these skills, paramount of which is adequate prejob education. Once on the job, the organization's resources must be used to fill the gap between what was learned in school and what is needed to perform the jobs required along the career path. Occasionally, lateral transfers or even selective use of downward transfers, as I shall shortly discuss, can be used to develop the appropriate skills for advancement. For the professional, reliance upon a mentor or sponsor, if not overused, is an important career strategy, as was discussed in the previous chapter. Likewise, the boss can be instrumental in shaping the individual's growth in the company.

Generally speaking, however, each organization creates its own benchmarks for advancement. Certain career paths are known to be the ones leading to the top. Others may be dead-ended. The professional has to know how long to spend on a given job and what level of performance is expected. One then has to know when to leave that job and which jobs are acceptable along the path to the top. Essentially, there are test points at each step of the way. Management might examine at these points, for example, how the employee handled interpersonal relationships, how responsibility was handled, how much initiative was taken, how the employee reacted to uncertainty, what decisions were made. If the employee passes the test, he or she can continue to move up the ladder. Each job, then, can be viewed as an opportunity providing "contacts, credentials, experience, exposure, and training/development."[14]

The first task in planning for a vertical promotion is to identify the most auspicious career path. This will likely present a number of alternatives for the next job, since there is typically more than one path to the top. The career path grid, if completed in Chapter Four (please refer to your Figure 4-1), identifies the next job in one's operational area along the vertical path. This job hopefully entails a higher degree of work-content, and perhaps functional skill than is required in the current job. Accordingly, the promotional skills analysis below should be completed. A promotion factor exercise follows.

EXERCISE 6-2

PROMOTIONAL SKILLS ANALYSIS. In Table 6-4, consider the skills necessary for successfully managing the job identified on the next rung of your vertical career path. (You may need to refer to the interest and skills assessment section of Chapter Two as well as Chapter Four to complete the exercise.) A job of greater responsibility in another suboperational or technical area may also be considered. In the next column over, rate yourself on how you currently perform these skills on a scale from one to five, one being poorly, five being very well. Then, rate how the organization — your boss, your peers, others whose opinion you respect — sees you with regard to your performance of these skills. Average both ratings for all three skill types. Finally, in the last column, try to derive some concrete developmental steps you can take to improve your performance on those skills which, in your opinion, received inadequate ratings. By developmental steps, I mean such activities as courses, counseling, meetings with key people, role modeling, awareness expansion, skilled practice, etc. Most likely the improvement plan will vary depending upon whether the low rating was in the personal or organizational column. Low ratings in the organizational column not reflected in the personal column, for example, may suggest a need to improve your political behavior to make your skills more known to others in your organization.

TABLE 6-4   Promotional Skills Chart

	My Current Rating	*Organizational Rating*	*Improvement Plan*
Work-Content Skills Required			
Average:			
Functional Skills Required			
Average:			
Self-Management Skills Required			
Average:			

EXERCISE 6-3

PROMOTION FACTOR EXERCISE. As indicated in the introduction to this option, although no empirical support has been found justifying the use of a given set of factors in promotion, general guidelines exist which can at least establish the relative importance of a variety of factors. In one study, executives from one hundred Fortune 500 companies were asked to indicate the relative importance in terms of advancement in their organization of 50 factors. These factors are presented in random order in Table 6-5. For each factor, you are to indicate your perception of its importance by rating the factor on a percentage or 100 point basis. Since this is not a ranking, you may use the same percentage any number of times for different factors. For example, if you believe "has a pleasant personality" is important all the time as a basis of promotion, give it a rating of 100. If "looks like a manager" is important nearly half the time, you might give it a rating of 46, etc. The executives' responses are given in Table 6-6. Do not turn to Table 6-6, however, until you have completed Table 6-5. Once you have finished, on Table 6-6 compute the difference for each factor (disregarding the minuses), and then add up all the differences to produce your total score.

After completing the exercise, examine any large differences closely. A large difference for any factor, from my experience with this exercise, is anything over 30 points, which approaches one standard deviation. Hence, any total difference score of 1500 or more shows significant disparity with the executives (although you should pay more attention to individual factors). Are you surprised by the executives' ratings? Do you feel they are accurate? What motivated them to answer in this way? Will this exercise in any way influence your perceptions regarding promotion in your organization? Will it induce you to make any concrete changes in your attitudes or behaviors? Make a short list of these changes now before completing this option.

Although, as I have pointed out, advancement in one's company is truly a hallmark of success, it may be approached too voraciously by some. Forcing a promotion may simply place you in too much stress by making excessive demands on your available skills and/or values. Further, promotions at too rapid a pace may not be acceptable from the company's point of view. Consequently, job advancement must be analyzed very carefully to ensure it meets your needs for long-term growth and satisfaction. Some questions along these lines are provided below:

TABLE 6-5 Your Rating of the Importance of Promotion Factors

Factor	Rating (based on % important)
1. Is willing to work more than 40 hours a week	
2. Regularly attends a house of worship	
3. Is a college graduate	
4. Has a wife who knows how to handle herself at social and company functions	
5. Has received job offers from other companies	
6. Has a pleasant personality	
7. Is tactful in making suggestions to superiors	
8. Lives in residential area similar in quality to those already at the top	
9. Works for a superior who is promotable	
10. Is willing to accept criticism, admits mistakes	
11. Is in good physical shape	
12. Belongs to the same club or lodge as those already at the top	
13. Has made few mistakes or errors	
14. Looks like a manager	
15. Is able to operate with a minimum of direction	
16. Is not considerably younger or older than others in the level to which he is to be promoted	
17. Has a good record of accomplishments	
18. Comes up with new ways to handle problems	
19. Is able to develop subordinates	
20. Is willing to express disagreement with superiors	
21. Is active in community affairs	
22. Is able to meet deadlines	
23. Doesn't complain about rules and procedures	
24. Is white	

220

25. Has never been divorced
26. Has the respect of colleagues
27. Is a Republican
28. Makes it clear that he wants a promotion
29. Has worked for superiors who have reputations for being good managers
30. Is able to sell his ideas
31. Goes strictly by the book
32. Is willing to make a geographical move when necessary
33. Is able to communicate clearly and concisely
34. Is married
35. Has a clean-cut appearance
36. Has a sponsor at a higher level
37. Is able to take suggestions from subordinates
38. Is cooperative, has the spirit of teamwork
39. Was born in the United States
40. Is able to see which way the wind is blowing accurately and quickly
41. Is able to argue logically
42. Understands the emotional makeup of people
43. Is willing and able to play organizational politics
44. Has a good academic record
45. Is an advocate of company policy
46. Is willing to take a risk
47. Is in a position that provides an opportunity to deal with higher level managers
48. Has the respect of subordinates
49. Has a similar social background to those already at the top
50. Is a graduate of a high prestige college

Source: Adapted from W. I. Meisler's article, "Promotion: What Does It Take to Get Ahead?" *Business Horizons* 21:57-63, 1978.

TABLE 6-6   Chief Executives' Ratings of the Importance of Promotion Factors

Factor	CEOs' Rating	Your Rating	Difference
1. Is willing to work more than 40 hours a week	94		
2. Regularly attends a house of worship	14		
3. Is a college graduate	80		
4. Has a wife who knows how to handle herself at social and company functions	56		
5. Has received job offers from other companies	23		
6. Has a pleasant personality	95		
7. Is tactful in making suggestions to superiors	98		
8. Lives in residential area similar in quality to those already at the top	5		
9. Works for a superior who is promotable	55		
10. Is willing to accept criticism, admits mistakes	96		
11. Is in good physical shape	93		
12. Belongs to the same club or lodge as those already at the top	8		
13. Has made few mistakes or errors	87		
14. Looks like a manager	57		
15. Is able to operate with a minimum of direction	100		
16. Is not considerably younger or older than others in the level to which he is to be promoted	38		
17. Has a good record of accomplishments	100		
18. Comes up with new ways to handle problems	100		
19. Is able to develop subordinates	97		
20. Is willing to express disagreement with superiors	95		
21. Is active in community affairs	64		
22. Is able to meet deadlines	99		
23. Doesn't complain about rules and procedures	84		
24. Is white	22		
25. Has never been divorced	14		
26. Has the respect of colleagues	98		

27. Is a Republican — 3
28. Makes it clear that he wants a promotion — 68
29. Has worked for superiors who have reputations for being good managers — 79
30. Is able to sell his ideas — 98
31. Goes strictly by the book — 26
32. Is willing to make a geographical move when necessary — 96
33. Is able to communicate clearly and concisely — 99
34. Is married — 24
35. Has a clean-cut appearance — 80
36. Has a sponsor at a higher level — 53
37. Is able to take suggestions from subordinates — 98
38. Is cooperative, has the spirit of teamwork — 100
39. Was born in the United States — 16
40. Is able to see which way the wind is blowing accurately and quickly — 80
41. Is able to argue logically — 100
42. Understands the emotional makeup of people — 98
43. Is willing and able to play organizational politics — 44
44. Has a good academic record — 76
45. Is an advocate of company policy — 81
46. Is willing to take a risk — 97
47. Is in a position that provides an opportunity to deal with higher level managers — 92
48. Has the respect of subordinates — 98
49. Has a similar social background to those already at the top — 22
50. Is a graduate of a high prestige college — 27

Total Difference Score:

Source: Adapted from W. I. Heisler's article, "Promotion: What Does It Take to Get Ahead?" *Business Horizons* 21:57-63, 1978. Percentages reported in article represent % of executives saying item is at least "somewhat important," but are used here to represent relative importance for purposes of the exercise.

1. What will your new boss be like? What's his or her work style like, his or her personality? Is he or she competent, at least from what you've seen or heard.
2. Will the new job involve relocation? If so, what will be the effects on your family?
3. Will the new job keep you visible in the organization, or will you be isolated? Does it, in turn, have a recognized career path?
4. Does the job give you real responsibilities?
5. Are you potentially giving up work activities you enjoy on your current job, or activities you do well? Will you be able to continue such activities in your new job?
6. Does your new job also take advantage of your past experience and skills?
7. Will it provide a healthy learning environment?
8. Think through your choice one more time. Are you changing jobs too quickly? Will a change throw you off balance? Have you been on your current job long enough to develop friends and supporters?

Lateral Option

As was suggested in the previous discussion, the vertical transfer is normally considered synonymous with success and fulfillment in an organization. Nevertheless, not every aspirant can find sufficient room at the top in which to move. In fact, certain conditions in our society militate against pure vertical movement.

For one, we have faced a deceleration in our economy in recent years. Even during times of recovery, some industries never make it back to full capacity. As organizations cut back in response to the surrounding economic environment, mobility certainly must decline. Further, the effect of inflation causes firms to look for ways to increase efficiency and eradicate waste. One method is to cut back on personnel at both middle and upper ranks.

Another condition which has dampened vertical opportunity is a liberalization in our retirement laws. This combined with the fact that our labor force is gradually aging suggests that competition for upper level jobs will indeed be stiff in the future.

Finally, the impact of our equal employment opportunity legislation is just as likely, if not more likely in the future, to be felt at the promotion point rather than at the selection point of our human resource systems. Newly hired minorities and women will be seeking to advance in their companies to positions heretofore bereft of fair representation. Management will be hard-pressed to deny them their right of advancement assuming their qualifications are appropriate. Minority advancement is likely to displace majority advancement, therefore, except in the most flourishing organizations, regardless of the hard feelings this might bring.

Given the barriers against vertical mobility, organizations are beginning to look to lateral transfers as a means of thwarting the disappointment and potential demotivation of plateaued workers. By lateral transfer, I mean moving to a job at the same level which demands the use of different technical skills. It is not equivalent to geographical transfers which may simply reassign workers to an identical job in a different location. Rather, it provides workers an opportunity to expand their repertoire of skills by learning the requirements of a different suboperational or entirely new operational area. Such transfers, if implemented according to the workers' needs and expectations, can keep them open to new learning and provide them with a broader perspective on the organization as a whole.

Most human resource analysts find little to discredit the use of the lateral option. There appear to be two main objections, however: (1) It still is not a vertical transfer, and may simply not substitute for the frustration experienced by some workers who for whatever reason don't find themselves moving up fast enough, and (2) It poses some administrative burdens on supervisors and management in general as it entails a good deal of time and planning. In fact, if not implemented fairly, supervisors may complain of having been "robbed" of some good workers.

In spite of these objections, lateral moves pose a number of distinct advantages both to the individual as well as to the organization. If you are considering a lateral transfer, can you identify which advantages apply to your personal situation?

Individual Advantages
1. The most important facet of the lateral transfer is the breadth of experience it provides to employees. Rather than becoming

locked into one specialty, employees undertaking a lateral transfer can become versatile in many areas. In turn, lateral movement can serve as a basis for ultimate promotion. In fact, McCaffrey[15] has reported that in some instances, workers can advance faster by selectively using the lateral as opposed to the vertical option.

2. The lateral transfer relieves employees from the potential monotony of doing the same job year after year. Hence, it allows for continual challenge on the job, for those who desire it, while at the same time providing an excellent learning experience.

3. It provides a means to reverse a dead end situation; in particular, employees who discover that they made a mistake in opting for a particular job, can get another chance.

4. It is oftentimes a superior alternative to dismissal; in fact, employees given a second chance might flourish in another technical area.

Organizational Advantages

1. Management can use the lateral transfer as an effective mechanism for identifying, testing, and extending employees' competence.[16] Capacity to handle upper level responsibilities is readily assessed when a worker has been challenged on a variety of different assignments.

2. The lateral transfer can stimulate innovation in an organization by bringing new perspectives into previously staid operational areas. People from different backgrounds transmit not only new ideas but new ways of handling problems.

3. It can create a more open organizational climate by revealing how people from different areas communicate. For example, an engineer attached to a product team could help the marketing people learn how to communicate their technical needs more effectively.

4. It can correct an erroneous placement by allowing professionals to move to an area where they might be more fulfilled compared to an original placement where they might be quite unhappy. Similarly, it can be used to resolve hopeless interpersonal incompatibilities.

It should be pointed out here that the lateral transfer is a qualitatively different concept from the technique of job rotation used by some organizations. Job rotation is normally considered a developmental tool only; consequently, its main purpose is to *expose* people to other job assignments for learning purposes. Consequently, the term of assignment is usually much less on a job rotation compared to a lateral transfer. Although, as we have seen, the lateral transfer is often used to develop some new skills, it is not undertaken solely as a temporary placement. Workers are expected to contribute fully to the job at hand and are not necessarily promised a higher placement at a later date.

To better assess any potential benefit from the lateral option, two exercises are provided in this section.

EXERCISE 6-4

TRANSFERABLE ACTIVITY ANALYSIS. As I discussed in Chapter Two, there are so-called functional skills and activities that are transferable from one job to another. Hence, if you undertake a lateral transfer, you may find some of the skill requirements to be quite familiar to you. On the other hand, some of the functional activities you confront may be entirely new or perhaps carried on more intensively than in your previous job. Below, a list is provided of some functional activities which, having transferable properties, are likely to be required to some degree in any new job.[17] Review the list carefully.

1. *Planning* — determining courses of action, establishing policies, procedures, and strategies
2. *Investigating* — collecting and preparing information usually in the form of records, reports, and accounts
3. *Coordinating* — exchanging information with people in the organization other than subordinates in order to relate and adjust programs
4. *Evaluating* — assessing and appraising proposals or performance
5. *Supervising* — leading and directing the work of subordinates
6. *Staffing* — engaging in activities that help maintain the workforce
7. *Negotiating* — contracting for goods and services, purchasing and selling
8. *Representing* — advancing the general interests of the organization through speeches, consultation, and contacts with individuals or groups outside the organization

Now consider these questions as you contemplate assignment to a lateral position, which you may have isolated in your career path grid (Figure 4-1).

1. In which of these activities do you spend a lot of time in your current job?
2. In a planned new job, in which of these activities do you wish to spend a lot of time?
3. In your current job and then in your planned new job, rate, using Table 6-7, each of these activities according to the following attributes: importance to you, satisfaction obtained, and your overall level of performance. Use the scale one to five, with five being the highest, one the lowest score. (On your planned new job, provide the expected ratings for these activities. You may obviously need to consult with colleagues or present job incumbents to complete these ratings.)
4. In the table above, are there significant differences (considered as 2 or more) between the scores of your current and planned new job? If so, think through your choice again. Might you be changing jobs too quickly? What are you giving up by the job change? Are activities formerly enjoyed, considered important, or done well going to be available in your new job?
5. Are you familiar with your potential new boss? What can be expected from his or her leadership?

TABLE 6-7   Transferable Activity Ratings

	Importance		*Satisfaction*		*Performance*	
	Current	*Expected*	*Current*	*Expected*	*Current*	*Expected*
Planning						
Investigating						
Coordinating						
Evaluating						
Supervising						
Staffing						
Negotiating						
Representing						

Source: Adapted from Andrew H. Souerwine, *Career Strategies*. New York: AMACOM, 1978, pp. 198-99.

6. What further options in terms of your career will be made available to you if you switch jobs? For instance, do you have an ultimate career goal that this lateral transfer will help you achieve? What new skill demands will be made if you switch and will you have the opportunity to learn them?

EXERCISE 6-5

TECHNICAL AREA ANALYSIS. A lateral transfer entails, by definition, the performance of different technical activities but at the same approximate level of responsibility within the organization. The list on Table 6-8 indicates some of the familiar operational or professional areas within an organization, each broken down by a number of suboperational areas.[18] Review the list briefly. Which area are you currently in? Which new operational and/or suboperational area are you planning to move into (try to be as specific as you can; perhaps the activity is not listed precisely)?

TABLE 6-8   Technical Area Chart

1. *Research and development*: basic research, applied research, development, production engineering – design, test, follow-up.
2. *Production*: plant engineering, industrial engineering, purchasing, production planning and control, manufacturing, inventory control, quality control
3. *Marketing*: marketing research, advertising, sales planning, sales promotion, sales operations, distribution
4. *Finance*: financial planning and relations, tax management, custody of funds, credit and collections, insurance
5. *Control*: general accounting, cost accounting, budget planning and control, auditing, systems and procedures
6. *Personnel administration*: recruitment and selection, training, wage and salary, benefits, industrial relations, organization planning and development, employee relations
7. *External relations*: public relations, creditor and investor communications, civic affairs, association and community relations
8. *Legal and corporate relations*: corporate legal matters, patents, employee legal questions, stockholder relations, board of directors' activities, corporation secretarial affairs

Source: Adapted from Andrew H. Souerwine, *Career Strategies*. New York: AMACOM, 1978, p. 199.

Now, using Exhibit 6-1, develop a list of 10 or more perceptions describing the nature of work in this new area — both formal and informal. Some attributes to consider as you develop your perceptions are provided in the exhibit. Conclude with a general statement of the opportunity afforded by this new area.

EXHIBIT 6-1   New Lateral Activity Perception List

Suboperational Area Identified:

Perceptions

1. Tasks expected —

2. Skills required —

3. Training provided —

4. Communication patterns —

5. Managing style —

6. Advancement potential —

7. Work climate —

8. Colleagues —

9. Reputation —

10. Other distinguishing characteristics —

General statement of opportunity:

Downward Option

Perhaps the most misunderstood of all the options is the downward option. This is because we are in a promotion-oriented society where *up* is considered to be a success, and *down* a failure. Nevertheless, under certain circumstances, moving downward in your company or agency can be an entirely appropriate career strategy.

Before reviewing the personal advantages and disadvantages of such a strategy, let's consider the basis for the downward option by examining both its personal and organizational conditions. In other words, let's ask the question: why would an individual or an organization consider this step which seemingly goes against the grain of societal norms. If considering a downward transfer yourself, you may wish to identify which of the conditions applies to you.

Individual conditions
1.   Obsolescence has occurred in the person's level of skills or knowledge. This can occur not only due to technical deficiencies, but as a result of aging and accompanying loss of energy or motivation.
2.   One's psychological needs or expectations have shifted from the success ethic to the drive for self-fulfillment.
3.   One has become less career-oriented and more interested in some of the other components of one's life space, i.e., the family, the community, hobbies.
4.   Intrinsic factors such as challenge, responsibility, or achievement on the job have become less important; on the other hand, such extrinsic factors as colleagueship, pay, benefits, working conditions, have become predominant.
5.   Opportunities for reemployment elsewhere have become scarce. This might occur particularly in instances when the company virtually controls all comparable jobs in the area.
6.   It has become increasingly unacceptable due to family preferences, community condition, age, or personal habits to make a geographic move.

Organizational conditions
1.   The nature of the work has changed, causing the obsolescence of the existing skills of an individual.
2.   The seasonal or contractual nature of the work (as in a job shop environment) has caused wide fluctuations in the work load.
3.   A shrinking market faced by the organization, either due to wider economic constraints or more internal financial difficulties, has caused work load reductions.

4. A merger has produced an oversupply of technical talent in certain job classifications.
5. An organizational restructuring has been conducted which, toward the goal of increased managerial efficiency, has forced the combination or elimination of certain jobs.

Any of the above conditions, singly or in combination, can lead to downward moves. As is apparent from the above list, the downward option can either be self-initiated or forced upon the individual. It is preferable, however, that the individual retain some choice in the selection of the option, even if it is not the most propitious choice but one which is inevitable due to circumstances outside of the individual's control. Being able to choose the downward option in and of itself presents certain advantages to the individual. There are many other advantages, however, which are worth mentioning. Hedda,[19] in her research of demoted managers, reported the following advantages: less strain on health, reduction in physical and mental burdens, and more opportunity to deal with interests unrelated to the job. Other advantages flow from the earlier cited conditions. From the individual's point of view, a downward transfer might offer an individual facing obsolescence of his or her current skills an opportunity to retool and learn new skills with the intent of moving up later on. Even barring obsolescence, an individual may use the downward option strategically as a way to negotiate a career shift. The downward option may also allow the opportunity to move to or stay in a select geographical area, or to stay simply where one is as a gesture of consideration to a working spouse who may be at a critical point in his or her career development. Downward strategies also accommodate the extrinsic or extracurricular concerns of people. Finally, a downward transfer may simply be a superior option compared to termination.

From the company's point of view, the principal advantage of the downward option is that it reverses the Peter Principle, allowing more capable individuals the opportunity to engage in more responsible work thereby increasing overall corporate effectiveness. Hence, it generally creates greater intraorganizational mobility and flexibility.[20] The person who actually takes a demotion does not necessarily have to be a poor performer, in fact, this individual may be a very capable person who is willing to move downward temporarily in order to develop skills which the company might subsequently call upon. Further, capable individuals might also be strategically located at lower-level positions to work on so-called hot spots. Finally, the downward transfer of capable individuals might be not only a more humane option but a more economically sound human resource policy than termination with its associated separation costs. Particularly if the company is in a temporary period of retrenchment, retaining capable people makes more sense than having to rehire them or their replacements at a future point when the company may be on sounder footing.

Although there are advantages, then, to downward strategies, the effects of *uninitiated* downward transfers, especially given the prevailing norm in our society of demotion signifying failure, tend to be negative for both the individual and the organization. Some of these effects or disadvantages are cited in the ensuing discussion.

Perhaps the first effect experienced by some individuals facing an involuntary downward transfer is a sense of ambiguity. Organizations, well aware of the stigma of a demotion, don't wish to do anything to jeopardize the motivation of their work force. Consequently, they often conceal downward transfers using ambiguous tactics. We are all familiar with the common usage of "kicking a man upstairs." Especially under growth conditions, there are many jobs to which less capable individuals can be shunted off.

Most demotions, however, become quite obvious to the individual. For some, it is only a matter of time before they learn to accept the inevitable. For many individuals, the effect of an involuntary demotion can be devastating. Demotion can severely damage self-esteem, resulting in such behavioral manifestations as withdrawal, apathy, sullenness, and even hostility. Some individuals, perhaps also in anticipation of a demotion, might use deviant/adaptive mechanisms which are antithetical to the precise behaviors which got them into a responsible position to begin with.[21] For example, they might stop exerting themselves to succeed or begin refusing to take risks. Anticipatory reactions of this type are especially prevalent among professional scientists, according to Glaser.[22] Young scientists, in comparing themselves not only to their peers, teacher, and supervisors, but also to the "great men" in their field, unwittingly set themselves up to become failures.

It is apparent that the negative effects of downward transfers on individuals tend to be psychological in character, at least according to the rather extensive literature on the subject. However, this should not serve to overlook the more objective effects such as loss of income, loss of responsibility, loss of challenge, or even loss of a current group of colleagues.

Organizational effects stem from the aforementioned individual disadvantages. Demoted individuals under psychological strain tend to be less productive. They also tend to react negatively to authority while attempting to retain control over their most immediate work environment. They might even vent their frustration on other workers, instilling a "we against them" attitude in the organization. Or, unable to accept the demotion psychologically, they might look down upon their new colleagues, damaging teamwork in the process. The overall effect on the company can be a loss of efficiency, decreased creativity, disloyalty, an increase in turnover, increased chronic illnesses and absenteeism, and an increase in privilege abuse.[23]

EXERCISE 6-6

PERSONAL ADVANTAGES OF THE DOWNWARD OPTION. Given the foregoing discussion, there are obviously advantages as well as disadvantages from choosing the downward option. Since your choice of this option is expected to be self-initiated, however, the personal advantages should outweigh the disadvantages.

Accordingly, I would next like you to brainstorm the advantages accruing to you from selecting this option. First, letting your ideas flow, just jot down below all the advantages which come to mind. If you know of some colleagues, whom you can trust, who may also be considering a downward transfer, you may wish to brainstorm advantages together. Simply have one person be the recorder for the group.

Now, begin to brainstorm advantages in the following list:

Advantages List

1.
2.
3.
4.
5.
6.
7.
8.

Having brainstormed the above advantages, you are now ready – if you haven't already – to focus on a specific job which as a downward transfer might capture many of the advantages cited. You may wish to consult your career path grid, Figure 4-1 in Chapter Four, to target this job. As you consider this prospective transfer, please reflect on the challenge questions of Exercise 6-7.

EXERCISE 6-7

DOWNWARD OPTION CHALLENGE QUESTIONS.

1. Are you sincerely ready to give up your present job? Are there activities which you enjoy doing and do well which you will be able to continue in your new job?
2. Do you believe this new position will take advantage of your past experience and skills?
3. What do you anticipate will be the reaction of your new colleagues at this new position? How will you react to them?
4. What things do you expect to learn on your new job?
5. What's your new boss going to be like? Do you expect you'll get along with him or her?
6. Once accepting this new position, what effect if any will it have on your reputation? How do you expect the company will view you? How will you view the company?
7. Will this job be less demanding on your time? If so, what use will you make of this time?
8. Think through your choice one more time. Is the move downward the most viable option for your career (in all its aspects) right now?

Enrichment Option

The enrichment option signifies an interest in retaining one's current job but changing its content to incorporate, what I referred to in Chapter Two as, the higher psychological needs of recognition, challenge, and responsibility. As was pointed out in that chapter, professionals, in particular, seek higher-order need satisfaction in their work, and among the various motivators, challenge seems to be the most often cited. In order to consider a job redesign incorporating an enrichment strategy, however, it is essential to clearly differentiate enrichment, implying vertical redesign, from horizontal job redesign. Enriching a job is *not* synonymous with giving the job occupant more things to do. For example, if you're a systems analyst working on quality assurance and upon asking for an enrichment option are simply given some additional work in inventory control, your job has not been vertically redesigned. However, if you are given some responsibility in designing some new standards rather than analyzing existing standards, your job in this instance has been conceivably enriched.

Exercise 6-8, which I shall present shortly, will facilitate making the distinction between vertical and horizontal enlargement schemes. Beforehand, though, in order to fully appreciate some of the alternatives available in undertaking an enrichment option, I would like to discuss five facets of job enrichment.

1. Autonomy — signifies the degree to which the job provides freedom, independence, or discretion in scheduling and carrying out work assignments. It is also associated with being able to set one's own goals, priorities, and pace. Assignments may be open-ended and may have a results orientation as well.

2. Responsibility — implies personal ownership over the final outcome of the job. It tends to be associated with high standards, increased problem solving and decision making, and often, responsibility for the work of others.

3. Growth — A job which provides growth offers opportunities for new learning and experimentation. One might have an opportunity, for example, to interact with others who have different or greater levels of expertise. The job might even be associated with augmented training or educational opportunities.

4. Significance — A significant job is one which has a perceivable impact on others whether they be in the immediate organization or in the community at large.

5. Recognition — implies being given credit or even status or compensation for doing good work. However, its principal attribute is receiving information from the job itself regarding how effective the worker's efforts were. It provides an opportunity to feel important.

EXERCISE 6-8

STOCKHOLDER COMPLAINTS. Now that you've had a chance to study the facets of job enrichment, I present this exercise to test your understanding of the difference between vertical job enlargement (job enrichment) and horizontal job enlargement.

In this exercise, you are to take the part of a productivity consultant assigned to study corrective actions suggested by management in response to turnover and morale problems in the job of stockholder complaints clerk. The clerk's job essentially entails answering, by letter or phone, complaints from stockholders. Complaints are made for many reasons, ranging from alleged mismanagement of the organization to lost or missing dividend checks. The current situation is as follows:

Five groups of women are divided among natural supervisory lines, with a total of 104 young women answering stockholder complaint letters and another group of 16 women handling phone calls from stockholders. The organization needs highly literate and intelligent employees (approximately 70 percent were college graduates) since the problems raised and the information sought by the stockholders can be very complex. After the letters are written, they are typed by clerk-typists.

The turnover rate is high and employee morale is low. Although the job is seen by management as complex and challenging, requiring many weeks of training, exit interviews indicate that the challenge of the job is more in the eyes of management than the workers. The quality of the stockholder service index is relatively poor. This index contains such items as speed of response, accuracy of details, and correctness of the response to a stockholder's letter.

In studying this case as a consultant, you have a number of objectives:

1. Improve the stockholder service index
2. Maintain or improve productivity
3. Reduce the turnover rate
4. Reduce costs
5. Increase worker satisfaction on the job.

Management has recommended a number of corrective actions that might result in improving the work performance of the clerks. Read through the list shown in Table 6-9 and decide whether or not the proposed corrective action involves either a vertical or horizontal redesign. Place a check indicating your choice next to each corrective action.

TABLE 6-9   Management's List of Corrective Actions

Corrective Action	Vertical	Horizontal
1. Set firm quotas of letters to be answered each day.		
2. Allow correspondents to sign their own names to letters from the first day on the job after training.		
3. Rotate the workers through the telephone unit, to units handling different customers and then back again to their own units.		
4. Develop better measures for verifying and catching errors.		
5. Let the correspondents type the letters themselves as well as compose them and take on such other clerical functions as reviewing the files or obtaining detailed information.		
6. Develop a better set of form letters, based on analysis of types of complaints.		
7. Have the work of the more experienced correspondents reviewed less frequently, at the desk of the correspondent.		
8. Encourage the verifiers and supervisors to be more alert in catching errors.		
9. Encourage correspondents to answer letters in a more personalized way, avoiding the form letter approach.		
10. Increase the number of supervisors and/or verifiers.		
11. Tell the correspondents they will be fully accountable for the quality of their work.		
12. Call the group together and impress upon them the necessity for increased production and reduced errors.		
13. Encourage the correspondents to check with the supervisor regarding questions.		
14. Encourage the correspondents to discuss questions with each other before involving the supervisor.		

Source: Adapted from Frederick Herzberg, "One More Time: How Do You Motivate Employees?" *Harvard Business Review* 46:53-62, 1968 and Robert N. Ford, *Motivation through the Work Itself*. New York: American Management Association, 1969.

To check your answers, refer to the key below:

Stockholder Complaints
Key to Correct Answers:

Λ	'ÞI	Λ	'L
H	'ƐI	H	'9
H	'ZI	H	'S
Λ	'II	Λ	'Þ
H	'OI	H	'Ɛ
Λ	'6	Λ	'Z
H	'8	H	'I

The choice of the enrichment option may well have been afforded through your balance-imbalance analysis or perhaps by an intuitive sense regarding the vertical potential of your present job. As another check regarding the enrichment option, review the results of your Needs Identification Questionnaire, Exercise 2-6 in Chapter Two. If your scores on the three categories of esteem, autonomy, and self-realization are high (above the national mean), that would indicate that these needs are quite important to you. If your job, however, is not fulfilling these needs, then perhaps this is a signal that a redesign of your job along the lines of enrichment would be personally fulfilling.

Before considering enriching your job, however, you are advised to use some caution. Even if a job can be technically enriched, there are many barriers to enrichment which you need to review before proceeding. Consider the following:

Personal Resistance

Even though enrichment may appear attractive at the outset, you need to really examine yourself and your work needs carefully to be sure that you really want more responsibility, etc., on your job. Katz,[24] for example, argues that job incumbents during the entry or acclimation stages of their organizational careers are typically more interested in enrichment to the extent of becoming a helpful and needed part of the overall operation, while as veterans they typically are more concerned with establishing and demonstrating competence. He further argues that job enrichment results tend to be rather short-lived. The implications of this latter point might be that you should be prepared to consider another option after a year or so of enrichment.

Management Resistance

Management has been a stumbling block to job enrichment efforts on a number of accounts.[25] First, managers may be uninformed or simply unskilled in the process of enrichment and may resist "enlightenment," especially if it comes from a subordinate. Related to this point is a general resistance to change among some managers. Further, if things go wrong, they may not wish to take the blame, but if things go right, they may not wish to have it implied that their past behavior was incorrect. Management may also resist job enrichment out of the basic belief that job fragmentation and rigid control over workers is necessary to achieve unit productivity standards. Until they can be shown that enrichment designs produce results, managers may see such an option as catering to the employee. Perhaps the greatest resistance by managers arises out of a fear that enrichment will require a loss of control, as job responsibilities formerly held by them will be placed in the hands of professional workers. Rather than see enrichment as an opportunity for them to get into *true* management, they fear that they'll wind up with little to do. Finally, managers tend to react against the anticipated time such an experiment may require.

Organizational Resistance

As organizations are made up of different work groups, any enrichment strategy adopted by one group which affects a second group will obviously have to be accepted by that second group. Similarly, as a personnel-related activity, job enrichment has to dovetail with other organizational support systems such as wage and salary administration. It might also have to be negotiated with a union if one is present. In the past, unions have typically resisted enrichment unless they can be guaranteed that it won't cause an overall reduction in jobs in their bargaining unit. Enrichment may also require technological changes and its accompanying expenses.

Finally, the enrichment option as a long-term strategy has been shown to produce results only after an initial period of worker and management reorientation. Many organizations unfortunately cannot afford the luxury of such long-term ventures.

Having considered these barriers but acknowledging the potential for a personal job enrichment strategy, you are invited to consider the eight job enrichment challenge questions in Exercise 6-9.

EXERCISE 6-9

JOB ENRICHMENT CHALLENGE QUESTIONS.

1. In light of all the information available to you on job enrichment, carefully write below how you specifically plan to enrich your current job.

2. Given the resistance you are likely to face in undertaking such a plan, state the specific barriers which you are likely to confront in your organization and how in each case you will plan to counteract these barriers.

3. Now consider the following additional questions:
   a. Is your superior likely to go along with your enrichment strategy? How can he or she be brought into the redesign process?

   b. Will enrichment of your job result in threatening the incumbent of the next most higher-up job? If so, what strategies can you use to reduce the threat?

   c. Are you really interested in more job responsibility, or is this a guise for more "extrinsic" aspects like better salary, work conditions, benefits, status, security, etc.?

   d. Is enrichment an option consistent with your company's organizational style?

e. Have you identified real responsibilities in your job enrichment plan?

f. How do you plan to measure the results of this change?

Adjustment Option

The choice of the adjustment option is guided by a personal philosophy which resists the risks entailed in a job change as well as the increased responsibilities resulting from a job enrichment strategy. Many individuals, due to a concern for other elements in their life space beyond work itself, have little interest in taking on the burdens of a job or career change. The vertical and the lateral option, for example, require additional time and energy to learn the new job indicated in one's evolving career path. Job enrichment by definition requires additional responsibility, even though one presumably remains in the same job.

In Chapter One, I talked at length about the dissonance experienced by professionals when having to conform to the goals and expectations of management. Deviant/adaptive behavior was cited as one type of response to the dissonance. Three other response patterns are to: (1) change your interpretation of your job, (2) change yourself, or (3) leave your organization.

According to Bailyn,[26] those who adjust (that is, those who do not engage in deviant/adaptive behavior) tend to be tolerant individuals who are concerned about the problems of society. She further characterizes the nonadjusters as being scientifically oriented, whereas the adjusters are humanistically oriented. In addition, adjustment was found to have significant advantages for family members, particularly spouses.

On the basis of the foregoing discussion, I view the adjustment option in two ways. First, adjustment can be achieved by a job change that results in greater overall job satisfaction. This type of change is just as likely to be extrinsic or contextual in nature in contrast to an enrichment change which, by definition, would be intrinsic or content-specific. Second, adjustment can be achieved by an increase in overall life satisfaction, in particular, by emphasizing other activities in the life space beyond the job itself. This entails taking the job for what it is and using extra time to pursue these other non-work-related activities.

I begin, then, with two exercises which address the first strategy of increasing overall job satisfaction. I shall address the life satisfaction strategy subsequently.

EXERCISE 6-10

JOB DIMENSION ANALYSIS. Edward Roseman[27] talks about three dimensions of the job which are critical to satisfaction. These dimensions are (1) like/dislike, (2) do well/don't do well, and (3) important/unimportant. The dimensions may be extrinsic or intrinsic depending upon the incumbent's interpretation. Eight combinations are mathematically possible, but only the combination *like, do well, important* is truly conducive to satisfaction.

Accordingly, please begin the exercise by reviewing your job description. (You will need to consult your Exercise 4-3.) In particular, write down all the separate tasks or procedures which you do (whether required or voluntary) on your job.

Your Job Tasks

Now consider the eight combinations of Roseman's job dimensions:

1. like, do well, important
2. like, don't do well, important
3. like, do well, unimportant
4. like, don't do well, unimportant
5. dislike, do well, important
6. dislike, don't do well, important
7. dislike, do well, unimportant
8. dislike, don't do well, unimportant.

As you review your job tasks, place the number after each one corresponding to one of these combinations. For instance, if you are responsible for arranging the department's typing assignments, and it's a task you dislike, but do well and consider important, you would place the number five after that task.

In general, the numbers five through eight placed after any task will indicate particular problem areas needing remediation of some kind. This is because these represent tasks which you dislike, a condition which is most intolerable of all. A task which you don't do well can be damaging to your credibility let alone organizational effectiveness. However, it is possible that you could improve your performance through some form of developmental activity, such as skills training. An unimportant task if required can be frustrating to carry out. Hopefully your organization or unit will be sufficiently flexible to at least hear your arguments regarding the task's insignificance.

Now, look at your completed list with numbered tasks. Consider all tasks with numbers other than one next to them. Record for each of these tasks one or more changes which might make this task less offensive. At this point, don't be concerned whether the change is practical or not. For instance, elaborating upon the example cited above, if one of your tasks is organizing the inflow of assignments from department members to the department secretary and you have given it a five, you might decide to work out a queuing procedure with department members and the secretary. This may have the effect of reducing the time you have been spending on this important but unpleasant task while at the same time enriching the secretary's job.

Next, review each task with its strategy for change. Is (are) the recommended change(s) feasible within the climate of your organizational unit? What other barriers are there against implementing your strategy? How can these be overcome? Discuss your strategies with a colleague whom you trust, who may or may not be performing the same job. If he or she agrees with your strategies, consider implementing your strategies for change one at a time. Establish a milestone for implementing all of the strategies. Be realistic. You don't want to move too fast, yet you must not delay. The result of your efforts should be greater job satisfaction.

EXERCISE 6-11

EXTRINSIC JOB OPTIONS. Another method to use to increase your job satisfaction is to review the extrinsic properties of your job and to create options from these contextual factors. In Table 6-10, a number of extrinsic properties are shown on the left side of the page. Next to each is a typical job-related option that might evolve from this extrinsic property. Below the option are spaces for you to write in suggestions which are specific to your situation and which, in a similar vein as the example option, respond to the extrinsic need indicated.

Besides, or in addition to, adjusting the job or perceptions of the job, adjustment can also include making changes in other aspects of one's life space. In particular, I refer to changes which may enrich family life, attention to self, and community and outside activities.

TABLE 6-10   Extrinsic Properties and Options for Change

Extrinsic Property	Options for Change
Monetary rewards	Attempt to get an increase in salary or benefits (write in your own options)
Security	Conduct a study of how others in the organization have gotten tenure
Peer relationships	Join a team project or task force
Job extension	Put in some extra effort on a promising proposal
Personal status	Share my technical knowledge and expertise by becoming a mentor
Working conditions	Rearrange my office
Learning	Participate in an interesting training course
Supervision	Get to know my boss more and how I can help him solve his work-related problems
Policy	Organize an effort to change a particularly troublesome organizational procedure
Personal attitude	Consider different ways of viewing my work
Sense of belonging	Join an after-work social group with some of my colleagues

These changes can be effected either in conjunction with or totally separate from work-related changes. In fact, one might decide simply to let the job stand for what it is (an income-producing vehicle, for example) and concentrate additional time and energy on leisure activities. In most cases, however, I expect that increasing life satisfaction will have salutary effects on job satisfaction and, in turn, job performance.

Below I have listed some sample activities in each of the nonwork life space areas which you could consider adopting. You will naturally be invited to add your own ideas to this list.

1. Family Activities
    a. Travel — plan a trip with your family members and follow through on their suggestions.
    b. Family meetings — organize and hold family meetings on a periodic basis to air gripes and search for solutions.
    c. Serious talk — set up a time to engage in serious talk with your spouse or some other close family member in order to share life issues and address ways of coping with those issues.
    d. Individual attention — plan special events to engage in with separate family members in order to get to know them more and to let them get to know you more as a person.
2. Self-Related Activities
    a. Self-learning — join a personal growth group or engage in psychotherapy as a means to discover more about yourself, such as your interpersonal abilities and perceptions, the roots of your behavior, or your true ambitions and needs.
    b. Relaxation — anticipate those situations in your life which produce stress and learn how your body reacts to this stress. Then, perhaps through reading or through relaxation training, learn how to select an appropriate muscle relaxation technique.
    c. Physical conditioning — on the advice of your personal physician, begin a program of steady exercise and conditioning, whether it be through athletic competition or running, walking, and/or dieting.
    d. Modeling — carefully select and observe a model who has achieved the goals you want and adapt your behavior accordingly.
3. Community Activities
    a. Political campaigning — become an active supporter and participant in a political campaign.

b. Civic organization — join a local civic organization and consider becoming an officer or at least an active participant in that organization.
c. Volunteer work — extend your time and expertise to the work of your favorite service or charitable organization.
d. Religion — actively pursue your faith through adherence to the teachings of your religion, through study or spiritual contemplation, and/or through efforts undertaken on behalf of your church or temple.

4. Outside Activities
a. Friendships — spend more time in either increasing the number of friendships available to you or by increasing the depth of the friendships you currently have.
b. Educational programs — augment your current skills in either a work-related or non-work-related area by taking courses in a continuing education program offered by your local school system, a self-help organization, or a nearby university.
c. Hobbies and avocations — develop your skills and abilities in newly formed or existing hobbies.
d. Sports — join an organized athletic team or simply find a steady partner or partners to play you in a regular sports activity.

As you review the list above, jot down your own ideas for expanding your involvement in non-work-related activities. Indicate the specific interests within each activity which appeal to you. You may wish to conduct this search with a partner (spouse, friend, adviser, etc.).

Exploratory Option

In selecting the exploratory option, the assumption is that time is still needed to find the most propitious career option. Therefore, the only path to take is to search for the right alternative. This may be a painful process because it encompasses no definitive solution, but it is essential in order to follow the path of choice as opposed to the path of chance.

Of course, the preceding chapters of this book have been designed to help in this search. Further, the preceding options each represent ways to approach a career decision. Hence, an initial preparatory activity in the exploratory option is to simply read the material on the five preceding options.

Dick Bolles[28] discusses six elements of the career search that should be included as agenda items in your personal exploration. These elements entail focusing on:

1. the values, purposes, or goals that you want your skills to serve
2. the subject matter you want your skills to work on
3. the people-environments that you do your best work in
4. the level of responsibility you desire in working with people
5. the working conditions that facilitate your best work
6. your preferred geographical location

On the basis of these six elements, a number of questions may be posed for you to consider carefully. An action step follows the questions.

EXERCISE 6-12
EXPLORATORY QUESTIONS AND ACTION.

1. Identify those elements of a career which are critical to you. (You may find it helpful to simply review the Table of Contents of this book as you contemplate your answer to this question.)

2. Can these elements be reasonably attained?

3. Do you have any long-range career goals? How committed are you to them?

4. How willing are you to sacrifice off-job activities to accomplish on-job tasks and career goals?

5. Can you foresee circumstances which might require you to change your career goals?

6. What are your key skills and how can they be successfully deployed in your organization?

7. What kind of job performance will earn you your career desires?

8. How will improved performance or skills increase your probability of success?

9. What personal deficiencies may hinder your achieving your career desires?

10. Might your personal values conflict with your job role or career expectations?

11. What kind of work setting is best for you; for example, do you work better alone or with others?

12. How much contact do you desire with work associates?

13. Do you desire to lead, to follow, or simply be a member of your work group?

14. How many hours a week are you willing to devote to your job?

15. Are you willing to work extra hours?

16. What salary and benefits are critical to your needs both on the job in terms of prestige and at home in terms of security?

17. How mobile are you? Are you willing to put where you live ahead of your career?

18. How does your family or other nonwork commitments affect your career plans?

After working through these questions, refer back to your career path grid of Chapter Four (Figure 4-1) and identify one, two, or three specific jobs which you might want to consider to further your career goals. You might well include your current job. If you do choose your present job, you might be doing so because you want to enrich or adjust it. If you are thinking of other jobs, then they might constitute vertical, lateral, or downward moves. In as many steps as it takes, specify exactly how you plan to accomplish the option which you have now chosen. This will entail working through the preceding material detailing the procedures for successfully implementing the respective option.

Removal Option

The removal option is expressly left at the end of the option list since it is the option of last resort. I should first clearly distinguish removal from retirement. In retirement, one presumably leaves an organization because the age has been reached where one is no longer either interested in working or capable of continuing to work productively. Removal, in contrast, in its barest form implies leaving to seek work elsewhere. Of course, one might also leave to pursue another kind of activity, such as education, but such an activity will normally end up in employment in one form or another. In choosing the removal option, one should be able to declare implicitly that all of the other options have been reviewed and resultingly have been considered infeasible. Otherwise, the choice of removal may be premature with but one other exception. That is when some kind of environmental condition has placed one's organization in jeopardy so that there is sufficient reason to fear being able to hold onto one's job. It is also premature to consider removal when there is reason to suspect that one will be laid off due to personal as opposed to organizational or environmental factors. This is because as a career option, removal cannot in most cases make up for deficiency in skills or for poor performance, it cannot necessarily smooth interpersonal difficulties, nor can it automatically solve personal problems. These issues should be first dealt with on the current job. Again, removal is the option of last resort.

The removal option may not only entail a change in organizations but a change of career as well. The risks entailed are clearly greater when one changes both organization and career. Nevertheless, people in the United States are quite prone to change both job and occupation; as a matter of fact, nearly one third of the entire work force did so at the last count.[29] Naturally, a new career is not typically started without some prior preparation. Some individuals, for example through moonlighting, may begin a second career while still pursuing their first.

What is it, then, that really induces people to leave their organization, probably at great risks to themselves? Williams[30] indicates that most people in fact prefer to stay with their present organization for some very good reasons. For one, they like the routine. People will resist change unless it is practically forced upon them. Normally, removal will entail a geographical change which has enormous effects on family and friends. There are also practical institutional reasons for staying. Although laws have recently required some fringe benefits, such as pensions, to be portable from one organization to another, some benefits are still very much tied to seniority with the original organization – for instance, vacations, bonuses, and profit sharing. Although these latter fringes may be negotiated at a new placement, former benefits are by no means guaranteed. The reasons that people give for leaving their organization, acknowledging the personal costs involved, vary an incredible amount. Generally, the search for a better job and for more pay reign at the top of the list. However, these reasons are not that cogent for professionals, who – as we have seen – would *not* tend to cite pay as one of their initial reasons for leaving. Although higher salary may be the second or third choice, the first reason for leaving given by professionals tends to be some kind of characteristic relative to the job itself or to the career. Gerstenfeld and Rosica[31] report the main reasons as being: change in career direction, more interesting work, and opportunity for advancement. Miller and Labovitz[32] find that professional turnover is very much based upon social conditions, in other words, one leaves if one's friends or colleagues do. Wilensky,[33] taking a more practical approach, bases removal on one's sense of security or market position which is in turn dependent upon alternative employment opportunities, skill replaceability, and connections inside or outside the organization.

In line with Wilensky's findings, it is apparent that turnover is greater among the more talented employees than among those for whom performance is declining. Turnover also tends to be lower among longer-service employees, among those whose careers have plateaued, or those who have few remaining career options.[34] This suggests that if removal is called for, it should be done while at the peak rather than at the bottom of the career. If one waits too long, it may no longer be a viable option. It is unlikely that a professional bordering on obsolescence, for example, would be attractive to another organization. Removal, then, can be an effective option for taking advantage of one's skills and competencies. It can stimulate individuals to seek new opportunities, to expand their horizons, and to grow. It can also provide an organizational climate more conducive to personal values than the current organizational setting.

Yet, the pitfalls of removal also must be considered. It is never a sure thing. In fact, it entails in most cases a need to start over again. This would include the development of a psychological contract with the new organization. Further, the climate in a new organization can never be fully deciphered through the interviewing process. Therefore, one would need to learn all of the cultural idiosyncrasies of the new organization, including its political processes, that perhaps were taken for granted in the old organization. Finally, a fall-back position cannot always be assured if things don't work out. The original organization may not be willing to take the worker back. One could always move again, but at the risk of being labeled a "job-hopper." In sum, the choice of removal has to be very carefully considered for it is less reversible than any of the other options.

EXERCISE 6-13

REMOVAL CHALLENGE QUESTIONS. On the basis of the foregoing discussion, I present a set of questions which you are asked to carefully work through before completing your plan for change.

1. Please list below all the dissatisfiers on your current job, i.e., the factors which have contributed to your dissatisfaction.

a. Now add to this list other factors which would not be considered dissatisfiers, but which nevertheless induce you to consider the removal option (i.e., company filing for bankruptcy, family move, loss of favor with the president).

b. Prioritize your list in order of the importance you would attach to each factor as a contribution to your potential removal from the organization.

c. Place a C in front of any factor which you would consider to be at least somewhat controllable (i.e., efforts by you or others that could mitigate that factor's impact).

d. Are any of the C's in front of some of your highest priority items? If so, please reconsider your choice of the removal option.

Will your prospective new job really respond to some of your unmet needs?

Are you potentially giving up work activities you enjoy or do well on your current job?

Will your new job take advantage of your past experience and skills? Will it provide a healthy learning environment?

Are you changing jobs too quickly? Have you really given your current job a chance?

2. What goals do you hope to accomplish in changing organizations and/or careers? What is the likelihood that you will achieve your goals?

3. What personal characteristics will help you in achieving your goals? hinder you?

4. What information do you have available on the new organization you might be entering? What do you know about your prospective new job? Do you have enough information to make a decision? Do you believe your information to be accurate?

5. Which influences have promoted your consideration of removal as a viable option? Who have you consulted about your move? Has their advice been objective or subjective?

6. Will removal facilitate the accomplishment of your ultimate life and career objectives? Is it a stepping stone? What is the likelihood that successful performance on your new job will lead to the next step?

7. Who will you be affecting in your potential move? Will they be better or worse off?

8. Who can you count on to support you in the implementation of this option?

Objective Setting

The presentation of the foregoing options was included as part of the option-setting task of the planning step in the plan for change model. Previously, I had briefly discussed the reflecting step. You are now ready to complete the plan for change. As noted, there is a second task in the planning step which should immediately follow the selection of an option for change. This task, referred to as *objective-setting*, commits the choice of an option to writing in the form of measurable, behavioral objectives. In preparing a behavioral objective, one focuses on the specific behaviors needed to accomplish the objective. Another attribute of a behavioral objective is that it becomes essentially a statement of intended outcome. Hence, it commits the individual to action and, as we shall see, encompasses the means by which to measure the results of the action. It is therefore a required planning vehicle which is anticipatory to the doing and evaluating steps.

EXERCISE 6-14

WRITING BEHAVIORAL OBJECTIVES. Although there is room for creativity in writing behavioral objectives, there are certain elements that must be included in any behavioral objective. These elements can be checked for their presence according to a handy memory aid, which is depicted below in Table 6-11.

TABLE 6-11   Behavioral Objective Memory Aid

WHO
WILL DO WHAT
WHEN
UNDER WHAT CONDITIONS
TO WHAT EXTENT   and
HOW WILL IT BE MEASURED

Using the memory aid, one can prepare an effective behavioral objective. Once the objective is written, you only need to insure that each of the six questions of the memory aid can be successfully answered. The six questions are discussed more in depth as follows:

1. Who — includes the person or actor — usually yourself — who is setting the objective and who will be performing the action specified in the objective.
2. Will Do What — specifies a behavior or set of behaviors which the actor will perform and which can be verified.
3. When — indicates the time frame for accomplishing the action.
4. Under What Conditions — states the means through which one will be able to accomplish the action. The conditions tend to incorporate development steps one will take preparatory to the action.
5. To What Extent — specifies the level of performance desired.
6. How Will It Be Measured — designates the criteria to be used to know whether the action was indeed attained at the desired level.

The behavioral objective can be developed from a short goal statement of what one wishes to accomplish. For example, let's assume after choosing the adjustment option, you make the following statement:

I'd like to reduce the boring parts of my job.

Although this goal statement is perfectly clear, it is not behavioral in the sense that there is no indication how one plans to accomplish the goal nor how one will know if in fact it was accomplished. It also does not satisfy the memory aid test on other criteria. Can you detect them?

Turning the goal statement into a behavioral objective using the memory aid becomes quite simple. For example, one might derive the following:

After a careful job inventory leading to a precise accounting of my job functions on the work-balance sheet, in six months I will have cut the "bugs" from my job ultimately by 50 percent of their time duration by developing personal efficiencies in my schedule.

A check against this objective can then be made as follows:

Who — I
Will Do What — cut the bugs from my job
When — in six months
Under What Conditions — after a careful job inventory . . . by developing personal efficiencies
To What Extent — by 50 percent
How Will It Be Measured — reduction in hours spent on bug activities each month, leading to a 50 percent reduction by the end of the sixth month

INSTRUCTIONS:
Prepare a set of goal statements which indicate how you plan to proceed with your career on the basis of the option which you selected. Your goals should flow naturally from your study and work on the selected option, including any exercises completed. Once you have written these goal statements, convert each one into a behavioral objective. Be sure to use the memory aid to check that your objectives have been accurately prepared. With the behavioral objectives in place, you will now be ready to carry out your plan for change.

DOING

The most obvious task in the plan for change is the doing or implementing stage. Its existence is practically tautological since one would hardly go through an extensive planning episode and then shun the effort to carry out one's plans. Yet, there is some evidence that even successful individuals dismiss this vital step by letting the environment take its course.[35]

I believe that implementing the plan for change is the most critical step in the entire process and one in which there should be absolutely no delay. It should be initiated after the behavioral objectives of the plan for change have been formulated. The objectives in fact establish a time period or milestones in which to accomplish the plan. Therefore, in order to attain one's objectives, the sooner one begins, the greater the likelihood of successful performance. Finally, most planning models, similar to this one, focus on success in accomplishing one's goals as a key motivator. Being able to accomplish goals has been linked to the enhancement of self-esteem as well as to greater career involvement.[36] Hence, in order to stimulate the whole career planning process, plans need to be acted on at the earliest possible time and all available resources need to be utilized to see that the goals specified in the original plan get carried out. As I indicated in the planning step, it is permitted and, in fact, encouraged that the plan be continually adjusted to respond to emerging circumstances. The doing step may even be the cause of such adjustments. It is not always possible to foresee personal reactions to an option, for example, without actually experiencing that option. It is through implementation, then, that the plan for change is put into operation, that the plan becomes truly fitted to the individual's needs, and that success in career planning can be achieved.

Implementation of a plan accordingly is a personal process. Nevertheless, it cannot be done without the involvement and even support of significant other people in one's life space. As you shall see in the final step, evaluating, people who are chosen to observe or even participate in the plan for change can also function as sources of useful feedback on one's progress. At implementation, these individuals serve three other initial purposes: (1) they become supporters not only of the individual per se but also of the personal plan for change, (2) they become problem solvers of the plan particularly if the plan involves them in some way, and (3) they provide short-term checks on how the plan is going.

EXERCISE 6-15

SUPPORT SYSTEM. In this short exercise, you are asked to develop a list of people who can become part of your support system during the implementation of your plan for change. Consider these sources:

Your manager —

Your former manager —

Your manager's manager —

An operational manager in
your area of interest —

Other managers you know who
may be acquainted with your
career interests or who may
know someone they can introduce you to —

Your family —

Your trusted friends —

Your professional colleagues —

Your subordinates —

An incumbent or former incumbent
of an identified job or career path —

Personnel people in your own or
other organizations —

Library research staff —

You are now ready to implement your plan for change. To assist you, a Personal Career Development strategy form is provided in Exhibit 6-2. This form constitutes your document of progress in developing your personal career development strategy. In this form, you essentially summarize the results obtained from all prior steps.

EXHIBIT 6-2   My Personal Career Development Strategy

INSTRUCTIONS:

Complete this form now but be sure to update it periodically to ensure that it remains a usable document of progress of your personal career development strategy. The form should also be used as an instrument for evaluating your plan within the time periods specified in your objectives.

Date Completed: _____

Date Revised: _____

Date Evaluated: _____

1. My goals for change related to the career option(s) I have chosen are:

2. My specific objectives related to each goal, including milestones are (use additional sheets if necessary):

Goal No. 1

Objective a:

Objective b:

Exhibit 6-2, continued

Objective c:

Goal No. 2

Objective a:

Objective b:

Objective c:

Goal No. 3

Objective a:

Objective b:

Objective c:

3. My support system includes:

4. I will know if I have succeeded in my personal career development strategy if:

5. Others will know if I have succeeded in my personal career development strategy by:

6. My current attitude towards my plan right now is:

EVALUATING

The evaluating step is the easiest to discuss since if the planning and doing steps were successfully completed, they furnish practically all the information needed to complete a full evaluation of the plan for change. The most critical of all the tasks leading up to the evaluation is the objective-writing task since the behavioral objective has contained within it not only the criteria of evaluation but also the time period specified in which to actually conduct the evaluation.

I shall discuss three related tasks in evaluating your personal career development strategy: assessment, feedback, re-assessment.

Assessment

The assessment task constitutes a review of your personal career development strategy based upon your original or revised set of objectives. The essence of the assessment process is a comparison between a planned objective and your actual performance. The value to be placed on performance will vary depending upon the degree of accomplishment and the unforeseen conditions which affect objective accomplishment. You might find, for example, that you did not meet your objectives. This does not necessarily imply failure. For one, it is conceivable that you set your sights too high, that the level of performance actually achieved, though lower than the expected performance, was nevertheless quite satisfactory. If this is the case, you should adjust the criteria to be applied to the ensuing objectives that are similar in nature. It is also possible that conditions, such as family or organizational constraints, interfered with the achievement of particular objectives. As underperforming does not necessarily imply failure, overperforming does not automatically imply success. Here, the criteria may have been set too low. Chance events may have facilitated the quick achievement of certain objectives. The point of this is to suggest that the assessment process is relative to the standards that have been set. Consequently, you must continually adjust your objectives to reflect the true conditions that are operating. Only by evaluating the objectives at the specified milestones can this adjustment be effectively made.

Consider these points as you conduct your personal assessment:

1. Did you underperform or overperform against your objectives?
2. What conditions may have caused you to underperform or to overperform?
3. Are you satisfied with your accomplishment? Why or why not?
4. Do you think the criteria and time period specified in your objectives were realistic?
5. What adjustments will you make in preparing your next set of objectives?

Feedback

Feedback entails an assessment of your personal career development strategy as reflected by the significant people whom you selected as part of your support system. It is initiated when you solicit the opinion of these other individuals regarding your progress. To begin with, you need to accurately communicate your accomplishments as well as your failures in meeting your objectives. It is likely in many instances that the individual providing the feedback will have observed you while pursuing your career option and may even have offered some unsolicited advice during the process.

Before initiating a feedback session, it is important to establish some ground rules to insure that the feedback is constructive. First, the feedback should be objective. This can only occur when there is a sufficiently trusting relationship established with the observer that the latter can report what has been observed without making a value judgment on you and without making generalizations about your motives or personality traits. This can only be accomplished if there are no hidden agendas regarding the observer's relationship with you. The sole purpose of soliciting the feedback is to generate useful, observable information which can be used to improve your performance of your career development strategy. Therefore, the observer cannot use this time to discuss his or her own problems.

The feedback session is consequently a private affair and one which requires an unusual degree of openness and nondefensiveness. If there is mutual respect between the parties, then a discussion of failures should be entertained as openly as a discussion of successes. Yet, the relationship should also be respectful to the extent that the observer understand the principle of changeability. There is little point in focusing on issues over which you have little control, or simply cannot change.

The feedback process can be a very critical element in the evaluating step since it constitutes a source from which information on one's progress can be truly derived. Accordingly, it is useful to solicit feedback from more than one person. Finally, although the discussion here presents feedback in its formal sense, I acknowledge the usefulness of obtaining informal, unsolicited feedback from your closest associates and family members as a normal life process.

Reassessment

We now come to the end but, at the same time, to the beginning of the plan for change, for in reassessment, you renew your personal career development strategy on the basis of the performance on your initial plan. The information obtained during assessment and feedback is now used to recycle the plan for change.

In reassessment, we remember that the career is not an end point of the work-related components of our life but a process that sequences these components. In undertaking a plan for change, we have made a statement that we wish to be actively involved in this process rather than simply letting it happen.

The accomplishment or near-accomplishment of your initial plans does not suggest that your career planning is over. Rather, it acknowledges achievement of a temporary milestone in a larger, ever-evolving plan of action. The second and ensuing plans should be easier to formulate since the completion of the initial plan serves as a base of information in which to develop your subsequent strategies. My hope is that the process will become natural enough to continue throughout the course of your entire professional life.

Notes

CHAPTER ONE

1. Seymour B. Sarason, *Work, Aging and Social Change* (New York: Free Press, 1977).

2. Ibid., p. xi.

3. Steven Kerr, Mary Ann Von Glinow, and Janet Schriesheim. "Issues in the Study of Professionals in Organizations: The Case of Scientists and Engineers," *Organizational Behavior and Human Performance* 18:329-45, 1977.

4. G. Ritzer, *Man and His Work: Conflict and Change* (New York: Meredith Corporation, 1972) p. 53.

5. Richard H. Hall, "Professionalization and Bureaucratization," *American Sociological Review* 33:92-104, 1968.

6. Kerr, Von Glinow, and Schriesheim, "Issues in Study," pp. 332-39.

7. Bernard Barber, "Some Problems in the Sociology of the Professions," *Daedalus* 92:669-88, 1963.

8. William Kornhauser, *Scientists in Industry* (Berkeley: University of California Press, 1962), pp. 5-6.

9. Ralph L. Blankenship, "Professions, Colleagues and Organizations," in *Colleagues in Organization*, ed. Ralph L. Blankenship (New York: John Wiley and Sons, 1977), pp. 1-50.

10. Everett C. Hughes, "Professions," in *The Professions in America*, ed. Kenneth S. Lynn (Boston: Houghton-Mifflin, 1963), pp. 1-14.

11. Blankenship, "Professions," p. 21.

12. Harold L. Wilensky, "The Professionalization of Everyone?" *The American Journal of Sociology* 70:137-58, 1964.

13. Kornhauser, *Scientists*, pp. 197-203.

14. Joseph A. Raelin and Betty B. Sokol, "Rethinking the Relationship Between Regulation and R&D Lag," *Business Forum* 7:11-13, 1982.

15. See, for example, Renato Taguiri, "Value Orientations, and the Relationship of Managers and Scientists," *Administrative Science Quarterly* 10:39-51, 1965.

16. Barber, "Some Problems," p. 681, and Kornhauser, *Scientists*, p. 201.

17. Kornhauser, *Scientists*, p. 45.

18. Theodore Caplow and Reece McGee, *The Academic Marketplace* (New York: Basic Books, 1958), p. 82.

19. Leon Festinger, *A Theory of Cognitive Dissonance* (Evanston, IL: Row, Peterson, 1957).

20. J. Richard Hackman and Greg R. Oldham, "Development of the Job Diagnostic Survey," *Journal of Applied Psychology* 60:159-70, 1975.

21. Wilensky, "Professionalization of Everyone?" pp. 137-58.

22. Gerald R. Salancik, "Commitment and Control of Organizational Behavior and Belief," in *New Directions in Organizational Behavior*, eds. B. M. Staw and G. R. Salancik (Chicago: St. Clair Press, 1977).

23. Sarason, *Work, Aging and Change*, pp. 2-8.

24. Joseph A. Raelin, "An Examination of Deviant/Adaptive Behavior in the Organizational Careers of Professionals," Paper presented at 43rd Annual National Meeting of the Academy of Management, Dallas, August 14-17, 1983.

25. More detail on the deviant/adaptive model shown in Figure 1-2 can be found in Raelin, "An Examination," Dallas, August 14-17, 1983.

26. Kornhauser, *Scientists*, pp. 1-15.

27. Todd R. La Porte, "Conditions of Strain and Accommodation in Industrial Research Organizations," *Administrative Science Quarterly* 10:21-37, 1965.

28. Philip Selznick, *Leadership in Administration* (Evanston, IL: Row, Peterson, 1957), pp. 74ff.

29. Chris Argyris and Donald A. Schön, *Theory in Practice* (San Francisco: Jossey-Bass, 1974), pp. 164-69.

30. Todd R. La Porte and James L. Wood, "Functional Contributions of Bootlegging and Entrepreneurship in Research Organizations," *Human Organization* 29:273-87, 1970.

31. Lotte Bailyn, "Involvement and Accommodation in Technical Careers: An Inquiry into the Relation to Work at Mid-Career," in *Organizational Careers: Some New Perspectives*, ed. John Van Maanen (London: John Wiley, 1977), pp. 109-32.

32. Cary Cherniss, *Staff Burnout* (Beverly Hills: Sage), 1980, esp. pp. 11-25.

33. A. W. Kornhauser, *Mental Health of the Industrial Worker* (New York: Wiley, 1965).

34. William H. Mobley, Stanley O. Horner, and A. T. Hollingsworth, "An Evaluation of Precursors of Hospital Employee Turnover," *Journal of Applied Psychology* 63:408-14, 1978.

35. Argyris and Schön, *Theory in Practice*, pp. 76-80.

36. William H. Mobley, *Employee Turnover: Causes, Consequences and Control* (Reading, MA: Addison-Wesley, 1982), pp. 22-26.

37. Sheldon E. Haber, "The Mobility of Professional Workers and Fair Hiring," *Industrial and Labor Relations Review* 34:257-64, 1981.

38. Douglas T. Hall, *Careers in Organizations* (Pacific Palisades, CA: Goodyear, 1976).

39. Harold L. Sheppard, "The Emerging Pattern of Second Careers," *Vocational Guidance Quarterly*, 20:89, 1971.

40. Arthur Gerstenfeld and Gabriel Rosica, "Why Engineers Transfer," *Business Horizons* 13:43-48, 1970.

41. Jay M. Gould, *The Technical Elite* (New York: Kelley, 1966).

42. Sharon Frederick, "More Older Engineers: Stuck in the Rut of Mid-Career," *Boston Sunday Globe*, May 23 1982.

43. Douglas T. Hall and Roger Mansfield, "Relationships of Age and Seniority with Career Variables of Engineers and Scientists," *Journal of Applied Psychology* 60:201-10, 1975.

44. See the summary report in James A. Bayton and Richard L. Chapman, "Making Managers of Scientists and Engineers," *Research Management* 16:33-36, 1973.

45. Larry E. Greiner and Alan Scharff, "The Challenge of Cultivating Accounting Firm Executives," *Journal of Accountancy* 150:57-61, 1980.
46. Meryl Reis Louis, "Managing Career Transition: A Missing Link in Career Development," *Organizational Dynamics* 10:68-77, 1982.

CHAPTER TWO

1. Walter D. Story, "Which Way: Manager-directed or Person-centered Career Pathing?" *Training and Development Journal* 32:10-14, 1978.
2. Joseph A. Raelin, *Building A Career: The Effect of Initial Job Experience and Related Work Attitudes on Later Employment* (Kalamazoo, MI: The W. E. Upjohn Institute for Employment Research, 1980).
3. Edward K. Strong, Jr., *Vocational Interests of Men and Women* (Stanford, CA: Stanford University Press, 1943).
4. Sidney A. Fine, *A Systems Approach to Manpower Development in Human Services* (Kalamazoo, MI: The W. E. Upjohn Institute for Employment Research, 1969).
5. Richard N. Bolles, *The Three Boxes of Life* (Berkeley: Ten Speed Press, 1978), pp. 146-47.
6. Henry G. Pearson, *Your Hidden Skills: Clues to Careers and Future Pursuits* (Wayland, MA: Mowry Press, 1981).
7. Elmer H. Burack and Nicholas J. Mathys, *Career Management in Organizations: A Practical Human Resource Planning Approach* (Lake Forest, IL: Brace-Park Press, 1980), pp. 223-24.
8. B. F. Skinner, *Science and Human Behavior* (New York: Macmillan, 1954).
9. Malcolm S. Knowles, *The Adult Learner: A Neglected Species* (Houston, TX: Gulf Publishing Company, 1973).
10. David A. Kolb, Irwin M. Rubin, and James M. McIntyre, *Organizational Psychology: An Experiential Approach*, Third Edition (Englewood Cliffs, N.J.: Prentice-Hall, 1979), pp. 37-42.
11. David A. Kolb, "Experiential Learning Theory and the Learning Style Inventory: A Reply to Freedman and Stumpf," *Academy of Management Review* 6:289-96, 1981.
12. David A. Kolb and Mark S. Plovnick, "The Experiential Learning Theory of Career Development," in *Organizational Careers: Some New Perspectives*, ed. John Van Maanen (London: Wiley, 1977), pp. 65-87.
13. Peter G. W. Keen, "Cognitive Style and Career Specialization," in *Organizational Careers: Some New Perspectives*, ed. John Van Maanen (London: Wiley, 1977), pp. 89-106.
14. David A. Kolb, *The Learning Style Inventory: Self-scoring Test and Interpretation Booklet* (Boston: McBer & Company, 1976).
15. A debate between Kolb and Freedman and Stumpf was played out in the Academy of Management's two principal publications, the *Journal* and the *Review*. See Richard D. Freedman and Stephen A. Stumpf, "What Can One Learn from the Learning Style Inventory?" *Academy of Management Journal*

21:275-82, 1978; "Learning Style Theory: Less Than Meets the Eye," *Academy of Management Review* 5:445-47, 1980; and "The Learning Style Inventory: Still Less than Meets the Eye," *Academy of Management Review* 6:297-99, 1981, and Kolb, "Experiential Learning Theory," pp. 289-96.

16. Abraham Maslow, *Motivation and Personality* (New York: Harper and Brothers, 1954), p. 13.

17. Clayton P. Alderfer, "An Empirical Test of a New Theory of Human Needs," *Organizational Behavior and Human Performance* 4:142-75, 1969.

18. Terence R. Mitchell, *People in Organization* (New York: McGraw-Hill, 1982), pp. 162-65.

19. Frederick Herzberg, *World and the Nature of Man* (Cleveland: World Publishing, 1966).

20. Andrew H. Souerwine, *Career Strategies: Planning for Personal Achievement* (New York: AMACOM, 1978), pp. 114-19.

21. Dale A. Seiler, "Job Needs of the Newly Hired Professional," *Personnel Journal* 49:923-25, 1970.

22. Robert Perrucci and Joel E. Gerstl, *Profession Without Community: Engineers in American Society* (New York: Random House, 1969).

23. Alvin W. Gouldner, "Cosmopolitans and Locals: Toward an Analysis of Latent Social Roles," *Administrative Science Quarterly* 2:281-306, 444-80, 1957 and 1958.

24. Barney G. Glaser, *Organizational Scientists: Their Professional Careers* (New York: Bobbs-Merrill, 1964), pp. 111-60.

25. William Kornhauser, *Scientists in Industry* (Berkeley, CA: University of California Press, 1962), pp. 117-56.

26. Gordon W. Allport, *Pattern and Growth in Personality* (New York: Holt, Rinehart and Winston, 1961), pp. 279-99.

27. Robert D. Doering, "Enlarging Scientist Task Team Creativity," *Personnel* 49:45-47, 1972.

28. Len Sperry, Douglas J. Mickelson, and Phillip L. Hunsaker, *You Can Make It Happen* (Reading, MA: Addison Wesley, 1977), pp. 30-35.

29. John L. Holland, *Making Vocational Choices: A Theory of Careers* (Englewood Cliffs, NJ: Prentice-Hall, 1973). See especially Appendix B, pp. 110-17.

30. Edgar H. Schein, *Career Dynamics: Matching Individual and Organizational Needs* (Reading, MA: Addison-Wesley, 1978), p. 125.

31. Thomas J. DeLong, "Reexamining the Career Anchor Model," *Personnel* 59:50-61, 1982.

32. Ibid., pp. 56-57.

33. Donald B. Miller, *Personal Vitality* (Reading, MA: Addison-Wesley, 1977), p. 101.

34. Rosabeth M. Kanter, *Work and Family in the United States* (New York: Russell Sage, 1977).

35. Lotte Bailyn, "Involvement and Accommodation in Technical Careers: An Inquiry into the Relation to Work at Mid-Career," in *Organizational Careers: Some New Perspectives*, ed. John Van Mannen (London: Wiley, 1977), pp. 109-32.

36. Talcott Parsons, "The Kinship System of the Contemporary United States," *American Anthropologist* 45:23-38, 1943.

37. Schein, *Career Dynamics*, pp. 50-52.

38. Bailyn, "Involvement and Accommodations: An Inquiry," pp. 109-32.

39. Perrucci and Gerstl, *Engineers in American Society*, p. 151.

40. Bailyn, "Involvement and Accommodation: An Inquiry," pp. 126-30.

41. Ibid.

42. William H. Whyte, Jr., *The Organization Man* (New York: Simon and Shuster, 1956).

43. Seymour B. Sarason, *Work, Aging, and Social Change* (New York: The Free Press, 1977).

44. Perrucci and Gerstl, *Engineers in American Society*, pp. 154-65.

CHAPTER THREE

1. See, for example, Barbara S. Lawrence, "Work Careers in Mid-Life," *The Career Development Bulletin* 2:13-14, 1980.

2. Erik Erikson, *Life History and the Historical Movement* (New York: Norton, 1975).

3. Roger Gould, *Transformations* (New York: Simon and Shuster, 1978).

4. Daniel J. Levinson, Charlotte N. Darrow, Edward B. Klein, Maria H. Levinson, and Braxton McKee, *The Seasons of a Man's Life* (New York: Alfred A. Knopf, 1978).

5. Michael E. McGill, "Facing the Mid-Life Crisis," *Business Horizons* 20:5-13, 1977.

6. Levinson et al., *Seasons of Man's Life*.

7. McGill, "Mid-Life Crisis," pp. 7-9.

8. Carl G. Jung, "The Stages of Life," in *The Portable Jung*, ed. J. Campbell (New York: The Viking Press, 1971).

9. Barbara S. Lawrence, "The Myth of the Mid-Life Crisis," *Sloan Management Review* 21:35-49, 1980.

10. Donald C. Pelz and F. M. Andrews, *Scientists in Organizations* (New York: John Wiley & Sons, 1966), pp. 174-99.

11. H. G. Kaufman, *Obsolescence and Professional Career Development* (New York: AMACOM, 1974), pp. 44-67.

12. Seymour B. Sarason, *Work, Aging, and Social Change* (New York: The Free Press, 1977), pp. 99-121.

13. Charles D. Orth III, "How to Survive the Mid-Life Crisis," *Business Horizons* 17:11-18, 1974.

14. Douglas T. Hall, *Careers in Organizations* (Pacific Palisades, CA: Goodyear, 1976), pp. 29-33.

15. Kurt Lewin, "The Psychology of Success and Failure," *Occupations* 14:926-30, 1936.

16. R. Richard Ritti, *The Engineer in the Industrial Corporation* (New York: Columbia University Press, 1971).

17. See, for example, Andrew Stedry and Emmanuel Kay, *The Effects of Goal Difficulty in Performance* (Lynn, MA: Behavioral Research Service, General Electric Company, 1962) and Emmanuel Kay and R. Hastman, *An Evaluation of Work Planning and Goal-Setting Discussions* (Crotonville, NY: Behavioral Research Service, General Electric Company, 1966).

18. Michael J. Driver, "Career Concepts and Career Management in Organizations," in *Behavioral Problems in Organizations*, ed. C. L. Cooper (Englewood Cliffs, N.J.: Prentice-Hall, 1979).

19. The table was adapted from material appearing in Mary Ann Von Glinow, Michael J. Driver, Kenneth Brousseau, and J. Bruce Prince, "The Design of a Career Oriented Human Resource System," *Academy of Management Review* 8:23-32, 1983.

20. Arnold van Gennep, *The Rites of Passage* (Chicago: The University of Chicago Press, 1960).

21. See, for example, John Van Maanen and Edgar H. Schein, "Towards a Theory of Organizational Socialization," in *Research in Organizational Behavior* 1, ed. Barry M. Staw (Greenwich, CT: JAI Press, 1979). Also, for a broader overview, see John Van Maanen, "Breaking in: Socialization to Work," in *Handbook of Work, Organization, and Society*, ed. Robert Dubin (Chicago: Rand McNally, 1976).

22. Edgar H. Schein, *Career Dynamics: Matching Individual and Organization Needs* (Reading, MA: Addison-Wesley, 1978), Chapter 7.

23. Ibid., pp. 81-82.

24. Mary Coeli Meyer, "Demotivation — Its Cause and Cure," *Personnel Journal* 57:260-66, 1978.

25. Edgar H. Schein, "The First Job Dilemma," *Psychology Today* 1:26-37, 1968.

26. Mark Abrahamson, *The Professional in the Organization* (Chicago: Rand McNally, 1967), p. 17.

27. Schein, "The First Job Dilemma," pp. 26-37.

28. Abrahamson, *Professional in Organization*, p. 57.

29. Meryl Reis Louis, "Surprise and Sense Making: What Newcomers Experience in Entering Unfamiliar Organizational Settings," *Administrative Science Quarterly* 25:226-51, 1980.

30. Abrahamson, *Professional in Organization*, p. 92.

31. Clifford Elliott and David Kuhn, "Professionals in Bureaucracies: Some Emerging Areas of Conflict," *University of Michigan Business Review* 22:12-16, 1978.

32. Mark Abrahamson, "The Integration of Industrial Scientists," *Administrative Science Quarterly* 9:208-18, 1964.

33. R. Richard Ritti, *The Engineer in the Industrial Corporation* (New York: Columbia University Press, 1971), p. 62.

34. Schein, *Career Dynamics*, p. 98.

35. Daniel C. Feldman, "A Practical Program for Employee Socialization," *Organizational Dynamics* 4:64-80, 1976.

36. Daniel C. Feldman and Jeanne M. Brett, "Coping with New Jobs: A Comparative Study of New Hires and Job Changers," *Academy of Management Journal* 26:258-72, 1983.

37. Schein, *Career Dynamics*, p. 104.
38. Simon Marcson, "Career Development of Scientists," in *Organizational Careers*, ed. Barney G. Glaser (Chicago: Aldine, 1968), pp. 133-38.
39. Bernard Barber, "Some Problems in the Sociology of the Professions," *Daedalus* 92:669-88, 1963.
40. Schein, *Career Dynamics*, pp. 104-06.
41. Schein, *Career Dynamics*, p. 108.
42. Schein, *Career Dynamics*, p. 113.
43. Schein, *Career Dynamics*, pp. 114-20.
44. Feldman, "A Practical Program," pp. 77-78.
45. Edgar H. Schein, "The Individual, the Organization, and the Career: A Conceptual Scheme," *Journal of Applied Behavioral Science* 7:401-26, 1971.
46. Kaufman, *Obsolescence*, p. 22.
47. Ibid., p. 23.
48. Alvin Toffler, *Future Shock* (New York: Random House, 1970).
49. J. L. George and S. S. Dubin, *Continuing Education Needs of Natural Resource Managers and Scientists* (University Park, PA: Department of Planning Studies, Pennsylvania State University, 1972).
50. Donald B. Miller, "Managing for Long-Term Technical Vitality," *Research Management* 18:15-19, 1975.
51. Kaufman, *Obsolescence*, p. 110.
52. Kaufman, *Obsolescence*, Chapter 6.
53. Kaufman, *Obsolescence*, p. 67.
54. Kaufman, *Obsolescence*, Chapter 8.
55. Gene W. Dalton, Paul M. Thompson, and Raymond L. Price, "The Four Stages of Professional Careers — A New Look at Performance by Professionals," in *Managing Career Development*, ed. Marilyn Morgan (New York: Van Nostrand, 1980), pp. 43-60.

CHAPTER FOUR

1. Edward Roseman, *Confronting Nonpromotability* (New York: AMACOM, 1977), pp. 209-19.
2. Patricia A. Renwick and Edward E. Lawler, "What You Really Want from Your Job," in *Managing Career Development*, ed. Marilyn Morgan (New York: Van Nostrand, 1980), pp. 13-24, reprinted from *Psychology Today Magazine*.
3. Ibid.
4. Douglas T. Hall and Benjamin Schneider, "Correlates of Organizational Identification as a Function of Career Pattern and Organizational Type," *Administrative Science Quarterly* 17:340-50, 1972.
5. M. K. Badawy, "Industrial Scientists and Engineers: Motivational Style Differences," *California Management Review* 14:11-16, 1971.
6. Chris Argyris and Donald A. Schön, *Theory in Practice: Increasing Professional Effectiveness* (San Francisco: Jossey-Bass, 1974), pp. 139-55.

7. Ralph Katz, "Job Enrichment: Some Career Considerations," in *Organizational Careers: Some New Perspectives*, ed. John van Maanen (London: Wiley, 1977), pp. 133-47.

8. Richard W. Beatty and Craig E. Schneier, *Personnel Administration: An Experiential Skill-Building Approach* (Reading, MA: Addison-Wesley, 1977), p. 65.

9. James W. Walker, *Human Resource Planning* (New York: McGraw-Hill, 1980), Chapter 13, pp. 308-24.

10. Ibid., p. 318.

11. Elmer H. Burack and Nicholas Mathys, "Career Ladders, Pathing and Planning: Some Neglected Basics," *Human Resource Management* 18:2-8, 1979.

12. James W. Walker, "Individual Career Planning: Managerial Help for Subordinates," *Business Horizons* 16:65-72, 1973.

13. Robert A. Rothman and Robert Perrucci, "Organizational Careers and Professional Expertise," *Administrative Science Quarterly* 15:282-93, 1970.

14. Simon Marcson, "Career Development of Scientists," in *Organizational Careers*, ed. Barney G. Glaser (Chicago: Aldine, 1968), pp. 133-38.

15. Rothman and Perrucci, "Organizational Careers," pp. 282-93.

16. Theodore Caplow and Reece J. McGee, "Publish or Perish," *Organizational Careers*, ed. Barney G. Glaser (Chicago: Aldine, 1968), pp. 227-29.

17. Edwin D. Smigel, *The Wall Street Lawyer* (New York: Free Press of Glencoe, 1965), pp. 50-65.

18. H. Dudley Dewhirst, "Impact of Organizational Climate on the Desire to Manage Among Engineers and Scientists," *Personnel Journal* 50:196-203, 1971.

19. "Providing Career Prospects for Engineers and Technicians," *AMA Forum* 70:29-31, February 1981.

20. H. G. Kaufman, *Obsolescence and Professional Career Development* (New York: AMACOM, 1974), pp. 124-26.

21. Fred H. Goldner and R. Richard Ritti, "Professionalization as Career Immobility," *The American Journal of Sociology* 72:489-502, 1967.

CHAPTER FIVE

1. Zandy B. Leibowitz and Nancy K. Schlossberg, "Training Managers for Their Role in a Career Development System," *Training and Development Journal* 35:72-79, 1981.

2. John J. Gabarro and John P. Kotter, "Managing Your Boss," *Harvard Business Review* 58:92-100, 1980.

3. Ibid., p. 98.

4. Ibid., pp. 98-99.

5. Andrew H. Souerwine, "The Boss: Committing Power to Help You Win," *Management Review* 67:57-65, 1978.

6. Eugene Raudsepp, "What 'Type' of Supervisor Are You?" *Supervision* 42:3-6, 1980.

7. Gene W. Dalton, Paul M. Thompson, and Raymond L. Price, "The Four Stages of Professional Careers — A New Look at Performance by Professionals," in *Managing Career Development*, ed. Marilyn Morgan (New York: Van Nostrand, 1980), pp. 43-60.

8. "Everyone Who Makes It Has a Mentor," (Interviews with F. L. Lunding, G. E. Clements, and D. S. Perkins.) *Harvard Business Review* 56:89-101, 1978.

9. Rudi Klaus, "Formalized Mentor Relationships for Management and Executive Development Programs in the Federal Government," *Public Administration Review* 41:489-96, 1981.

10. Gerald R. Roche, "Much Ado About Mentors," *Harvard Business Review* 57:14-16, 1979.

11. Eugene M. Jennings, *Routes to the Executive Suite* (New York: McGraw-Hill, 1971).

12. Daniel J. Levinson with Charlotte N. Darrow, Edward B. Klein, Maria H. Levinson, and Braxton McKee, *The Seasons of a Man's Life* (New York: Alfred A. Knopf, 1978).

13. Dalton et al., "Four Stages of Careers," pp. 43-60.

14. Lawton Wehle Fitt and Derek A. Newton, "When the Mentor Is a Man and the Protegee a Woman," *Harvard Business Review* 59:56-60, 1981.

15. Theodore J. Halatin and Rose E. Knotts, "Becoming a Mentor: Are the Risks Worth the Rewards," *Supervisory Management* 27:27-29, 1982.

16. George G. Gordon and Bonnie E. Golberg, "Is There a Climate for Success?" *Management Review* 66:37-44, 1977.

17. Gordon and Golberg, "Climate for Success?" pp. 37-44, and John A. Drexler Jr., "Organizational Climate: Its Homogeneity Within Organizations," *Journal of Applied Psychology* 62:38-42, 1977.

18. Richard W. Woodman and Donald C. King, "Organizational Climate: Science or Folklore?" *Academy of Management Review* 3:816-26, 1978.

19. John D. W. Andrews, "The Achievement Motive and Advancement in Two Types of Organizations," *Journal of Personality and Social Psychology* 6:163-69, 1967.

20. William R. LaFollette, "How Is the Climate in Your Organization?" *Personnel Journal* 54:376-79, 1975.

21. Ibid.

22. Climate types were developed by McBer and Company, Boston, MA, and are reported in Andrew H. Souerwine, *Career Strategies: Planning for Personal Achievement* (New York: AMACOM, 1978), pp. 223-29. They have been adapted for use here.

23. Ibid.

24. Rensis Likert, *New Patterns of Management* (New York: McGraw-Hill, 1961), pp. 223-33.

25. See, for example, Jay W. Lorsch and John J. Morse, *Organizations and Their Members: A Contingency Approach* (New York: Harper & Row, 1974).

26. Theodore M. Alfred, "Checkers or Choice in Manpower Management," *Harvard Business Review* 45:157-68, 1967.

27. David G. Moore and Richard Renck, "The Professional Employee in Industry," *The Journal of Business* 28:58-66, 1955.

28. Bernard Barber, "Some Problems in the Sociology of the Professions," *Daedalus* 92:669-88, 1963.

29. See, for example, George T. Gmitter, "The Industrial R&D Scientist and His Environment," *Research Management* 9:115-31, 1966; and Paula Goldman Leventman, *Professionals Out of Work* (New York: Free Press, 1981).

30. H. G. Kaufman, *Obsolescence and Professional Career Development* (New York: AMACOM, 1974), pp. 93-95.

31. R. Richard Ritti, *The Engineer in the Industrial Corporation* (New York: Columbia University Press, 1971), pp. 106-07.

32. Leventman, *Professionals*, pp. 80-82.

33. Gmitter, "Scientist and His Environment," p. 119.

34. Arthur Gerstenfeld and Gabriel Rosica, "Why Engineers Transfer," *Business Horizons* 13:43-48, 1970.

35. H. G. Kaufman, *Factors Related to the Utilization and Career Development of Scientists and Engineers: A Longitudinal Study of Involuntary Termination*, (Washington: National Science Foundation, Report No. SRS 77-20737, March 1980).

36. Ibid.

37. Ritti, *Engineer in the Corporation*, p. 217.

38. Leonard I. Pearlin, "Alienation from Work: A Study of Nursing Personnel," *American Sociological Review* 27:314-26, 1962.

39. Ibid.

40. Lotte Bailyn, "Involvement and Accommodation in Technical Careers: An Inquiry into the Relation to Work at Mid-Career," in *Organizational Careers: Some New Perspectives*, ed. John Van Maanen (London: Wiley, 1977), pp. 118-19.

41. Frederick Herzberg, "One More Time: How Do You Motivate Employees?" *Harvard Business Review* 46:53-62, 1968.

42. Kaufman, *Obsolescence*, pp. 115-19, and Ritti, *Engineer in the Corporation*, pp. 143-49.

43. Kaufman, *Obsolescence*, pp. 113-15.

44. Robert Perrucci and Joel E. Gerstl, *Profession Without Community: Engineers in American Society* (New York: Random House, 1969), pp. 119-25.

45. Harvey F. Kolodny, "Managing in a Matrix," *Business Horizons* 24:17-35, 1981.

46. James D. Thompson, "Decision-Making, the Firm and the Market," in *New Perspectives in Organizational Research*, eds. W. W. Cooper, H. J. Leavitt, and M. M. Shelly II (New York: Wiley, 1964), pp. 335-48.

47. Peter F. Drucker, *The Age of Discontinuity* (New York: Harper & Row, 1969).

48. Marlys C. Hanson, "Implementing a Career Development Program," *Training and Development Journal* 35:80-90, 1981.

49. George C. Bucher and John E. Reece, "What Motivates Researchers in Times of Economic Uncertainty," *Research Management* 15:19-32, 1972.

50. Douglas T. Hall and Roger Mansfield, "Organizational and Individual Response to External Stress," *Administrative Science Quarterly* 16:533-47, 1971.

51. Jeffrey Gantz and Victor V. Murray, "The Experience of Workplace Politics," *Academy of Management Journal* 23:237-51, 1980.

52. Nicholas W. Weiler, *Reality and Career Planning* (Reading, MA: Addison-Wesley, 1977), p. 22.

53. Ibid., pp. 171-72.

54. Edgar H. Schein, *Career Dynamics: Matching Individual and Organizational Needs* (Reading, MA: Addison-Wesley, 1978), pp. 116-17.

55. Robert W. Allen, Dan L. Madison, Lyman W. Porter, Patricia A. Renwick, and Bronston T. Mayes, "Organizational Politics: Tactics and Characteristics of Its Actors," *California Management Review* 22:77-83, 1979.

56. R. Richard Ritti and G. Ray Funkhouser, *The Ropes to Skip and the Ropes to Know* (Columbus, Ohio: Grid, 1977), pp. 238-40.

57. Stands for electrically erasable read-only memory.

CHAPTER SIX

1. Donald E. Super, *The Psychology of Careers* (New York: Harper & Row, 1957).

2. John L. Holland, *The Psychology of Vocational Choice* (Waltham, MA: Blaisdell, 1966).

3. Chris Argyris, "Human Relations in a Bank," *Harvard Business Review* 32:63-72, 1954.

4. Walter D. Storey, "Which Way: Manager-directed or Person-centered Career Pathing?" *Training and Development Journal* 32:10-14, 1978.

5. Irving Janis and Dan Wheeler, "Thinking Clearly About Career Choices," in *Managing Career Development*, ed. Marilyn A. Morgan (New York: Van Nostrand, 1980), pp. 209-16.

6. Douglas T. Hall, "A Theoretical Model of Career Subidentity Development in Organizational Settings," *Organizational Behavior and Human Performance* 6:50-76, 1971.

7. George C. Thornton III, "Differential Effects of Career Planning of Internals and Externals," *Personnel Psychology* 31:471-76, 1978.

8. Kurt Lewin, *Field Theory in Social Science* (New York: Harper & Row, 1951).

9. Donald B. Miller, *Personal Vitality* (Reading, MA: Addison-Wesley, 1977), p. 254.

10. Beverly L. Kaye, "How You Can Help Employees Formulate Career Goals," *Personnel Journal* 59:368-73, 1980.

11. C. Wright Mills, *White Collar* (Oxford: Oxford University Press, 1951).

12. Melville Dalton, "Informal Factors in Career Achievement," *American Journal of Sociology* 56:407-15, 1951.

13. Edwin O. Smigel, *The Wall Street Lawyer* (New York: Free Press of Glencoe, 1965), pp. 50-65.

14. Gary K. Himes, "Your Upward Steps," *Supervision* 41:5-7, 1979.

15. William T. McCaffrey, "Career Growth Versus Upward Mobility," *Personnel Administration* 26:81-87, 1981.

16. Ibid., p. 82.

17. Adapted from Andrew H. Souerwine, *Career Strategies* (New York: AMACOM, 1978), pp. 198-201.

18. Ibid.

19. Laurids Hedda, "Demotivation . . . or De-escalation?" *Across the Board* 16:23-25, 1979.

20. Douglas T. Hall and Francine S. Hall, "What's New in Career Management," *Organizational Dynamics* 4:17-33, 1976.

21. Fred H. Goldner, "Demotion in Industrial Management," *American Sociological Review* 30:714-24, 1965.

22. Barney G. Glaser, "Comparative Failure in Science," in *Organizational Careers: A Sourcebook for Theory*, ed. B. G. Glaser (Chicago: Aldine, 1968), pp. 280-86.

23. Douglas M. More, "Demotion," *Social Problems* 9:213-21, 1962.

24. Ralph Katz, "Job Enrichment: Some Career Considerations," in *Organizational Careers: Some New Perspectives*, ed. John Van Maanen (London: Wiley, 1977), pp. 133-47.

25. David Sirota and Alan D. Wolfson, "Job Enrichment: What Are the Obstacles," *Personnel* 49:8-18, 1972.

26. Lotte Bailyn, "Involvement and Accommodation in Technical Careers: An Inquiry into the Relation to Work at Mid-Career," in *Organizational Careers: Some New Perspectives*, ed. John Van Maanen (London: Wiley, 1977), pp. 110-19.

27. Edward Roseman, *Confronting Nonpromotability* (New York: AMACOM, 1977), pp. 66-72.

28. Richard N. Bolles, *The Three Boxes of Life* (Berkeley, CA: Ten Speed Press, 1978), pp. 286-87.

29. Leon B. Sager and Richard E. Kipling, "The Alchemy of Career Changes," *Business Horizons* 23:23-30, 1980.

30. Crawford Williams, "Why Workers Say 'I Quit,'" *Supervisory Management* 13:2-8, 1968.

31. Arthur Gerstenfeld and Gabriel Rosica, "Why Engineers Transfer," *Business Horizons* 13:43-48, 1970.

32. Jon P. Miller and Sanford Labovitz, "Individual Reactions to Organizational Conflict and Change," *The Sociological Quarterly* 14:556-75, 1973.

33. Harold L. Wilensky, *Intellectuals in Labor Unions* (New York: Free Press of Glencoe, 1956), pp. 226-30.

34. James W. Walker, *Human Resource Planning* (New York: McGraw-Hill, 1980), p. 270.

35. Sam Gould, "Characteristics of Career Planners in Upwardly Mobile Occupations," *Academy of Management Journal* 22:539-50, 1979.

36. Douglas T. Hall, "Potential for Career Growth," *Personnel Administration* 34:18-30, 1971.

APPENDIX: Complete Definitions of Fine's Functional Job Analysis Scales

DATA FUNCTION SCALE

Data are information, ideas, facts, statistics, specification of output, knowledge of conditions, techniques, mental operations.

Level 1 — COMPARING
Selects, sorts, or arranges data, people, or things, judging whether their readily observable functional, structural, or compositional characteristics are similar to or different from prescribed standards, for example, checks oil level, tire pressure, worn cables; observes hand signal of worker indicating movement of load.

Level 2 — COPYING
Transcribes, enters, and/or posts data, following a schema or plan to assemble or make things and using a variety of work aids. Transfers information mentally from plans, diagrams, instructions to workpiece or work site, for example, attends to stakes showing a grade line to be followed while operating equipment.

Level 3A — COMPUTING
Performs arithmetic operations and makes reports and/or carries out a prescribed action in relation to them. Interprets mathematical data on plans, specifications, diagrams, or blueprints, for example, reads and follows specifications on stakes.

Level 3B — COMPILING
Gathers, collates, or classifies information about data, people, or things, following a schema or system but using discretion in application, for example, considers wind, weather (rain or shine), shape, weight and type of load, heights and capacity of boom in making lift.

Level 4 — ANALYZING
Examines and evaluates data (about things, data, or people) with reference to the criteria, standards, and/or requirements of a particular discipline, art, technique, or craft to determine

interaction effects (consequences) and to consider alternatives; for example, considers/evaluates instructions, site and climatic conditions, nature of load, capacity of equipment, other crafts engaged with in order to situate (spot) crane to best advantage.

Level 5A — INNOVATING

Modifies, alters, and/or adapts existing designs, procedures, or methods to meet unique specifications, unusual conditions, or specific standards of effectiveness within the overall framework of operating theories, principles, and/or organizational contexts; for example, improvises using existing attachments, or modifies customary equipment to meet unusual conditions and fulfill specifications.

Level 5B — COORDINATING ˴

Decides times, place, and sequence of operations of a process, system or organization, and/or the need for revision of goals, policies (boundary conditions), or procedures on the basis of analysis of data and of performance review of pertinent objectives and requirements. Includes overseeing and/or executing decisions and/or reporting on events; for example, selects/proposes equipment best suited to achieve an output considering resources (equipment, costs, manpower) available to get job done.

Level 6 — SYNTHESIZING

Takes off in new directions on the basis of personal intuitions, feelings, and ideas (with or without regard for tradition, experience, and existing parameters) to conceive new approaches to or statements of problems and the development of system, operational, or aesthetic *solutions* or *resolutions* of them, typically outside of existing theoretical, stylistic, or organizational context.

PEOPLE FUNCTION SCALE

The people scale measures live interaction between people, communication, interpersonal actions.

Level 1 – *TAKING INSTRUCTIONS/HELPING*

Attends to the work assignment, instructions, or orders of supervisor. No immediate response or verbal exchange is required unless clarification of instruction is needed.

Level 2 – *EXCHANGING INFORMATION*

Talks to, converses with, and/or signals people to convey or obtain information, or to clarify and work out details of an assignment, within the framework of well-established procedures; for example, requests clarification of a signal, verbal (in person or on radio) or hand signal.

Level 3A – *COACHING*

Befriends and encourages individuals on a personal, caring basis by approximating a peer or family-type relationship either in a one-to-one or small group situation; gives instruction, advice, and personal assistance concerning activities of daily living, the use of various institutional services, and participation in groups; for example, gives support or encouragement to apprentice or journeyman on unfamiliar piece of equipment.

Level 3B – *PERSUADING*

Influences others in favor of a product, service, or point of view by talks or demonstrations; for example, demonstrates safety procedures required on a piece of equipment for compliance with new regulations.

Level 4A – *CONSULTING*

Serves as a source of technical information and gives such information or provides ideas to define, clarify, enlarge upon, or sharpen procedures, capabilities, or product specifications; for example, informs project managers of effective and appropriate use of equipment to achieve output within constraints (time, money, etc.).

Level 4B – *INSTRUCTING*

Teaches subject matter to others or trains others including animals, through explanation, demonstration, and test.

Level 5 – SUPERVISING

Determines and/or interprets work procedure for a group of workers; assigns specific duties to them (delineating prescribed and discretionary content); maintains harmonious relations among them; evaluates performance (both prescribed and discretionary) and promotes efficiency and other organizational values; makes decisions on procedural and technical levels.

Level 6 – NEGOTIATING

Bargains and discusses on a formal basis as a representative of one side of a transaction for advantages in resources, rights, privileges and/or contractual obligations, *giving and taking* within the limits provided by authority or within the framework of the perceived requirements and integrity of a program.

Level 7 – MENTORING

Works with individuals having problems affecting their life adjustment in order to advise, counsel, and/or guide them according to legal, scientific, clinical, spiritual, and/or other professional principles. Advises clients on implications of analyses or diagnoses made of problems, courses of action open to deal with them, and merits of one strategy over another.

THINGS FUNCTION SCALE

Physical interaction with and response to tangibles – touched, felt, observed, and related to in space; images visualized spatially.

Level 1A – HANDLING

Works (cuts, shapes, assembles, etc.), digs, moves or carries objects or materials where objects, materials, tools, etc., are one or few in number and are the primary involvement of the worker. Precision requirements are relatively gross. Includes the use of dollies, handtrucks, and the like. (Use this rating for situations involving casual use of tangibles.)

Level 1B – FEEDING/OFFBEARING

Inserts, throws, dumps, or places materials into, or removes them from, machines or equipment which are automatic or tended/operated by other workers. Precision requirements are built in, largely out of control of worker.

Level 1C – TENDING
Starts, stops, and monitors the functioning of machines and equipment set up by other workers where the precision of output depends on keeping one to several controls in adjustment, in response to automatic signals according to specifications. Includes all machine situations where there is no significant setup or change of setup, where cycles are very short, alternatives to non-standard performance are few, and adjustments are highly prescribed. (Includes electrostatic and wet-copying machines and PBX operations.)

Level 2A – MANIPULATING
Works (cuts, shapes, assembles, etc.), digs, moves, guides, or places objects or materials where objects, tools, controls, etc., are several in number. Precision requirements range from gross to fine. Includes waiting on tables and the use of ordinary portable power tools with interchangeable parts and ordinary tools around the home, such as kitchen and garden tools.

Level 2B – OPERATING/CONTROLLING I
Starts, stops, controls, and adjusts a machine or equipment designed to fabricate and/or process data, people, or things. The worker may be involved in activating the machine, as in typing or turning wood, or the involvement may occur primarily at startup and stop as with a semiautomatic machine. Operating a machine involves readying and adjusting the machine and/or material as work progresses. Controlling equipment involves monitoring gauges, dials, etc., and turning valves and other devices to control such items as temperature, pressure, flow of liquids, speed of pumps, and reactions of materials. (This rating is to be used only for operations of one machine or one unit of equipment.)

Level 2C – DRIVING/CONTROLLING
Starts, stops and controls (steers, guides) the actions of machines/ vehicles in two-dimensional spaces for which a course must be followed to move things or people. Actions regulating controls require continuous attention and readiness of response to traffic conditions.

Level 2D – STARTING UP

Readies powered mobile equipment for operation, typically following standard procedures. Manipulates controls to start up engines, allows for warm-up and pressure buildup as necessary, checks mobility where movement is involved, and working parts (as in construction equipment), brakes, gauges indicating serviceability (fuel, pressure, temperature, battery output, etc.) and visually checks for leads and other unusual conditions. Includes reverse shutdown procedures.

Level 3A – PRECISION WORKING

Works, moves, guides, or places objects or materials according to standard practical procedures where the number of objects, materials, tools, etc., embraces an entire craft and accuracy expected is within final finished tolerances established for the craft. (Use this rating where work primarily involves manual or power hand tools.)

Level 3B – SETTING UP

Installs machines or equipment; inserts tools, alters jigs, fixtures, and attachments, and/or repairs machines or equipment to ready or restore them to their proper functioning according to job order or blueprint specifications. Involves primary responsibility for accuracy. May involve one or a number of machines for other workers or for worker's own operation.

Level 3C – OPERATING/CONTROLLING II

Starts, stops, controls, and continuously modifies setup of equipment designed to hoist and move materials in multidimensional space, reshape and/or pave the earth's surface. Manipulation of controls requires continuous attention to changing conditions, and readiness of response to activate the equipment in lateral, vertical, and/or angular operations.

---

*Note: Three of the seven FJA Scales are included; the others are Reasoning, Math, Language, and Instruction. The definitions are drawn from empirical work with equipment operators and are, consequently, most appropriate for engineering professionals.

Source: Reprinted by permission of Sidney A. Fine, Copyright 1979.

Index

281

IBM, 151
identification, 5, 7-8, 14, 85 (*see also* professional characteristics)
imbalance between individual and organization: symptoms of, 211
inadequate internal search, 25
incentives, 14 (*see also* motives)
indifference, 24
interactionists, 94
interest assessment, 44-46
interests, 42-46
internal inactivity, 25
interpersonal sabotage, 22
interpersonal skills, 83
intrinsic needs, 186

Janis, Irving, 207
Jennings, Eugene M., 165
Jewel Tea Company, 164
job dissatisfaction, 7, 108, 137
job enlargement procedures, 186
job enrichment, 235-42: facets of, 236; management resistance to, 240; organizational resistance to, 240; personal resistance to, 239-40
job inventory: elements of, 130-31
job performance, 23, 138
job responsibility, 139
job satisfaction, 36, 105, 134-37: extrinsic factors of, 135; facets of, 134-36; intrinsic factors of, 135
"join" organizations, 181-82
Jung, Carl, 77, 158

Katz, Ralph, 135, 239
Kaufman, H. G., 104, 121, 122
Kaye, Beverly, 214
Keen, Peter G. W., 62
Kerr, Steven, 5, 7
King, Donald C., 169
knowledge environment, 121
Kolb, David A., 59, 62, 64
Kornhauser, William, 9, 20, 76
Kotter, John P., 157

Labovitz, Sanford, 251
Lafollette, William R., 170

LaPorte, Todd, 20, 23
Lawrence, Barbara S., 103
lawyers, 5, 9, 150, 188, 195, 216
learning climate, 58
learning style evaluation, 67
learning style inventory, 64
Leibowitz, Zandy B., 154
leisure activities, 24
Levinson, Daniel J., 96, 102, 165
Lewin, Kurt, 107, 209
librarians, 5, 6
life space (*see* personal space)
life space sociogram, 89
Likert, Rensis, 176
locals, 75
Louis, Meryl Reis, 33, 114
loyalty, 22

manager-directed career development, 35
Mansfield, Roger, 190
Marcson, Simon, 148
Maslow, Abraham, 68
McCaffrey, William T., 226
McGee, Reece J., 16, 150
McGill, Michael E., 102
McIntyre, James M., 59
medical schools, 15, 117
mental illness, 24
mentoring, 126, 164-68; risks and benefits of, 165-68
Meyer, Mary Coeli, 112
Mickelson, Douglas J., 78
mid-life crisis, 101-07; reasons for: achievement-aspiration gap, 102; the dream, 102; empty nest, 102-03; limits to life, 103; physiological changes, 103; role-status, 103; stagnation-growth, 103
mid-life crisis traps, 105-06
Miller, Donald B., 85, 211
Miller, Jon P., 251
Mills, C. Wright, 216
Mitchell, Terrance R., 70
Mobley, William H., 25
moonlighting, 250
motives, 30-31, 70, 71, 235

About the Author

JOSEPH A. RAELIN is associate professor of management at the Boston College School of Management where he teaches in the Departments of Administrative Sciences and Organizational Behavior. His special research interest is the field of human resources management where he is recognized for his pioneering work in such topics as the first job experiences of youth, part-time employment, public service employment, and most recently, the career concerns of professionals. Dr. Raelin concurrently serves as Director of Boston College's Institute for Public Service which has completed grants in such areas as R&D decision making for the National Science Foundation, and early youth careers for the W. E. Upjohn Institute for Employment Research. The latter resulted in Dr. Raelin's path-breaking volume, *Building A Career*.

Dr. Raelin has also been a management consultant for over 12 years, having served organizational clients of all varieties, both private and public, and having worked with all types of occupational groups. His specialty is working with professionals and in fact many of the materials appearing in this book have been successfully used with professionals in a workshop called "Career Motivation Within the Organization."